The Moral Capital of Leaders

NEW HORIZONS IN LEADERSHIP STUDIES

Series Editor: Joanne B. Ciulla
Professor and Coston Family Chair in Leadership Ethics,
Jepson School of Leadership Studies, University of Richmond, USA
and UNESCO Chair in Leadership Studies,
United Nations International Leadership Academy

This important series is designed to make a significant contribution to the development
of leadership studies. This field has expanded dramatically in recent years and the series
provides an invaluable forum for the publication of high quality works of scholarship
and shows the diversity of leadership issues and practices around the world.

The main emphasis of the series is on the development and application of new and
original ideas in leadership studies. It pays particular attention to leadership in business,
economics and public policy and incorporates the wide range of disciplines which are
now part of the field. Global in its approach, it includes some of the best theoretical and
empirical work with contributions to fundamental principles, rigorous evaluations of
existing concepts and competing theories, historical surveys and future visions.

Titles in the series include:

The Moral Capital of Leaders

Why Virtue Matters

Alejo José G. Sison

University of Navarre, Spain

NEW HORIZONS IN LEADERSHIP STUDIES

Edward Elgar

Cheltenham, UK • Northampton, MA, USA

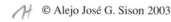 © Alejo José G. Sison 2003

Published by
Edward Elgar Publishing Limited
Glensanda House
Montpellier Parade
Cheltenham
Glos GL50 1UA
UK

Edward Elgar Publishing, Inc.
136 West Street
Suite 202
Northampton
Massachusetts 01060
USA

A catalogue record for this book
is available from the British Library

Library of Congress Cataloging in Publication Data
Sison, Alejo G.
    The moral capital of leaders : why virtue matters / Alejo José G. Sison.
        p. cm. — (New horizons in Leadership series)
        1. Business ethics. 2. Leadership—Moral and ethical aspects. 3. Social capital
(Sociology) I. Title. II. Series.

    HF5387.S5784 2003
    174'.4—dc21

2003045752

ISBN 1 84376 046 0 (cased)
Printed and bound in Great Britain by MPG Books Ltd, Bodmin, Cornwall

Contents

Foreword

Political scientists, leadership scholars, historians and ordinary people have always been fascinated by the way leaders obtain and use power. The standard sources of power for leaders are their position or legitimate power, the power to reward or punish, their knowledge or expertise, and charisma. Leadership scholars contrast transactional leadership, which is based on rewards and punishments, with transformational leadership which is based on moral values and the personal qualities of leaders. In business and in public life, most people would like to have effective leaders who know how to create social capital and build communities of trust and networks of good will that are based on shared values and goals.

Yet all too often scholars and the media pay more attention to the achievements of leaders, not the ethics of how they lead or the moral value of their achievements. Hence in history, Hitler and Gandhi are both considered great leaders, despite the moral differences between the means they used to bring about change and the results that they achieved. Similarly in the business world, the quality of leaders is usually based on how effective they are at making profits for the firm or reaching organizational goals – not on their ethics. For example, Wall Street once thought Al Dunlop was a great business leader because of his ability to raise the stock price of a company. The ethics of leaders often only comes to the forefront when they get in trouble. The big business scandals, such as Enron's, remind us of why the moral character of leaders matters. Despite the way we often talk about such cases, companies like Enron do not act immorally, its leaders do.

In this provocative and engaging book, Alejo Sison demonstrates why even with social and intellectual capital leaders and their constituents cannot flourish without moral capital. His goal is to integrate the notion of moral capital into the way we think about leadership. While Sison's focus is largely on business, his message and argument holds for leadership in a variety of contexts. By drawing on Aristotle's profound insights into the social dynamics of ethics, Sison offers us a helpful way to think about how everyday actions, habits, and the personal discipline of leaders, shape or undermine the moral resources of organizations today. Richly illustrated with real examples and case studies, Sison demonstrates the importance of moral capital and the personal and professional perils of those who lead without it.

Ethics is an underlying theme in the New Horizons of Leadership series. While there is nothing new about the subject of ethics, the ethical aspects of leadership have not been fully explored in the leadership literature. Sison's book, with its emphasis on the quiet power of morality, offers us a more comprehensive understanding of leadership and makes a significant contribution to both leadership studies and business ethics.

Joanne B. Ciulla, Ph.D.
Series Editor, New Horizons in Leadership Studies
December 27, 2002

Introduction and acknowledgements

In recent years there has been a flood of articles and books on the role of social capital or trust among economic actors. These works generally conclude that a high degree of trust and trustworthiness is an important key to achieve success in most, if not all, business endeavors.

Social capital may be considered a stage in how the human contribution to wealth creation has been understood historically. At first human labor was simply conceived of as a commodity, as manpower. As appreciation for the many unique human characteristics grew, and knowledge about the influence of each of them on worker productivity became clearer, manpower evolved into some sort of branded good that behaved like capital, human capital. Subsequently we came to know of the different modalities of human capital, from intellectual capital to emotional capital, and from cultural capital to social capital. Although social capital as a trait can be attributed to both individuals and groups, it could best be studied perhaps as a feature of the personality of a leader. A problem that one immediately encounters, however, is that social capital is morally ambivalent in its uses and effects: that is, social capital could equally serve the purposes of a mafia clan as those of a philanthropic NGO.

If business ethics is to be taken seriously, a way has to be devised in order to take stock of the 'moral value' generated by workers and firms. This moral value could then be related to the ends that employees and businesses jointly pursue, such as wealth-creation and the attainment of overall well-being. Several initiatives from both the public and the private sectors have arisen to capture this moral value: the elaboration of codes of conduct for professions and organizations; the provision of ethical training within firms; the institution of corporate ethics offices; the design of social, ethical and environmental standards and accounting systems; and the passing of enabling legislation such as the US Foreign Corrupt Practices Act or the US Federal Corporate Sentencing Guidelines and their counterparts in different countries the world over.

At times, however, these measures are perceived to be superficial and cosmetic, as mere publicity gimmicks. The deeper intentions of those who put them into effect are not trusted. Furthermore, global civil society certainly demands compliance with its just laws, but aside from that it also requires a strong commitment to values and integrity from workers, managers and firms. This is especially the case when individual and corporate actions do not violate – strictly speaking – any law, but are still nevertheless morally censurable.

In other words, beyond mere legal compliance, business ethics needs to be institutionalized in such a way that it permeates even apparently isolated individual practices, eventually forming part of a particular organization's wider corporate culture.

This book responds to the aforementioned challenges of overcoming the moral ambivalence of social capital and integrating moral value operatively into corporate culture. It seeks to achieve these twin goals by grounding itself on an aristotelian anthropology and by proposing guidelines or indicators for effective moral capital management.

This volume on moral capital rests on two basic analogies. The first one deals with a parallelism between persons and firms or organizations of whatever type. Human beings may be studied, both structurally and operationally, as living units that could be divided into at least four major levels: actions, habits, a unique temperament or character, and a singular lifestyle or biography. Similarly, the organizations which human beings constitute may also be said to be comprised of certain products (goods and services), protocols or standard operating procedures, a distinctive corporate culture and a particular corporate history. As we shall later explain, there is a striking correspondence between each of the levels that make up a human being and those that are found in a firm: between a person's actions and a firm's products, between a person's habits and a firm's procedures or protocols, between a person's character and a firm's culture, and finally, between a person's lifestyle choice or biography and a firm's corporate history.

The second analogy refers to the excellence or virtue of each of the previously mentioned levels on the one hand, and a specific institution of capital on the other. Thus, the good in a person's actions or in a firm's products may be conceived of as the basic currency or asset of moral capital; the good in a person's habits or in a firm's protocols as the compound interest; the good in a person's character or in a firm's culture as an investment bond; and the good in a person's lifestyle choice or in a firm's corporate history as an estate or legacy.

The development of these two analogies gives rise to some very enlightening and fertile insights on the true nature and meaning of human work within organizations. I have tried to amplify these points on the basis of what Aristotle had to say in the *Nicomachean Ethics* regarding the constitution and dynamics of the human being, and on what modern economic thinkers have taught with reference to capital.

In the course of writing this book I've also had the chance to examine a handful of recent business stories in search of examples in moral capital management. Almost always, I've focused my analysis on the figure of the corporate leader, trying to gauge how his or her initiatives and responses to the ever-changing environment have resulted in the growth or diminution of moral capital in the individuals and in the firm under his care.

How could the decades of neglect in the selection, training and pay of US airport security screeners by contractors such as Argenbright and ITS have contributed to the September 11 tragedy? Regarding the Enron executives and their associates, why weren't the extraordinary human capital holdings that they possessed – ivy-league MBAs – sufficient to prevent them from falling into such gross errors of professional and ethical judgment? While accommodating every outstanding quality that conventional human capital can offer – especially in terms of professional training and competence – moral capital certainly seems to require something more, such as internal rectitude.

The significance of actions and products as the elementary units of value and measure of moral capital will be discussed within two contexts. In the first one we shall look into the experiences of Ford and Firestone, in their joint denial of responsibility over a series of deadly accidents related to the use of their products, the Explorer SUVs and the ATX and Wilderness series tires, respectively. In the second, we shall be following the Cantor Fitzgerald CEO, Howard Lutnick, as he tried to cope with the consequences of the World Trade Center attacks and readily assumed responsibility over the welfare and well-being of the families of the workers who had perished. To begin with, something as simple as taking his son to kindergarten saved his life.

Both Ford and Firestone certainly got themselves into serious legal and financial trouble over the hundreds of deaths and injuries resulting from tire blow-outs and SUV rollovers in the 1990s. To what extent was each of these corporations responsible for the accidents? What did each of them know regarding the safety risks of their products? When and where did they first take notice of them? How did these safety risks or manufacturing defects come about? And most important of all, what could each of these companies have done to avoid so much suffering and loss of life?

This long string of accidents has caused a fallout not only in the top management of both Ford and Firestone but also in their century-old partnership. Most of these negative consequences could have been avoided if only the companies had owned up to their responsibilities for their products and actions squarely and in a timely fashion.

Cantor Fitzgerald could probably have been the firm worst affected by the 9-11 attacks, having lost 70 per cent of its workers. Its CEO, Howard Lutnick, however, set aside his personal grieving and promptly took charge – so to speak – of the victims' families, which he began to address and consider his own. But why did he immediately drop the missing employees from the payrolls? Was he not being hypocritical in his leadership?

In turn, personal habits and corporate procedures – which represent moral capital's compound interest – will be explained by way of Microsoft's history of antitrust suits.

As corporate vices go, Microsoft stands out for its serial abuse of market dominance. The continuous denial of these charges by its leaders, together with their lack of repentance, have only caused these faults to worsen, both in scale and in scope. This may be the reason why any remedy other than the court-ordered structural break-up would always foreseeably fall short of its goal. Will the dragon from Redmond ever be slain or will it again just prove itself to be more powerful and cunning than its adversary?

The impact of personal character and corporate culture – the investment bonds of moral capital – will be shown through an analysis of Hewlett-Packard (HP)'s takeover attempt of Compaq Computers.

Normally, a clash of cultures could be expected each time a merger between companies is under way; but that often takes place between the acquiring firm and the one that is acquired. In this case, however, the merger triggered off a culture crisis in the heart of the acquiring company itself, HP. It was a no-holds-barred standoff between the heirs of the founding families and the old guard, represented by Walter B. Hewlett, and the group of professional managers and investors who rallied around the figure of the current CEO Carleton (Carly) S. Fiorina. This strategic corporate move rapidly turned into a contest over who among the two major characters was more credible and trustworthy in his or her vision of the HP way. Although as a matter of fact, Fiorina did pull the merger through by a 'slim but sufficient margin', the jury is still out as to whether the combined company would actually be a success. What repercussions will this drastic change of direction in management imply for the HP way?

And lastly, lifestyle choices or personal biographies together with corporate histories – the estates of moral capital – will be considered through an account of the auditing firm Arthur Andersen's downfall and a revision of Jack Welch's record at GE.

Andersen had gone through incredibly rough sailing throughout the latter half of the 1990s. During that time, it seemed to have abandoned strict compliance measures with its auditing standards for short-term gains in other activities such as consulting. What followed was a rapid breakdown of its corporate reputation, and consequently, the flight of its clientele. Once the reputation of an auditing firm is gone, there is hardly anything left in it of value. It just may have taken Andersen's last American CEO, Joseph Berardino, too long to realize this fact.

Apart from Jack Welch, it would be hard to find anyone in the corporate world who would better fit the definition of a living legend. But historical revisionism has caught up even with the corporate world and Jack Welch's record at GE has now come under close scrutiny. Just how much truth is there behind the avowed success of Jack Welch's stint at GE? What was his real personal impact on the company? What impact did GE in turn have on Jack Welch's own personal life?

This whole project would not have come to light were it not for the help of some very special people and institutions. I owe my thanks in the first place to Professor Rafael Alvira, for his unwavering confidence in my work, and to the *Instituto Empresa y Humanismo* of the University of Navarre, for its unstinting support. I would also like to express my gratitude to Professor W. Michael Hoffman and to the Center for Business Ethics at Bentley College for having provided me with a very congenial environment to bring this work to conclusion. And lastly, I would like to thank Professor Joanne Ciulla of the Jepson School of Leadership at the University of Richmond, and Alan Sturmer, my editor, for their encouragement as well as for their invaluable comments and suggestions.

Alejo José G. Sison
Elmbrook
Cambridge, MA
4 September 2002

1. Understanding labor.
From manpower to social capital

I. 9-11 FROM AN AIRPORT SCREENER'S VIEWPOINT

I would have wanted to begin this book differently, but the events surrounding 11 September 2001 somehow prevent me from doing as I had originally planned. That morning three commercial jets were hijacked and crashed as fire-bombs into the Twin Towers of the World Trade Center in New York and into the Pentagon in Washington, DC. A fourth one, supposedly headed towards the White House, after a heroic struggle between the passengers and the hijackers finally hurtled down into a rural Pennsylvania field. The questions that immediately arose in most people's minds were, understandably, 'Why?' and 'Who's behind this?' The exact responses to these questions lie far beyond the scope of this work. Later on would come the query 'How did this happen?', or better still, 'How could this have been avoided?' Although we may never know with certainty how such a disaster could have been averted, a close look at the working conditions of the airport screeners and at the management practices of the firms that employed them provide very telling clues.

Since the late 1970s, it was common knowledge among federal regulators and members of the air transport industry that the airport screeners represented the weakest link in the security chain in the US. The situation only grew worse with the passing of years. Federal Aviation Administration tests in 1978 revealed that 13 per cent of the time screeners repeatedly failed to detect and intercept guns and pipe bombs before these were brought on board the aircraft; in similar tests conducted in 1987 screeners missed identifying dangerous objects by a full 20 per cent (Greenhouse and Drew 2001). Expensive, high-tech screening machines with a capacity for up to 225 bags an hour may have been installed in major airports, but they were no good since workers barely used them. Security doors were only effective to the extent that they remained guarded, not abandoned, as had often occurred. Even graver, though, than this spate of human errors was the passiveness and the conspiracy of silence in the face of such a serious and widespread threat.

Screeners in American airports comprised a legion of poorly selected, inad-equately trained and underpaid workers. A significant number suffered from bad vision, some were immigrants unable to speak English and many had criminal records. At least until November 2001, 8 to 12 hours of classroom and 40 hours of on-the-job training were sufficient for screeners in the US, whereas in the Netherlands, security personnel underwent 40 hrs of classroom and two months of on-the-job training (*The Economist* 2001). US screeners received hourly wages of $6, barely clearing the legal minimum, with no provisions for sick days, nor health or pension benefits. Their European counterparts, on the other hand, enjoyed generous, government-mandated benefits aside from the equivalent of $15 hourly wages. In consequence, American airport screeners had an average turnover rate of 126 per cent; 200 per cent at Boston's Logan Airport, from where two of the four ill-fated flights had departed, and a whopping 400 per cent at other air terminals. In Europe, by contrast, average turnover rates were a mere 5 per cent.

Having a dead-end job that was boring, frustrating, tiresome and – specially since 9-11 – highly stressful, it's easy to understand the dearth of motivation among US screeners. Consider how mind-numbing the experience of searching bags for weapons or explosives – which almost always aren't there – for hours on end can be; or how agitating it is to have to ask suspicious-looking passengers to step aside in one's halting English and frisk them for body checks. One is inevitably risking their annoyance, if not their outright indignation. Under these circumstances it was preferable just to let people and bags pass in order to avoid getting into a confrontation.

Problems, however, were not confined to the performance of screeners at American airports; they extended to the management practices of their employers as well. To begin with, government supervision of airport security contractors was considerably more lax in the US than in Europe. Despite the fact that three of the four dominant contractors in American airports were actually owned by European companies (Argenbright by Securicor of Britain, Globe Aviation by Securitas of Sweden and Huntleigh by ICTS International of the Netherlands), with only International Total Services as a US-based firm, their operations on either side of the Atlantic yielded completely different results (Oppel 2001). This should somehow lead us to think that the issue wasn't really firm ownership, nor the conflict between nationalization and privatization, but rather more effective oversight and management.

Argenbright, the dominant player with 40 per cent of the American market, was found guilty by a Philadelphia court in 2000 of conspiracy to falsify records, and for having failed to run adequate background checks on prospective employees. Normally, background investigations took 30 to 45 days for each applicant, perhaps much too long a wait given the abnormally high turnover rates in the sector (Pear 2001). At least 14 Argenbright workers turned out to have convictions for offences such as burglary, firearm possession, assault and drug dealing (Firestone 2001). The court then ordered Argenbright to pay $1.55

million, aside from putting the company on probation and meting a 30-month jail term for its Philadelphia supervisor, Steven E. Saffer.

Far from being isolated cases, these misdeeds happened to fall into a pattern of conduct within the company founded by Frank A. Argenbright, Jr in 1979 as a small polygraph operation. By 1997, Argenbright had grown into a diverse holding with 60 offices and annual revenues of $200 million. Philadelphia prosecutors claimed that for many years Argenbright did not have internal controls or audit systems, and that as a result a great number of its workers were hired without taking aviation agency tests or despite failing them. In June 2000, after its plea bargain in Philadelphia, Argenbright was once more obliged to pay a $10,000 fine to the Illinois Department of Professional Regulation for having failed to file registration forms on behalf of 97 employees. A former Argenbright employee in the mid-1990s, Michael B. Cantor, recalled some questionable tactics the company employed in order to win business from the airlines, ranging from invitations to sumptuous steakhouse dinners to free Super Bowl tickets. Once, they even considered sending the airlines a $100,000 check that could be cashed in as 'transition money', just in case Argenbright did a bad job and a change in security providers became necessary (Moss and Eaton 2001). According to John J. Pease, the Assistant US Attorney who prosecuted the Philadelphia case, Argenbright desperately needed a 'change in corporate culture'. Unfortunately, however, the company failed to take advantage of the opportunity afforded by the court-ordered probation and instead stuck to its old ways.

In November 2001, David Beaton, until then an executive at Securicor, Argenbright's British owner, replaced Frank A. Argenbright, Jr as chief executive in an unabashed effort to salvage the company's reputation.

Like Argenbright, International Total Services (ITS) was another beleaguered airport security firm (Moss and Eaton 2001). Given the tight labor market in the late 1990s, it could hardly hire enough workers and those whom it did quickly left. In August 1999, when its headcount in one airport slipped from 90 to 60 employees, the firm resorted to raising salaries by more than a third, just to try to stem the outflow. But it meant losing $80,000 a month on that contract alone, although on the positive side, recruitment increased, turnover plunged and screening significantly improved at the site. That same year, however, the company was forced to delist from Nasdaq and declared a $7.3 million loss in its SEC filings, despite reporting a $1 million *pro forma* profit to shareholders.

On that fateful morning of 11 September 2001, Mark D. Thompson, ITS president, was in his lawyer's Midtown Manhattan office preparing to file for the company's bankruptcy. A week later, perhaps in search of someone on whom to pin the blame, the company brought a lawsuit against Robert A. Weitzel, its founder and former president until late 1999. Among other charges,

Weitzel had allegedly underpaid workers' compensation premiums by $2.6 million since 1995.

By the time of the 9-11 tragedy the airport screening and security business had long been suffering from dangerously misplaced and conflicting incentives. In 1973 the US government decided to hand security control over to the airlines. The carriers, however, immediately realized that this was a money-losing proposition and outsourced the job as soon as they could. Airline deregulation brought along with it aggressive cost-cutting, to the extent that security contracts were routinely awarded to the lowest bidder regardless of track record. Even in the aftermath of 9-11, some airlines still instructed security contractors to slash costs by another 15 per cent. The only reason firms such as Argenbright or ITS put up with these strictures was in order to gain access to other, more lucrative, airport contracts, such as baggage or wheelchair handling and cabin cleaning. The airport security business in itself was completely unappealing from the economic viewpoint. No wonder airport security and screening workers were such an uncared for and hapless bunch.

Airport security tasks – and by extension, airport security workers – were grossly taken for granted by the government, by airlines and by contractors. No one really cared about the screeners. The contractors were distracted by other more profitable airport deals, even as they battled with their own managerial incompetence and were kept occupied by their occasional brushes with the law. The neglected security and screening staff simply reciprocated this lack of concern from their employers by leaving as soon as a better work offer came along or by pretending – at best – to do the job for which many of them were unfit or unprepared. The decades of neglect of the plight of American airport screeners had as their direct consequence, in a very material sense, the gaping holes at Ground Zero, in the Pentagon and in the Pennsylvania farmland.

So the question stands, 'How could all this have been avoided?' Because of their criminal convictions, many of the screeners were not eligible for security jobs in the first place; others should have been declared unfit due to poor eyesight, inability to concentrate or inadequate language skills. Granted that low pay in a tight labor market did not help to attract workers or retain the better qualified, but this should never have been an excuse for airport terminals to be understaffed or tended by incompetent, unmotivated personnel. The labor shortage and the high turnover rates aside, the companies themselves failed to provide sufficient training; even worse, several members of their management team were engaged in fraud and other illegal dealings, on occasions to cover up the tracks of their own negligence and incompetence. So it just was not just a string of bad human resource and management decisions, nor simply a case of poor corporate culture compounded by financial straits in a complicated industry. These incidents point to a serious lack of what I call 'moral capital' among security workers and the firms that employed them. But before explaining what moral capital is, perhaps we should first of all try to establish what is meant by capital itself.

II. THE MAGIC OF CAPITAL

According to the doctrine received from economists of the classical school, wealth results from the interplay of a triad of production factors; namely, land, labor and capital. From among these, the idea of capital is what has most staunchly resisted definition. Even an authority as William Nassau Senior himself concluded in the early 1800s that 'capital' may not have any generally accepted meaning (Fisher 1997b: 81). Irving Fisher was certainly no less skeptical when he remarked in the first of a series of works that he dedicated to the topic at the turn of the 19th century, 'Of economic conceptions few are more fundamental and none more obscure than capital' (Fisher 1997a: 299).

Initially, capital is almost always associated with wealth and property. In the words of Fisher, by wealth we mean 'material appropriated objects', and by property, 'rights in these objects' (Fisher 1997b: 79). Whereas by wealth we normally refer to things in themselves, property indicates a relation between things and an owner who, by law, has the right to them. Thus far hardly any difficulty. Disagreements arise as soon as one tries to distinguish capital from other kinds of wealth, taking the cue from Adam Smith, the father of modern economic science. For Adam Smith capital was the productive part of wealth, the class of wealth that yielded revenue, the stock that was saved for future – as opposed to immediate – consumption. However, the eminent economists who followed Adam Smith – Mill, Marx, Ricardo and Walras, to name a few – could not agree later on as to the exact kinds of wealth that qualify as capital; instead they ended up attributing to capital all sorts of irreconcilable characteristics (Fisher 1997a: 301–2). The failure of these attempts led Fisher, like Alfred Marshall before him, to conclude that no clear dividing line between wealth and capital could be drawn, and that in consequence the mystery of capital could not be solved by a mere effort to classify wealth (Fisher 1997b: 85, 89).

A better way of solving the mystery of capital seems to begin by adopting a business person's viewpoint, in place of that of an economist's. Popular business usage understands capital to be synonymous with wealth, with wealth understood as a stock and not any specific kind or part of it. Among merchants and accountants capital indicates the net value of wealth, the assets that remain once liabilities have been discharged. Etymologically, capital comes from *capitalis pars debiti*, a Latin phrase meaning the 'principal part of a debt'. Although the medieval usage of capital was confined to money loaned or principal, excluding interest accrued or income, it nevertheless proves very enlightening.

Fisher's seminal work, *The Nature of Capital and Income*, explains wealth – which he takes to be capital's synonym – by relating it to the human experience of time (Fisher 1997b: 79). Any amount of wealth could be measured with respect either to (1) a particular instant of time, as the money that I have in my pocket right now, or to (2) a period of time, as the money that I have earned, spent or saved within a given month. The first quantity speaks of wealth as a stock or a fund, the second as a flow or a stream. A stock or fund is expressed in terms of just one magnitude, $10.00, while a flow or stream requires two, as for example, a net of $3,100.00 for the month of December 2001. From the amount of flow ($3,100.00) divided by the duration of flow (31 days) one could derive a third figure which is the rate of flow (approximately $10.00 per day). If we recall the original Latin sense of capital as the principal or amount of money loaned, we realize that capital is a stock or fund of wealth, in the same way that interest accrued or income earned is a flow or stream of wealth. Hence, Fisher's definitions: 'A *stock of wealth* existing at an instant of time is called *capital*. A *flow of services* through a *period* of time is called *income*' (his italics, Fisher 1997b: 80). A commentator as qualified as James Tobin sums up Fisher's view of capital as one that comprehensively 'embraces all stocks of material objects that yield services that human beings like' (Fisher 1997b: 4).

Capital is an instantaneous snapshot of wealth, while income gives a continuing story of wealth. Capital simply refers to a quantity of wealth, while income recounts the production, consumption, exchange and transformation of wealth within a given time frame. In his most elaborate formulation, Fisher identified four senses in which 'capital' could be used: (1) as a stock of wealth or 'capital-wealth'; (2) as a stock of property or rights to wealth, 'capital-property'; (3) the value of a stock of wealth or 'capital-wealth-value'; and (4) the value of a stock of property or 'capital-property-value' (Fisher 1997a: 341–2). Two observations are important here: the first is the distinction between capital-stock and its value which is expressed in monetary terms and the second is the relation between capital and income, between stocks and flows. This second relation explains how capital (stocks of wealth or property) yields income (flows), and inversely, how income may be capitalized or fixed into a stock. Underlying either process is the difficulty of calculating the capital or ready money that is equivalent to a given income.

As Hernando de Soto recently reminded us in *The Mystery of Capital* (de Soto 2000), despite the very close relation between these concepts, wealth by itself does not behave as capital, nor is capital always enabled to yield income. Although in theory there should be no difference between capital and income, except for the human experience of time, in practice, this is not the case. As the majority of people in non-Western societies and the disenfranchised classes of the West could attest, the meager wealth they manage to earn, produce or possess hardly provides them with any benefit; it does not contribute as significantly to their well-being as one would expect. Hence the subtitle of de Soto's work, *capitalism triumphs in the West and fails elsewhere.* Why so?

After conducting extensive fieldwork in third world countries such as the Philippines, Peru, Haiti and Egypt, de Soto and his team concluded that the problem of the poor does not lie in an absolute lack of resources or assets, that could be loosely termed wealth, but rather in their inability to capitalize such wealth. In these regions, the poor held assets but in 'defective forms', such as houses built on land with inadequately recorded ownership, unincorporated enterprises with undefined liabilities, or cottage industries beyond the reach of financiers and investors. For example, towards the close of the 20th century, untitled rural and urban real estate holdings – a major form of 'dead capital' – in the Philippines amounted to nearly \$133 billion, equivalent to four times the market value of listed companies in the Philippine Stock Exchange, seven times the total of savings and time deposits in domestic commercial banks, or fourteen times the inflow of foreign direct investment between 1973 and 1988 (de Soto 2000: 27). Because these assets were not capitalized, they could not be bought or sold except in very narrow local circles. Neither could they be used as collateral for loans, nor mortgaged for further investments. This anomalous but unfortunately widespread situation indeed provided a sharp contrast to circumstances in Midtown Manhattan or in the City of London where, presumably, every parcel of land, every building or empty space, and every piece of equipment would be registered in some sort of property document. This document would then indicate precisely who had which rights over what. That way, alongside an asset's physical existence, it was able to lead a gainful, parallel life as capital, producing other sorts of utilities. At the root of this socioeconomic disorder endemic to the third world is a serious deficiency in legal property systems: 'The poor inhabitants of these nations – the overwhelming majority – do have things, but they lack the process to represent their property and create capital' (de Soto 2000: 6).

It is not enough just to have resources, assets or wealth; it is also imperative that one be able to capitalize such wealth. And capitalization is to a large extent simultaneous with the conversion of that wealth into some form of property or bundle of socially recognized and legally protected rights. In the same way that time becomes utterly difficult to manage unless represented by a clock or a calendar, wealth, if not properly embodied in property, could hardly function as capital. A clock or a calendar adds nothing real, in the physical sense, to time, but merely represents it, thanks to a shared agreement or convention. Similarly, property adds nothing tangible to wealth, but merely formalizes or symbolizes it. This formalization however is crucial, inasmuch as it permits one to identify, describe, capture and organize in a user-friendly way the economically meaningful aspects of a resource. 'It is formal property that provides the process, the forms and the rules that fix assets in a condition that allows us to realize them as active capital' (de Soto 2000: 39).

Thanks to property, the invisible becomes visible, the informal, formal; what otherwise would have been considered a dead or dormant resource comes to life, to a life of capital. As de Soto would have it, the formal property system is 'the place where capital is born' (de Soto 2000: 40).

For his account of capital de Soto makes use of another popular etymology related to 'heads (*capita*) of cattle'. Cattle and other livestock were used as measures of wealth in older nomadic and agricultural communities, because they served not only as sources of meat, but also of milk, leather, wool and even fuel. Furthermore, they are easy to count and, being mobile, readily exchangeable or tradeable. Hence, the most important characteristic of capital for de Soto seems to be, aside from being readily consumable or fungible, its capacity to generate additional wealth or surplus value (de Soto 2000: 33–4). The value of capital is not exhausted in its actual uses, because it has other potential uses in production and consumption.

Therefore, although one may rightly say with Fisher that all wealth is capital, nevertheless, due to de Soto's observations, we realize that wealth first needs to undergo a certain process of transformation or conversion into property, before it can actually function as capital. However, such conversion process is, in truth, basically a shared mental representation or formalization, which in no way alters the physical state of the resource. This change, no matter how slight, is nonetheless sufficient to unleash the magic of capital, enabling that resource to lead a parallel life in the creation of additional wealth and surplus value. The conditions for the transformation of wealth into property and capital undoubtedly exist in the physical asset, but the transformation itself is the result of human mind and ingenuity. In other words, without the intervention of human beings, no property nor capital could exist as such, for our mental powers are essential in the transformative processes of 'propertization' and capitalization: the capturing and fixing of the socioeconomically relevant information about a resource. Yet, during much of the history of economic science, labor – the distinctively human contribution to the production of wealth – has surprisingly been conceived as a factor not only separate, but even diametrically opposed to capital. This was arguably Karl Marx's foremost contention. Now, then, how could human effort or labor and capital be conceptually reconciled?

III. CAPITALIZING LABOR

In societies with predominantly agricultural or early industrial economies, labor, consisting largely of illiterate and unskilled manual workers, tended to be abundant and for that reason, cheap. It was also of low quality and productivity. Labor was valued exclusively for its brute force, and measured in terms of manpower, which was the human equivalent of horsepower, the unit of measure for energy in physics. Energy in physics is defined simply as the 'capacity to do work' or the 'application of a force through a distance'. With labor or the human contribution in such low regard, the greater part of economists' attention was directed toward the other production factors, land and (financial) capital.

Ever since *The Wealth of Nations*, however, Adam Smith (1776) had already included all the acquired and useful abilities of the inhabitants of a country in its capital. In proposing an all-inclusive concept of capital, Irving Fisher, more than a century later, did nothing else but follow Adam Smith. Nevertheless, it was Theodore Schultz who first effectively bridged the gap between capital and labor through a precise formulation of the notion of 'human capital'.

In the preface of his book *The Economic Value of Education*, Schultz narrated his dissatisfaction and dismay at the dominant theories of the 1950s used to explain productivity increases and economic growth in the US (Schultz 1963: vii). More particularly, he found the terms capital and labor to be empty, and the pervasive recourse to technological change more of an obstacle than a help in explaining growth. On the other hand, he observed that Americans were investing heavily in their own education and he thought that this could very well be the key in explaining their success as economic agents. In the beginning, there was certainly a lot of resistance to Schultz's proposal of submitting education to hardcore economic analysis. The general opinion was that as the repository and vehicle for the transmission of human values, education should be placed beyond the reach of economic calculus. Education was supposed to belong to the realm of intrinsic ends, desirable in themselves and not to the domain of means, which was economics' proper concern. Nevertheless, faithful to Smith's intuition, Schultz insisted on his query, 'Is it permissible to extend the concept of capital to man, specifically to include the acquired skills and knowledge of the human agent that augment his economic productivity?' (Schultz 1963: x).

To give a more credible account not only of economic growth but also of the overall well-being that derived from progress, Schultz suggested that the concept of capital be broadened to include investments in education, health and training. Whatever money and resources were dedicated to these activities should be considered as investments in human capital formation. Labor is not capital-free nor is the number of labor-hours worked the only thing that matters in productivity. The knowledge and skills, absent at birth, which human beings acquire through years of schooling have enormous economic value. Education lends itself to economic analysis inasmuch as it is something that human beings produce and consume. They invest in themselves by undergoing instruction and they benefit immensely from what they have learned, not only at the very moment of learning, but also in the future. Contrary to Marx's belief, once we have accepted the notion of human capital laborers could then behave as true capitalists, accumulating knowledge and other useful skills at work, if not acquiring equity stakes in the firms for which they work. Like other forms of capital, human capital is a product of investment; it is a means of production that is itself produced: 'We thus "make" ourselves and to this extent "human resources" are a consequence of investments among which schooling is of major importance' (Schultz 1963: 10).

How does Schultz understand education, the activity that best represents human capital formation? After allowing some margin for its culture-bound aspects, he states:

> to educate means etymologically to educe or draw out of a person something potential and latent; it means to develop a person morally and mentally so that he is sensitive to individual and social choices and able to act on them; it means to form him for a calling by systematic instruction; and it means to train, discipline or form abilities, as, for example, to educate the taste of a person (Schultz 1963: 3).

Notice that Schultz's construal of education is refreshingly broad. It applies equally to vocational and professional training as well as to the development of moral and aesthetic qualities. In a more pragmatic light, education may be conceived as a set of services that could ultimately be broken down into teaching and learning, either in organized institutions such as schools, or in less formal, unorganized environments such as the home (Schultz 1963: 4).

Just like any other set of economic activities, the production and consumption of education or human capital formation involves costs and benefits. That education entails costs means that it is not free, although oftentimes, the greater part of its costs is borne by the state, as in the case of publicly funded schools, or by other not-for-profit private institutions. Seldom does the student or the student's family bear all the costs of his education. Aside from the obvious costs of schooling reflected in the salaries of teachers, there are also hidden costs as the opportunity costs corresponding to foregone earnings when one chooses to study rather than work (Schultz 1963: 4–5; 20–23). Schultz informs us that although the cost of schooling rises more than the cost of living over long periods, the income of workers (or the rewards of labor) normally always rises faster than that of the other factors of production (Schultz 1963: 9).

Regarding the benefits of education, a large part is captured by the student himself in the form of increased future earnings. However, a great amount of these benefits also accrues to others, as the members of the student's family, his employers and co-workers, and the other members of his community (Schultz 1963: 56–7). Education, therefore, has a significant shared or social value. Education is also desirable for its positive effects on the non-economic spheres of human existence, such as on the cultural and the political domains, which contribute to a more global sense of well-being. Compared to other economic goods, the human capital created through education is unique in that as such it cannot be sold (Schulz 1963: 4). An entirely different matter is the income flowing from that capital or the services that an educated person renders: these could be readily put up for hire.

The consumption of education or schooling provides satisfaction in three ways (Schultz 1963: 8, 38). Firstly, through the immediate enjoyment that one experiences in closely associating with learned colleagues; secondly, through the possibility of future enjoyment, such as in the appreciation of literature after having mastered the rudiments of a language; and thirdly, through enhanced future production capacities, such as when one becomes able to write works of literature oneself, after having acquired the pertinent skills. The two latter forms of consumption clearly display the marks of an investment, because they defer enjoyment. As a consumer good, education is special because it is far more enduring than most consumer durables; in principle its benefits should last a person's lifetime (Schultz 1963: 9).

In the wake of Schultz's research, Gary Becker conducted a series of studies on the rates of return of human capital investments. By investments he meant activities such as schooling, on the job training, medical care, migration, price-canvassing, and so on that affect people's skills, knowledge, health and ultimately, their future monetary or psychic incomes (Becker 1993: 11). These expenditures primarily influence human capital rather than capital of the physical or financial kind because the knowledge, skills, health and values they produce are inseparable from the person himself (Becker 1993: 15–16).

These investment activities differ in at least three ways: in their effects on earnings and consumption, in the amounts of other forms of capital that they typically absorb, and in the size and perception of their returns. For example, the average money rate of return on a college education of white males is between 11 and 13 per cent, with higher rates on a high school education and still higher rates on an elementary education (Becker 1993: 7). On the other hand, although there are higher money rates of return for urban white males than for black rural males, in the case of women rates are higher for black than for white females (Becker 1993: 9). However the case may be, the fact is that improved investments in knowledge and health always raise people's productivity and income.

Becker showed through US age–wealth and age–earnings profiles that education and training are the most important investments in human capital, with at least equal or even superior rates of return than physical or financial capital (Becker 1993: 17). This general tendency is confirmed while controlling for other factors such as sex, race, place of residence (urban or rural), inherited abilities, culture, economic systems and historical periods (Becker 1993:12). Until then, economists were somehow at a loss in explaining many of their own observations. Some examples of these observations were: the distribution of earnings is positively skewed, especially among professionals and other skilled workers; earnings typically increase with age at a decreasing rate, with both the rate of increase and the rate of retardation positively related to the level of skill; unemployment rates tend to be inversely related to the level of skill; younger persons change jobs more often even as they receive more schooling and on the job training than older persons (Becker 1993: 30). Becker's statistical analyses provided a solid scientific basis for what were, up to that moment, mere conjectures regarding the impact of human capital investments, particularly education, on wealth and earnings (Becker 1993: 12).

Thanks to Becker, therefore, factors such as sex, age, race, and family backgrounds – aside from education – were included to enrich the notion of human capital. This signaled a clear break from what was then the dominant theory, that workers were mere 'labor commodities'. Furthermore, he provided an empirical framework through which the influence of such factors in wealth and income could be studied, in particular by way of varying rates of return on education investments. And regarding the common charge that human capital analysis disproportionately stresses the economic or monetary effects of education, Becker responds that nothing in his theory states that cultural effects are less important; they are simply harder to quantify (Becker 1993: 12–13, 21).

It was Carl Menger, the father of the Austrian School of Economics, who back in the late 19th century first drew our attention to the importance of knowledge in business. Nevertheless, it wasn't until the 1960s – when Schultz and Becker carried out their work on human capital – that Fritz Machlup, a 'third-generation' Austrian economist, first coined the term 'knowledge-industries' and began to study this sector. Machlup identified knowledge as the crucial element in human capital formation, and endeavored to explain its role in raising productivity and promoting economic growth.

In the initial volume of his work, *Knowledge: Its Creation, Distribution, and Economic Significance*, Machlup cited the major reasons for his interest in the knowledge production industry (Machlup 1980: 9–10). First of all, he observed that an increasing share of the US budget was being allocated to the 'production of knowledge', however widely this term was understood. The trend proved problematic because a growing portion of these expenses was already being financed by government, even when their effects on national income and welfare were still not distinctly known: 'Because of the nonmeasurability of the product, the consequent lack of productivity data, and the absence of market prices, one cannot even state with assurance that an increase in the expenditures for knowledge, relative to GNP, will result in more knowledge being provided to society' (Machlup 1980: 226). Until then, the only justification for this policy was a generalized belief that the public or social benefits of knowledge production outweighed its private benefits. Still much had to be done in the direction of identifying and quantifying the spillover effects or externalities of these investments, specially the nonpecuniary ones (Machlup 1980: 211).

Another difficulty that Machlup faced consisted in the selection of the relevant actors – apart from government – in knowledge production. In principle, one could either follow an industry approach that singles out the firms, institutions, organizations, departments or teams that produce knowledge, information goods or information services, or an occupation approach that considers chiefly the gainful or costly activities designed to generate, transmit or receive knowledge. An industry approach defines the knowledge sector by its output, independently of input, whereas an occupation approach does so by the input or the kinds of work performed, regardless of output or product (Machlup 1980: 227–9). Hence, according to the first criterion, a janitor, as long as he worked for a university, would be considered a knowledge worker; while according to the second criterion, he would not be counted as one. Correspondingly, a shoe designer would not be considered a knowledge worker by the first measure; whereas by the second measure, he would be accounted for as one. Corollary to the concern over the metric of the knowledge sector was a preoccupation with its efficiency, especially with regard to institutions of formal education. The productivity of such institutions proved arduous to measure, mainly because the psychic income and social benefits they provided were very hard to determine.

Machlup's interest in the knowledge sector was stimulated, in second place, by the changes he perceived in the production of many goods and services brought about by technological progress. Above all, technological development seemed to result in shifts of demand from physical labor to 'brain workers' or 'knowledge workers'. Consequently, the share of knowledge workers in the total US labor force increased, with important implications for the employment of physical labor, the demand for which decreased. However, Machlup's understanding of both knowledge and knowledge production were reassuringly broad. Knowledge referred to 'anything that is known by somebody' (Machlup 1980: 7), regardless of whether it be theoretical or practical (Machlup 1980: xiii); knowledge was also taken to be synonymous with information (Machlup 1980: 9). On the other hand, knowledge production designated 'any activity by which someone learns something he or she has not known before' (Machlup 1980: 7), thereby including all forms of generation, dissemination and use of knowledge. Specifically, generation related to the production of 'socially new knowledge', that which nobody knew before, while dissemination corresponded to 'subjectively new knowledge', the production of old knowledge in new minds (Machlup 1980: 7, 158). Therefore, not only researchers, scholars and scientists, but also executives, managers and secretaries take part in knowledge production. The use of knowledge occurred whenever the activity carried out is guided or influenced by the knowledge received (Machlup 1980: 174). Hence, by watching, listening, reading, experimenting, inferring, discovering, inventing, interpreting, computing, processing, translating, analyzing, judging, evaluating, and so on, knowledge was used, either as an end product (consumption) or as an intermediate product (investment). With such descriptions it was easy to see how – aside from education and research and development – other activities in print, broadcast and electronic media, telegraph, telephone, and information industries qualified for a place within the knowledge sector (Machlup 1980: xv–xvii).

In consonance with Machlup's teachings, how did knowledge, in particular, display the basic attributes of capital? Above all, knowledge was capital because, like other forms of wealth, it satisfied human needs, wants and desires. Knowledge was capital too because it could exist either as a stock or fund, in the case of knowledge stored in the mind or in any other record, or as a flow or stream, whenever knowledge was communicated from transmitters to recipients or beneficiaries (Machlup 1980: 161). Furthermore, knowledge flows, as with any flow of income, were subject to accumulation, replacement, current input, investment, consumption or waste (Machlup 1980: 176). There was accumulation when knowledge flows resulted in a net addition to the stock of knowledge; replacement when they offset or compensated for parts of the stock that had been lost; current input when they served present production; investment when they contributed to future production; consumption when they were used for current enjoyment; and finally, waste when they fulfilled none of the above.

That knowledge was the prime embodiment of human capital could also be seen from the experience of the knowledge production sector. It so happens that we could only avail of the services of educators and researchers thanks to previous knowledge production that has been capitalized in the guise of human capital. Past investments in human resources equipped workers with the knowledge, skills and other capacities required to effectively and efficiently fulfill their tasks, not only at present, but also in the future. A positive feedback loop therefore exists in the formation of knowledge or in the formation of human capital through education. As Machlup succinctly noted, 'the production of knowledge through education and research relies on flows from the human capital accumulated in the past. At the same time, the process of education largely serves the production of human capital for the sake of benefits in a remote future' (Machlup 1980: 172).

Machlup unapologetically admitted that part of his purpose in studying the economic significance of knowledge production was to affix dollar tags on items such as education, research and art (Machlup 1980: 23). Nevertheless, there was a long stretch between admitting this and accepting accusations of materialism and insensitiveness to moral and cultural values. As Machlup himself convincingly argued, one could have a healthy interest in learning exactly how much – in dollar terms or as a fraction of GNP – was spent on knowledge-producing activities, without necessarily falling into a normative judgment (that is, that too little was being spent) about the expense, or without pretending to quantify the total value of the benefits that these activities bestowed upon society (Machlup 1980: 23–4). On the contrary, it could indeed be very helpful to engage in such an exercise, if only to provide a more solid economic basis for one's preference or for society's policies.

It took a very short step from Machlup's ruminations on knowledge as the prime element of human capital to arrive at the current emphasis on intellectual capital as the decisive factor for success in the post-industrial or information economy. Nowadays, a country's wealth no longer depends primarily on agriculture or massive industrial capacities but on the delivery of value-rich services in finance, telecommunications, information and entertainment media content sectors. In consequence, an ever smaller fraction of society's workers is dedicated to the land growing food, or manufacturing heavy machinery, and more and more begin to engage in knowledge production as knowledge workers (Drucker 1968) or as symbolic analysts (Reich 1992).

The award-winning writer and consultant, Thomas A. Stewart, probably offers us the best account of intellectual capital in his book, *Intellectual Capital. The New Wealth of Organizations* (Stewart 1997), although an earlier work by Annie Brooking, *Intellectual Capital. Core Asset for the Third Millennium Enterprise* (Brooking 1996) also provides valuable insights. Both authors agree that intellectual capital refers above all to the intangible assets that allow a company to function. What differentiates intellectual capital from more conventional assets is that it is not tangible or physical, in the way of something that one could lay one's hands on. This does not mean, however, that intellectual capital is not real. Although managers and accountants cannot count it directly, as they could cash, equipment or inventory, nevertheless its presence has always been acknowledged in the form of goodwill. In accounting terms, goodwill signifies the difference between a firm's book value and its market value. In recent years, driven mainly by the interest in a firm's intellectual capital, there have been attempts at a finer discernment of intangible assets through the introduction of different pro forma accounting methods.

The major difficulties surrounding the use of intellectual capital in business concern its recognition and classification. Regarding its recognition, aside from the lack of a physical presence, much of a company's intellectual capital also happens to be tacit, unexpressed or informal, just like a great amount of the valuable knowledge that it uses. As for its classification, three basic types have been proposed (Stewart 1997: 75–8): human capital, structural capital and customer capital. Human capital stands for the attributes or inputs of individual workers, such as their competencies, knowledge, skills, talents and other productive qualities, to the extent that these contribute to the creation of different forms of intellectual property, such as patents, copyrights, industrial designs, trade secrets and the like. Stewart adopts a three-grade scale for human capital, where 'commodity skills' (for example typing or telephone manners) that are not specific to any business occupy the lowest rung, 'leveraged skills' (such as programming for an IT consultancy or working as a partner in a law firm) specific to an industry but not to a company fill the intermediate slot, and 'proprietary skills' (for instance creative programming for a software company) around which it is possible to build up a business, rank highest.

Structural capital depends on human capital put at the service of an organization; it concerns assets which no longer belong exclusively to an individual, but already form part of a firm's portfolio, such as a unique corporate culture, standardized processes, proprietary methods and so forth. The synergies that make the whole organization greater than the sum of its individual workers would constitute its structural capital. Being intangible, structural capital may not refer to the hardware or the software of a computer system, for example, but to the knowledge involved in customizing that system to a company's needs or to the manner in which the users take advantage of the computer system to the fullest. Brooking prefers to call these elements 'infrastructure assets', inasmuch as they provide the context within which a company's employees communicate and work with each other (Brooking 1996: 16). It is hard to overestimate the importance of structural capital, which could most likely explain why – for instance – a group of individually brilliant university researchers could work less productively than the kitchen crew at the local McDonald's franchise, presumably composed of people of average intelligence. Perhaps the above-mentioned university researchers are too reluctant or simply do not know how to communicate their knowledge, and as a result each one of them feels the need to 'reinvent the wheel' in order to go forward. Under the guise of 'communities of (best) practice', structural capital becomes the source of innovation, knowledge-transfer and continuity or tradition within an organization.

Customer capital is management and accounting shorthand for the value of an organization's relationships with the people with whom it does business. It is a token in what is normally known as market share, qualified through a triple dimension of width (coverage, extension), depth (degree of penetration) and attachment (strength of loyalty to a brand or a company). In a large measure, good publicity and repeat business orders come as the result not only of superior products and competitive prices but also of employee savoir faire in dealing with clients. By contrast, any instance of poor treatment at the hands of a company representative is more than enough reason for a customer to move on to another supplier in today's highly competitive market. At present, customer capital or that particular kind of 'emotional intelligence' (Goleman 1995) related to the ease of dealing with other people has become nothing less than essential.

Thomas Sowell took another significant step forward in the study of human capital in his book *Race and Culture. A World View*, where he dwelt on the notion of cultural capital (Sowell 1994). By this term he understood the distinctive cultural skills and values which explain the differences in wealth and economic development of specific ethnic groups and countries. These values referred concretely to work habits, thrift, appreciation of education and entrepreneurial drive, among others. On account of their cultural capital, for example, ethnic Chinese tended to be more successful in their business ventures than their Malay co-nationals, be it in Malaysia, Indonesia or the Philippines. According to Sowell, this was because the Chinese see virtue in thrift or saving, which is capital-forming, while the Malays considered it a vice, finding liberality more desirable. Similarly, the strength of family ties and the value that Asian families generally placed on education seemed to be the key to better school accomplishments among their children, as compared to those belonging to other minorities in the US.

In order to capitalize labor, we have had to first of all identify what was truly valuable in the human contribution to the production process. As societies and economies evolved we realized that it was not physical strength, but human intelligence, that really counted. But human intelligence or knowledge could not be developed independently of health, an adequate family environment and proper training.

Human capital is a concept that binds all these traits and characteristics together, while stressing the importance of education as the primary form of investment. From an economic viewpoint, education forms part of the knowledge production sector or industry, and its principal products are the different forms of intellectual capital. The various kinds of intellectual property (or rights to that capital) are conveniently included herein. Knowledge is capital – intellectual capital – because it accumulates and it can be stored for future use. However, neither intelligence nor knowledge exists in the abstract; that is, they always refer to the intelligence and knowledge of a concrete person, living in a specific time, place and culture. In other words, intellectual capital is also culturally nuanced, just like the human being who possesses it. And this cultural shading that influences a person's productivity is similarly subject to development and investments, precisely as cultural capital is.

IV. SOCIALIZING CAPITAL

If human and intellectual capital are cultural, then they likewise have to be social; that is, recognizable attributes not only of isolated individuals, but also of groups of persons, however they may be related. Thus we turn to social capital.

In his book *Bowling Alone. The Collapse and Revival of American Community*, Robert Putnam proffers a brief history of the term 'social capital' (Putnam 2000: 19–20). It first surfaced at the turn of the 20th century in the writings of L.J. Hanifan, a state school supervisor in Western Virginia, as the object of some loosely connected formulations. Hanifan's intent was to underscore the need for community involvement (fellowship, sympathy, good will, social intercourse) in order to ensure the success of local educational institutions. In the 1950s social capital gained currency among Canadian sociologists to describe the club memberships of arriviste suburbanites. In the following decade, the urbanist Jane Jacobs used social capital to indicate neighborliness and other related qualities that act as the ferment of life in modern cities. The economist Glenn Loury then employed the term in the 1970s in his analysis of the social legacy of slavery. And finally, in the 1980s, European social scientists such as Pierre Bordieu and Ekkehart Schlicht referred to the economic resources embedded in social networks as social capital, while the American sociologist James Coleman resurrected the term within its original context of education.

Returning to Putnam, we find that he defines social capital as the connections among individuals in so far as these enhance community or civic life; it particularly refers to social networks and the reciprocal norms of conduct that dominate them, foremost of which is an attitude of mutual trust (Putnam 2000: 19, 21). Social capital is closely related though not identical with civic virtue, for – as Putnam understands both terms – it is possible to have a society of virtuous yet isolated individuals, a society which, precisely for this reason, is poor in social capital. On the other hand, the civic virtue of individuals seems to have a multiplier effect and bear most fruit when lived within the context of a dense web of social relations. The need to sustain and develop social connections spontaneously gives rise to rules of behavior consisting of mutal obligations of the type 'I'll do this for you now, in the hope that you (or someone else) will return the favor' (Putnam 2000: 20). Hence, social capital could be seen as resulting from a combination of short-term altruism and long-term self interest on the part of social actors. Such a behavioral norm differs from legal contracts in that its fulfillment, or the sanction for breaking it, does not in any way depend on or involve the state; rather, the pressure exerted is mainly social or pre-legal.

In his own version of social capital in *Trust. The Social Virtues and the Creation of Prosperity*, the political scientist Francis Fukuyama stresses 'the ability of people to work together for common purposes in groups and organizations'; this in turn depends on 'the degree to which a community shares norms and values and subordinates individual interests to those of larger groups' (Fukuyama 1995: 10). Fukuyama's contribution lies, firstly, in pinpointing social capital as the key factor not only for wealth creation but also for social prosperity. Secondly, in a manner reminiscent of Sowell, Fukuyama understands social capital or trust as a cultural trait, because the level of trust tends to be homogenous in a given sociocultural group.

The most significant criteria in gauging the degree of trust in a group are its family structure, the strength of associationism (spontaneous sociability) among its members, and the degree of state intervention in its affairs (Fukuyama 1995: 10–12). Among these, spontaneous sociability alone is always positively correlated with trust. When family ties are too strong, they may impede the formation of meaningful connections with those outside of the kinship circle, and when they are too weak, they may prevent an individual from bonding with anyone whomsoever, since he lacks the preparation for such relationships ordinarily acquired from the home. Similarly, an overbearing state stifles social capital formation since it establishes itself as the exclusive channel of communication and exchange among citizens, whereas a feeble one would also be incapable of building social bridges when these are needed to remedy generalized deficits of trust. At most, both the family and the state could only play a supporting role and never supplant nor substitute spontaneous sociability in social capital formation.

Without trust, a borderless global economy – such as the one we have at present – would incur spiraling insurance, legal and litigation costs, given the uncertainty of jurisdictions. Ronald Coase (1960) had earlier pointed out these 'transaction' or 'social costs': the extra costs – meaning beyond the price of the purchase – associated with economic exchange, be it in terms of money, time or other resources. According to Coase, the rationale behind the organization of production processes into firms was precisely to gain efficiency by keeping social or transaction costs to a minimum. In principle, it is always easier to trust – and thereby obtain lower transaction costs – when one works with an internal provider instead of with an external one. Due to the necessarily repetitive or reiterative nature of transactions, the incentives for opportunism and malfeasance are significantly reduced, and as a consequence cooperation and trust are built up among actors. In a business environment where one's word is one's bond, where every actor delivers on his promises, smooth working relations and even success could almost be guaranteed. Furthermore, as Putnam tells us, social capital has measurable and well documented positive effects on child welfare and education, on the health and happiness of adults, on democratic citizenship and government performance, aside from on a society's general well-being (Putnam 2000: 290). Lastly, as we have seen in the case of human, intellectual and cultural capital investments, the collective or public benefits of developing social capital also far outweigh the individual or private ones.

Putnam distinguishes between two kinds of social capital (Putnam 200: 22–3). He calls one 'bonding social capital' which is inward-looking and reinforces the identities of narrow, homogenous groups (in terms of race, religion, social class, and so on) by excluding the different others. Then there is 'bridging social capital' which is outward-looking and connects people of diverse backgrounds within a broad, inclusive group. Each kind seems to be more effective depending on the specific purpose of an endeavor: for example, bonding social capital is better for activities such as poor relief, fundraising or any intent to mobilize solidarity, while bridging social capital is more productive for job-seeking and similar efforts to tap into external resources or assets. Another way of expressing the contrast is that bonding social capital is good for getting by, while bridging social capital is crucial for getting ahead.

These two kinds of social capital underscore the moral ambivalence and the dangers that accompany trust. For it is not at all uncommon for the in-group loyalty identified with bonding social capital to degenerate into a form of out-group antagonism, nor for the outreach fomented by bridging social capital to cause the dilution and disappearance of one's identity and distinctiveness. What some call social capital, others would call sectarianism, ethnocentrism and corruption (Putnam 2000: 351–2). Whereas a case could always be made in favor of diversity and tolerance, it should never be at the expense of losing one's true and idiosyncratic self. (As happens with linguistic terms, extension is indirectly proportional to comprehension or content.) Both the Ku Klux Klan and the Mafia are groups that would rank high in a social capital index, but we could hardly say that society has ended up all the better for their existence. Trust could thus produce a host of negative externalities, including the self-exclusion of a group from mutually beneficial interactions with the broader society.

Social capital appears to be the best solution to the difficulties of collective action described in such various formulations as the Prisoner's Dilemma, the Free-rider Problem or the Tragedy of the Commons. Social capital acts as some sort of institutional mechanism that guarantees individual compliance with the collectively desirable modes of behavior (Putnam 2000: 288). Moreover, social capital – more than any other form of capital heretofore considered – tells us of the extent to which our fates as human beings are inextricably linked in the common pursuit of prosperity and well-being.

Earlier we mentioned that despite their many points of contact, social capital is not the same as civic virtue. As Putnam comments, honesty – an extremely valuable trait in business and all sorts of social dealings – could really be the best policy, if only others lived by the same maxim; otherwise, it may give rise to an attitude of gullibility and spell one's own economic ruin in the end (Putnam 2000: 135). Furthermore, as Kenneth Arrow (1974) correctly observed, trust is not a commodity traded in the open market. The moment one believes he has bought trust, he should already begin to doubt the true nature of merchandise he has just purchased. It is not so much trust, therefore, as trustworthiness that makes the difference. But if trust is social capital, then what is trustworthiness?

We began this chapter with some reflections regarding the 9-11 tragedy. We focused on the role that the systematic neglect of what has come to be described as the human, intellectual, cultural and social capital of airport screeners and security firms could have contributed to the dreadful turn of events. Fortunately, four months after the disaster, the US Department of Transportation enacted measures to correct past negligence (Firestone 2002). It would now be offering salaries of up to $150,000 a year – one of the highest in government service – to the directors of the country's 81 largest airports, aside from preferring that they possess advanced degrees and extensive experience in law enforcement and crisis management before receiving appointments. These directors would have immediate responsibility for the security of passengers, baggage and cargo at their airports and they would be in charge of all law enforcement activities therein. More importantly, they would have the power to close an airport and shut down operations in case of serious security breaches. Such was the change of heart that federal airport authorities even entrusted the recruitment of directors to Korn/Ferry International, an executive search firm. The interest these jobs generated was incredible, so much so that within a day of the applications web site's activation more than 1,200 inquiries were received. Perhaps the best piece of news, however, was the simultaneous announcement that the legion of 28,000 airport screeners running the X-ray machines and metal detectors would begin to earn about $35,000 a year, when they become federal government employees in November, 2002. This goal was finally met by the Transportation Security Administration on 19 November, 2002 (*The New York Times* 2002).

V. IN BRIEF

- All wealth – whatever satisfies human needs, wants and desires – broadly qualifies as capital; although strictly speaking, capital refers to wealth understood as a stock or fund, while wealth as a flow or stream is called income (Fisher).
- Wealth needs to be transformed into property, with defined rights of ownership and use, in order to behave as capital and produce income (de Soto). Property is a legal fiction, a product of the human mind that adds nothing physical to wealth.
- The notion of human capital, originally formulated by Schultz, bridges the gap between labor and capital as factors of production. Human capital allows the capitalization of labor. Labor is no longer viewed as a commodity measured in terms of brute force (manpower), but as the

object of investments in the form of education, health and training. These investment activities are all meant to improve worker productivity.

- In Becker's version, factors such as sex, age, race and family background enrich the notion of human capital. These factors also affect the rates of return of human capital investments such as education.
- Machlup not only singled out knowledge as the primary ingredient of human capital, but also studied the growing significance of knowledge production and consumption in the economy. Knowledge, like other forms of capital, is subject to accumulation, replacement, investment, consumption and waste.
- In today's post-industrial, service-oriented, information economy, knowledge has gained protagonism under the guise of intellectual capital. Intellectual capital refers to the hard-to-quantify, intangible assets responsible for a firm's competitive edge (Stewart, Brooking). Basically, there are three types of intellectual capital: human capital, structural capital and customer capital.
- Insofar as knowledge and intelligence are not abstract entities but capacities of real people, they too possess a sociocultural dimension. Cultural capital refers to the distinctive values and skills that explain the differences in wealth and economic development among ethnic groups (Sowell).
- If human, intellectual capital is cultural, then it also must be social, that is, an attribute of the community and not only of isolated individuals. Social capital refers to social networks and reciprocal norms of conduct, specifically to an attitude of trust (Putnam, Fukuyama). It lowers transaction costs and holds the key to the solution of collective action problems. However, social capital also accounts for the success of groups such as the Mafia. This prods us to a finer analysis of its real contribution; in the first place, to distinguish between trust and trustworthiness.

REFERENCES

Arrow, Kenneth (1974), *The Limits of Organization*, New York: Norton Publishers.
Becker, Gary S. (1993), *Human Capital: A Theoretical and Empirical Analysis with Special Reference to Education*, Chicago and London: The University of Chicago Press.
Brooking, Annie (1996), *Intellectual Capital: Core Asset for the Third Millennium Enterprise*, London: International Thomson Business Press.
Coase, Ronald (1960), 'The problem of social cost', *Journal of Law and Economics*, **3**, 1–44.
de Soto, H. (2000), *The Mystery of Capital*, London: Bantam Press.
Drucker, Peter F. (1968), *The Age of Discontinuity*, New York: Harper & Row.

Economist, The (2001), 'The end of the line', 15 September, 21.

Firestone, D. (2001), 'The leader in airport security, and in lapses', *The New York Times*, 9 November.

Firestone, D. (2002), 'Top credentials sought for airport security jobs', *The New York Times*, 13 January.

Fisher, I. (1997a), *The Works of Irving Fisher*, William J. Barber, Robert W. Dimand, Kevin Foster and James Tobin (eds), vol. 1, *The Early Professional Works*, London: Pickering & Chatto.

Fisher, I. (1997b), *The Works of Irving Fisher*, William J. Barber, Robert W. Dimand, Kevin Foster and James Tobin (eds), vol. 2, *The Nature of Capital and Income*, London: Pickering & Chatto.

Fukuyama, Francis (1995), *Trust: The Social Virtues and the Creations of Prosperity*, New York: The Free Press.

Goleman, Daniel (1995), *Emotional Intelligence*, New York: Bantam Books.

Greenhouse, S. and C. Drew (2001), 'Even workers can see flaws in airlines' screening system', *The New York Times*, 14 September.

Machlup, Fritz (1980), *Knowledge: Its Creation, Distribution, and Economic Significance*, vol. I, Princeton, NJ: Princeton University Press.

Moss, M. and L. Eaton (2001), 'Federal interest varies, but cost-cutting is constant for security firms', *The New York Times*, 15 November.

New York Times, The (2002), 'Airport security, 14 months later', 19 November.

Oppel, R., Jr (2001), 'Airport security companies talk of lawsuits if U.S. takes over their duties', *The New York Times*, 25 October.

Pear, R. (2001), 'Racing to offer the details of a plan on airline security', *The New York Times*, 17 November.

Putnam, Robert S. (2000), *Bowling Alone: The Collapse and Revival of American Community*, New York: Simon & Schuster.

Reich, Robert (1992), *The Work of Nations: Towards 21st Century Capitalism*, New York: Knopf.

Schultz, Theodore W. (1963), *The Economic Value of Education*, New York and London: Columbia University Press.

Smith, Adam (1776), *An Inquiry into the Nature and Causes of the Wealth of Nations*, reprinted in W.B. Todd (ed.) (1976), *Glasgow Edition of the Works and Correspondence of Adam Smith*, vol. I, Oxford: Oxford University Press.

Sowell, Thomas (1994), *Race and Culture: A World View*, New York: Basic Books.

Stewart, Thomas A. (1997), *Intellectual Capital: The New Wealth of Organizations*, New York: Doubleday.

2. Moral capital and leadership

I. ENRON: PRIDE COMES BEFORE THE FALL

At first it seemed as if Enron was just too big, just too important and just too valuable to fail (Walker 2002). It ranked seventh among the world's largest corporations in the Fortune 500 list, and for six consecutive years since the mid-1990s, it was voted 'America's Most Innovative Company'. During that period, Enron reported an almost eight-fold increase in sales from $13.3 billion to $100.8 billion, with a market capitalization of $63 billion. Its financial statement in 2000 reported a record-setting net income of $1.3 billion, with recurring earnings per share up by 25 per cent, and a total return to shareholders of nearly 89 per cent. Even as late as 2001, Enron's board of directors was named the third best board in the US by *Chief Executive* magazine. Yet on 3 December 2001 the unbelievable became inevitable and Enron became the largest corporation ever to file for bankruptcy in American history (Oppel and Sorkin 2001). Enron and its affiliates sought Chapter 11 court protection for assets worth $49.8 billion and debts of $31.2 billion. The air was heavy with accusations of accounting fraud, insider trading and other securities law violations.

Until its untimely demise, Enron was the epitome of a new-economy company, a thinking-outside-the-box, paradigm-shifting, market-making firm (Keller 2002). Founded in 1983, Enron got its big break when state-regulated monopolies in the production, distribution and sale of natural gas and electricity in the US were broken up, and a trading platform became necessary. According to Paul R. Kleindorfer, public policy professor at the Wharton Business School, 'In the early 1990s the company [Enron] single-handedly produced the backbone infrastructure that has led to a whole industry of broker intermediation' (*Knowledge at Wharton* 2001). Enron transformed energy supplies into financial instruments or 'derivatives' that could be traded online like stocks and bonds. Thanks to Enron's intervention, the market could be guaranteed a steady supply of energy at a predictable price. However, instead of sticking to its core competence as an energy broker, Enron figured that it could expand into buying and selling everything else, such as newsprint, television advertising time, insurance risk and high speed data transmission, in the new virtual marketplace. Enron poured billions into these trading ventures, and as could be expected, some of them precipitously failed. Although the company was excellent in inventing businesses, it turned out to be terrible in managing them, judging by its appalling internal audit practices. So far, there was hardly any wrongdoing, except perhaps for some erroneous business judgments for which one could always give the benefit of the doubt.

But instead of coming out in the open and declaring its losses in public – something that could have readily stripped the firm of its mystique, not to mention the havoc such an action would have wrought on stock price – Enron chose a less than honest solution. It set up thousands of partnerships that allowed it to hide its losses – thereby avoiding credit rating downgrades – and to generate fictitious revenues. By the time those debts and losses were properly recorded on Enron's books in October 2001, they meant a reduction of about $1.2 billion in shareholder equity, a large chunk of which was in employees' 401(k) plans. Furthermore, the corrected financial statements also wiped out close to $600 million in net income between 1997 and 2000. That triggered the beginning of Enron's downward spiral.

The chief architect and strategist of such partnerships was Andrew S. Fastow, Enron's senior vice president of finance since 1990 and, since 1998, its chief financial officer until his dismissal in October 2001 (Barboza and Schwartz 2002). Securities and accounting regulations allowed debts accumulated by a subsidiary to be kept off a parent company's records as long as the parent did not own more than 50 per cent of the subsidiary. Exploiting this loophole, Fastow created a myriad of such unconsolidated entities. In principle, there was nothing wrong with the constitution of these subsidiaries. They reflected a common financing technique consisting of decreasing a company's risk by moving its holdings into separate entities which in turn could be sold to outside investors. Cactus, the first one created way back in 1991, was so successful that Calpers, the California Public Employees' Retirement System, even approached Enron to form a joint venture called Jedi, or Joint Energy Development Investment, in 1993. Later on, however, Fastow seemed to have abused these accounting provisions and created partnerships that served no other purpose than to shuffle accounts and keep debts and losses off the balance sheet. It was not clear to what extent Enron directors were aware of these initiatives and had authorized them.

Certainly there were instances of conflicts of interest, for Fastow and some other Enron executives served as managing partners – if not ultimate controllers – of many of these supposedly independent subsidiaries. In recompense for his efforts in the LJM Cayman and LJM Co-Investment partnerships, for example, Fastow was able to pocket at least $30 million; while in the Southampton Place partnership he held with other Enron employees an initial investment of $25,000 netted him $4.5 million after only two months (Eichenwald 2002). Besides a hefty salary, Fastow also earned around $23 million in 1999 and 2000 from the sale of Enron stock options. So much for a man honored by *CFO* magazine in

1999 for having invented a groundbreaking financing structure and praised by Jeffrey K. Skilling, then Enron president and CEO, in the following words: 'We needed someone to rethink the entire financing structure at Enron from soup to nuts. We didn't want someone stuck in the past, since the industry of yesterday is no longer. Andy has the intelligence and the youthful exuberance to think in new ways. He deserves every accolade tossed his way.'

No one could ever doubt Fastow's financial wizardry and, up to a point, this served Enron well. But only up to a point, because soon enough Fastow used his skills to mislead the public about Enron's finances. He also neglected his fiduciary duties toward the company's investors, dedicating himself to deals resulting in self-enrichment through those complicated partnerships instead of maximizing investor returns.

On 14 August 2001, a mere six months after his appointment as Enron CEO, Jeffrey K. Skilling announced his sudden resignation for personal reasons. On that occasion he made the following remarks: 'We built a company that 10 years from now, 20 years from now, is going to be a factor to be reckoned with in the energy business' (Zellner 2001). Three and a half months later, Enron's bankruptcy filing proved this once lauded visionary CEO dead wrong. Was it possible that even up to the moment of his resignation he did not have the slightest inkling of what was going on?

Skilling first came in contact with Enron in the late 1980s as a McKinsey consultant (Schwartz 2002). In 1990, he jumped ship from the consultancy and began to take charge of Enron's nascent trading operations. By 1996, he had risen to the post of COO, and in February, 2001, as the chairman Kenneth L. Lay's protégé, he was named CEO. As a hands-on, down-to-the-details manager, Skilling was perceived to be complementary to Lay's more detached, more congenial and highly political leadership style. Some co-workers called Skilling Darth Vader, a moniker that he didn't mind, and even seemed proud of. However, other executives thought that for the lack of scruples he was more comparable with Machiavelli than with the *Star Wars* villain. Apparently, in a meeting of corporate vice presidents in 2000, Skilling had singled out a certain Louise Kitchen for praise. Ms Kitchen's merit consisted in starting out the company's Internet trading operation, Enron Online, despite Skilling's repeated refusals to allow her. Kitchen stealthily used funds allocated for other purposes and set up the network just the same. The moral of the story then, as a senior manager put it, was that one could break the rules, cheat or lie, but as long as he made money – at least in Enron, with Skilling – this mode of conduct was perfectly alright.

Between 1999 and 2000, Skilling earned $10.3 million in salary and bonuses, and a few months before Enron's collapse, during the blackout period that prevented employees from trading their holdings, he cashed in the equivalent of around $30.6 million in stock options (Oppel 2001).

Unlike many former Enron colleagues, Skilling did not invoke his Fifth Amendment rights against self-incrimination when called upon by Congress to testify in February 2002 (Labaton and Oppel 2002c). At issue was his knowledge and oversight of the partnerships and the transactions carried out by Fastow. Skilling admitted that the structure of the initial Fastow partnerships were approved by the board. The board then appointed members of top management – the chief accounting officer, Richard A. Causey, the chief risk officer, Richard B. Buy, the CEO (Skilling himself) and the Chairman (Lay) – to closely monitor the transactions of these partnerships.

As early as March 2000, Jeffrey McMahon, then Enron's treasurer and a subordinate of Fastow, supposedly warned Skilling of conflicts of interest and self-dealing in one of the partnerships. This resulted in a confrontation between Fastow and McMahon, and the latter's replacement by a Fastow chum and co-investor in one of the partnerships, Ben F. Glisan. Skilling acknowledged having met McMahon in March 2000, but he said that the topic of conversation was simply whether McMahon's compensation would be affected by his tense relations with Fastow and nothing more. Two Enron directors, Robert K. Jaedicke and Herbert S. Winokur, Jr, claimed that in a board meeting in October 2000, Fastow affirmed that Skilling had reviewed and approved the subsequent partnership deals. The minutes of the meeting confirm Jaedicke's and Winokur's account. Skilling said that he had no such recollection and that he was probably distracted because during that meeting the lights had gone out. Lastly, on 22 May 2001, a senior Enron lawyer, Jordan Mintz, supposedly sent a memo to Skilling expressing his concern about some unsigned approval sheets pertaining to the transactions of the Fastow partnerships for the year 2000. Mintz offered to send the approval sheets to Skilling for signature but he got no response whatsoever.

Therefore, in the face of contradictory testimonies and despite his reputation as a micromanager, all that Skilling could summon in his defense before the Congress committee was that Enron was a very large corporation and that it was impossible – even for a CEO like himself – to know everything that was happening.

What about Kenneth L. Lay, Enron's Chairman and since Skilling's resignation in August 2001, its CEO as well? What did he know about the Fastow partnerships and the state of the company's finances? On 14 August 2001, immediately after Skilling's departure, Lay sent the following message to all Enron employees: 'I want to assure you that I have never felt better about the prospects for the company' (Herbert 2002). And almost two weeks later, on 27 August, came this follow-up e-mail, 'One of my highest priorities is to restore investor confidence in Enron. This should result in a significantly higher stock price.'

At around this time, however, Lay had already received an explicit warning through an unsigned letter that was later on traced to Sherron S. Watkins, a vice president of corporate development at Enron (van Natta and Berenson 2002). Watkins began her letter by saying, 'Has Enron become a risky place to work? For those of use who didn't get rich over the last few years, can we afford to stay?' She then continued expressing her anguish over the dubious accounting practices of which members of senior management were aware but didn't seem interested in stopping. She concretely referred to one of the Fastow partnerships, 'we booked the Condor deals in 1999 and 2000, we enjoyed a wonderfully high stock price, many executives sold stock, we then try to reverse or fix the deals in 2001 and it's a bit like robbing the bank in one year and trying to pay back two years later.' All that Lay did in reaction was to forward the letter to the Vinson & Elkins law firm. The lawyers limited themselves to examining whether the letter offered new information, without looking into the veracity of the claims, and a few months later they concluded that Enron had committed no wrongdoing and gave it a clean slate.

While the e-mails and the warnings transpired, and well before the definitive collapse of Enron stock, Lay had already sold around $40 million worth of shares – at a profit of about $21 million – during the first half of 2001 (Herbert 2002, Norris 2002). This figure nevertheless paled in comparison with his previous earnings of $131.7 million in 2000, $49 million in 1999, and more than $300 million cumulatively since 1989.

Not until November 2001 did Lay publicly admit that all was not well with Enron, 'Enron became overleveraged' (*The New York Times* 2001). Lay said that he basically understood what was going on, but that he left crucial details to others who have since departed and as a result he no longer fully grasped the reality of Enron. On 23 January 2002, Lay announced his resignation as chairman and CEO, although he clarified that he would remain on the board (Yardley and Schwartz 2002). Scarcely a couple of weeks later, on 10 February 2002, Lay decided that he would exercise his right against self-incrimination and refused to testify before Congress (Oppel 2002c). He may have been influenced in his decision by a special committee report released on 2 February 2002 alleging that Lay had failed to properly oversee Enron and that he bore significant responsibility for the deals that brought the company down.

Thus far has been the story of Kenneth L. Lay, a man who dedicated at least the last three decades of his life to championing the cause of energy deregulation, while accumulating vast amounts of political influence (Yardley 2002). His friendly nature and polite, engaging manners were definitely a big help. In the mid-1990s, he even came to be known as Mr Houston, for the enormous amount of money he had spread all over the city, including the local football and baseball stadium which came to be called Enron field. But by far his most rewarding investments were those made on 'reputational capital', especially among politicians. Way back in 1994, Lay and Enron donated nearly $575,000 to George W. Bush's political race to the Texas Governorship; and for the

Bush campaign for presidency in 2000, another $100,000 was raised, aside from an additional $300,000 for the inauguration ceremonies (Eichenwald and Henriques 2002). Around two-thirds of the incumbent members of Congress could also be counted as beneficiaries of Enron's and Lay's financial largesse. Cultivating a high-profile public image and dispensing financial favors among the members of the political class were the wings that propelled this modern day Icarus to undreamt-of heights. But flying high and getting close to the sun were one and the same thing and, due to an excess of hubris, in the end Lay got singed.

How about the auditors, the accountants from Arthur Andersen? Were they, like Nero, just fiddling away while their client Enron burned to ashes? Well, almost. The last five years have proven specially tumultuous for Arthur Andersen, one of the Big Five auditing firms. Apart from its acrimonious divorce from its consulting arm, now known as Accenture, it has also been involved in a series of prominent and very costly scandals (Weber et al. 2001). In 1996, the SEC ruled that Andersen had engaged in improper professional conduct and that its reports on the firm Waste Management were materially false, having overstated income by more than $1 billion from 1992 to 1996. Without either admitting or denying responsibility, Andersen accepted an antifraud injunction, shelling out $7 million as a civil penalty and agreeing to pay part of a $220 million class action settlement as well. Once more, in 1997, the SEC accused Andersen of having certified statements containing false sales and profits on behalf of the Sunbeam company. True to form, without admitting or denying any wrongdoing, Andersen this time disbursed $110 million to settle shareholder litigation. Then came Enron.

Aside from potentially crippling financial damages, Andersen faced a formidable challenge to its already tarnished reputation. Joseph F. Berardino, Andersen's CEO, acknowledged in an interview, 'The integrity of this firm is in question... Our reputation is our most important asset' (Oppel and Eichenwald 2002). During Congressional hearings, Berardino was careful to portray Andersen's role as that of an auditor that stuck by the rules but was unfortunately lied to, thereby pinning the blame on its client, Enron, in the first place, and possibly on regulators as well, since they had set accounting standards that later on proved too lax. Never mind that Enron happened to be Andersen's second biggest client in 2000, from which it received combined auditing and consultancy revenues of more than $50 million.

This might have been a plausible defense of Andersen's innocence. However, since August, 2001 its chief auditor for Enron, David B. Duncan, had already been advised about possible illegal transactions by Sherron Watkins, the same executive who had sent a letter to Enron chairman Lay (Oppel 2002a). Apparently, even in February of that same year, some Andersen officials had already discussed dropping Enron from its list of clients due to concerns about questionable accounting practices. Nevertheless, Andersen just decided to look the other way and carry on with Enron's account, giving the company its seal of approval.

Meanwhile, once Enron figures were restated in the third quarter of 2001 and the SEC inquiries commenced, Andersen auditor Duncan, with the knowledge of in-house legal counsel Nancy Temple, entered into a frenzy of computer file purging and document shredding (Oppel 2002b). A parallel operation transpired within Enron itself (Glater and Brick 2002). The destruction of what was potentially incriminating evidence did not stop until further notice was given by an Andersen lawyer, Temple, in November 2001. On 15 January 2002, Duncan was fired from Andersen, together with four other partners who had worked on the Enron audits (Oppel and Eichenwald 2002). Finally, on 24 January 2002, after having admitted participation in the destruction of records, Duncan sought refuge in the Fifth Amendment and declined to respond to questions fielded by the members of Congress (Oppel and Labaton 2002).

At this point, no one knows for sure when and to what extent Andersen CEO Berardino became aware of the destruction of Enron audit documents by Duncan. In any case, if the auditing firm did not have anything to hide, and all its transactions with Enron were above board, why the rush to get rid of records?

What did characters such as Fastow, Skilling, Lay and Duncan have in common? We could say that among them, they undoubtedly held tons of human and intellectual capital. They were all educated in the country's premier business schools, had received excellent professional training, and each one was an over-achiever and a star performer in his own right. They also enjoyed huge endowments of social capital in terms of networks of influence and amount of public trust. Mainly for these reasons, they had always been held to a higher standard, because they were thought to be beyond suspicion – initially, at least – by their investors and employees, the regulators, government and society at large. But all of these assets which at first powered their rocket-like ascent, were in the end squandered and turned mercilessly against them. They lacked nothing but honesty, the bias of putting the interests of the people whom they were supposed to serve before their own, diligence in the performance of their oversight duties, and trustworthiness. In short, they lacked moral capital.

As we have seen, social capital builds up on the gains or merits of human capital, intellectual capital and cultural capital, like a nest of tables or a collection of Russian dolls. But insofar as social capital could sometimes lead to disastrous consequences, there must be something else beyond trust that is the true source of value among persons working in a corporation. This seems to be the role that moral capital is meant to play.

II. VIRTUE AS MORAL CAPITAL

Moral capital may be defined as excellence of character, or the possession and practice of a host of virtues appropriate for a human being within a particular sociocultural context. Nowadays, its meaning could also be expressed by the word 'integrity', a trait suggesting wholeness and stability in a person as someone on whom others could depend or rely. Having virtues or an excellent character may be considered moral capital not only because they are a form of wealth, but also because they are productive capacities or powers that accumulate and develop in an individual, through proper investments of time, effort and other resources, including financial ones. But unlike human, intellectual, cultural or social capital that perfect the person in just a limited aspect – be it in health, knowledge, an aptitude or skill, or through an advantageous acquaintance or relation – moral capital is unique in that it perfects the human being as a whole person. Moral capital is not what makes a person strong, or smart, or thrifty (instead of being liberal or generous); it is not even what makes a person successful in business. Rather, moral capital is what makes a person good as a human being. This doesn't mean that a person well-endowed with moral capital, by this very measure, is necessarily devoid of bodily strength, or health, or intelligence, or has to reject profit in business ventures. It only means that such a person would never readily sacrifice his moral excellence as a condition to gain health, knowledge, social connections, or profit.

How do we know what excellence of character or integrity – one's moral capital – consists in? With a great deal of common sense, Aristotle advises us that first we would have to examine what human beings are and what human beings are for. What human beings are refers to their nature, their distinctive activity or function (*physis*) (*Nicomachean Ethics*, henceforth NE, 1097b–1098a); whereas what human beings are for points out to their last or final end (*eudaimonia*) (NE1094a). Virtue (*arete*) etymologically denotes what is best for human beings from the viewpoint of both their nature and their end.

Human nature is described as that belonging to a 'political animal' or that proper of a 'living creature that uses words'. The first description simply attests to the fact that, unlike other animals or living beings capable of self-movement, humans live and thrive in complex, organized structures generally called cities (*poleis*, the plural form of *polis*). What is natural in human beings, therefore, is not to live alone as individuals, nor even to live confined within the very limited sphere of blood relations or families, but to carry on with life's basic activities together with their like in a wider community or society. Such an arrangement, of course, demands a minimum number of members, aside from a certain degree of specialization of functions and a discrete amount of coordination or government, in order to adequately provide for life's necessities. It is easy to see how the firm fits within the Aristotelian framework.

To say that human beings are the only creatures that make use of words means, before all else, that we are the only ones capable of rational thought (*logos*) in the material world. This distinguishes us from other animal species that may have the equivalent of a voice (*phone*), but are incapable of speaking. All they can express are biological needs and their corresponding satisfaction; the sounds they emit are never products of abstract reasoning or deliberation. A lot of evolutionary preparation was required before human beings were able to think and speak meaningfully, and every step up the ladder signified an increase in the amount of freedom, a weaning away from the immediate dependence on the material conditions of our nature.

Regarding our last end as human beings or *eudaimonia*, we can never suffi-ciently insist on its finality (NE 1094a). Whenever human beings engage in an activity in accordance with their rational nature, they do it with an end or purpose in mind. For example, the majority of us would say, when asked about why we work, that we do it in order to earn a living, that we do it for money. After all, nowadays, no one could deny that money is vital. Money is therefore an end. But perhaps what isn't as rational is to consider money as the one final end: that which we seek with a view to nothing other than itself, the sole purpose for which we do absolutely everything that we do. Imagine that, because of an inheritance, you had all the money you could ever need in your lifetime, fully guaranteed and without conditions. Would you still continue working? Chances are that you would, and perhaps we could all agree on the reasonableness of this decision. Thus, there is more to work than just earning money or making a decent living. You would continue working even if you didn't need the money, because work gives you an opportunity to develop yourself and relate to others, which are equally worthwhile goals. At the very least, this example demon-strates that money does not qualify as the final end for human beings. Whatever *eudaimonia* is, it cannot consist in just having money.

Aristotle says that *eudaimonia* consists in an activity, in a flourishing life within the *polis* or city (NE 1095b). This stresses the need for an appropriate sociocultural context or community, with its web of relationships and friend-ships forged in a variety of spheres (familial, educational, religious, economic, civic or political, and so on). There has to be a fit or an agreement between what one conceives as the best for himself and what the other members of his community believe in this regard. Happiness – which is *eudaimonia*'s most common translation – makes us dependent on others, on the members of our community, and perhaps we can never really achieve it unless the other people with us do so as well. Hence, happiness could only be attained as the result of a common effort; it is a goal that could be reached only with the help of others, together with others, with their cooperation.

At this point, it should be fairly easy to see how moral capital or virtue relates to intellectual capital on one hand, and to social and cultural capital on the other. Since reason and intelligence define our human nature, whatever is best for us – that is, knowledge – has to cater to the demands of these, our superior powers, and perfect them. That we could only attain full human flourishing in close cooperation with others, with whom we share common cultural traits, values, and norms of conduct, underscores the importance of social and cultural capital, so with community living. Thus, although virtue perfects the human being as a whole, it has a special influence on a person's rational powers. Virtue creates a proper disposition in one's intellect. At the same time, although virtue is primarily ascribed to an individual person as a trait, it needs an adequate sociocultural context or community in order to be practiced.

As Socrates untiringly affirmed and Plato faithfully attested – among other places, in the dialogue *Protagoras* (318e) – virtue is knowledge. Virtue is knowledge because it perfects that non-material principle in human beings which is the soul; more concretely, it perfects the superior power of the soul, reason. If virtue is knowledge, then there cannot be but just one virtue, in the same manner that there cannot be but just one knowledge and just one soul for every human being, in accordance with both Socrates' and Plato's accounts. There is just one knowledge because ultimately there is but one object of knowledge or idea, although it manifests itself in multiple forms, as truth, good, beauty, the one, and so on. In consequence, virtue-knowledge is one, although not monolithically one, because it adapts a variety of forms: it is some sort of 'unity-in-the-diversity' kind of knowledge, present in many singular objects.

That virtue is knowledge raises the question of its teachability. In principle, knowledge could both be learned and taught. There seems to be no doubt that virtue could be learned or acquired, but can it also be taught or transmitted? Virtue seems to be special in that, unlike other forms of knowledge, it cannot as readily be taught or transmitted. Most knowledge tends to be of the theoretical kind, while virtue is more of a skill or practice that one learns or acquires by doing. Certainly, rules may be laid down for the acquisition of virtue, in the same way that they may be set for playing chess or driving a car. But learning these rules is not quite as effective as actually playing a game of chess or driving a car in order to gain the pertinent skill. In any case, we should not confuse knowledge of the rules of chess-playing or driving with excellence or virtue in the specific skill or practice. In this class of affairs, it is skill or practice, not abstract knowledge that matters in the final analysis.

Another interesting corollary to the proposition that virtue is knowledge is that no one does evil voluntarily, that all wrongdoing is committed out of ignorance (Protagoras 357d–e, 358c–d). This is a point of particular dissent between Socrates and Aristotle. Socrates upholds the principle that evil is done out of ignorance, while Aristotle considers this an error, an instance of 'intellectualism' (NE 1144b). In Socrates' view, evil in itself exercises no attraction of any sort over the human mind or soul, which is by its very nature inclined to what is true and good. Therefore, one could only commit evil under a false or erroneous impression that he is actually doing good; had one known better, he wouldn't be doing it, or he would be doing otherwise. It could only be due to ignorance or the absence of the necessary knowledge that one commits evil; nobody knowingly does evil things.

Aristotle thinks that Socrates – or at least, the Socrates whom he knew through Plato – has somehow been misled by taking the equivalence between virtue and knowledge too seriously. Of course virtue has a knowledge component, but it cannot be purely knowledge for it also requires, among other things, action or practice. While in Socrates' thinking theory and practice comfortably share the general category of knowledge, which as such is readily applicable to virtue, for Aristotle this is no longer the case. Instead, Aristotle proposes a clear-cut distinction between knowledge or theory, on one hand, and practice, on the other. As a result, unitary Socratic virtue is divided within the Aristotelian framework into intellectual virtues, which perfect thought, and moral virtues, which denote excellence in character and action (NE 1103a). Another argument in support of Aristotle's stance against Socratic intellectualism is the difficulty – if not outright impossibility – of attributing responsibility to the agent of any wrongdoing: ignorance takes away responsibility from the agent because it converts an action into a non-human act. Yet experience abundantly shows that human beings are capable and, as a matter of course, do commit evil acts willfully and knowingly.

Regardless of whether Socrates or Aristotle was right on the issue of willful wrongdoing, both agree that it is better to suffer evil than to commit it. Clearly, evil-doing inflicts a lot of pain and suffering, both physical and moral, on other people. But to a certain extent, this harm will always be superficial. The greatest damage that evil causes is in the person himself that commits it, for above all, his evil acts damage his soul, and a person's soul is his most valuable possession. From this perspective, it would be preferable, therefore, to suffer physical or material pain as the result of other people's wrongdoing to committing such wrongdoing oneself. So long as one does not succumb to evil actions, although he may suffer from their effects, his soul remains pure and intact.

Earlier we witnessed how virtue relates to the other forms of capital; intellectual capital, cultural capital and social capital. We have also seen virtue's main characteristics in dialogue with thinkers of the School of Athens: virtue is knowledge; it is one; it is teachable, although in a very special way; its contrary – evil – is the result of ignorance; and that given the option, it is always better to suffer evil – and thereby preserve virtue – than engage in wrongdoing. However, the fundamental difference between virtue and the other forms of capital is that virtue can never be used to do wrong. In other words, moral capital does not share that ambivalence, or equal usefulness for the good or the bad, that the other forms of capital display. Previous examples culled from the

Enron cast of characters showed us how people with talent, schooling, wealth and the right social connections could use all these qualities to commit wrongdoing, transforming these assets into serious liabilities that ultimately work against themselves. This is precisely the kind of thing that virtue can never do, it can never be used to further evil purposes.

Despite the currently fashionable talk about the importance of values in business, moral capital, however, does not arise from mere lip-service or a superficial commitment to values. Rather, as excellence of character, moral capital depends primarily on cultivating the right habits or virtues. As Aristotle informs us, on the occasion of the etymology of the word ethics, 'Virtue of character results from habit; hence its name "ethical", slightly varied from "ethos"' (NE 1103a). A virtuous character comes from the cultivation of virtuous habits, virtuous habits result from the repeated performance of virtuous actions, and virtuous actions spring from a person's having nurtured suitable inclinations or tendencies in accordance with his nature and final end.

Part of human nature is the feedback mechanism among these different levels of character, habits, actions and inclinations. Normally, we might say that concrete actions arise from a person's inclinations or tendencies, found on a more basic level; although we would also be right in saying that the performance of certain actions themselves may in turn alter, weaken or reinforce particular inclinations. Similarly, habits do not only constitute character, but character of a specific type may equally predispose or disengage a person from acquiring certain habits. Hence the circularity in the Aristotelian teaching that a virtuous action is that which a virtuous person (in terms of habits and character) performs. Later, we shall return in greater detail to the reciprocal dynamics among the different levels of character, habits, actions and inclinations, which together constitute moral capital. Before this, however, we have to establish the link between moral capital and leadership.

III. LEADERSHIP: CHARACTER OR CHARISMA?

As we go about our daily work, in the ordinary exercise of our profession, there comes a point in which, either individually or as an organization, we seem to enter into uncharted territory, a no-man's land where there are apparently no rules, or at least where the rules we knew no longer apply. Previously, we could just go with the flow, driven by routine and bureaucracy, but all of a sudden, these guides seem to have disappeared or they plainly prove themselves useless. Although we may not want to admit it, we can find ourselves at a crossroads, without the slightest clue about where to go... We're simply lost!

This is the time for leadership. It is that defining moment when, without the help of external guides or rules, someone has to make a crucial decision, and then summon sufficient strength to put that decision into effect. Leadership necessarily involves discretionary acts or the exercise of prerogatives; notwithstanding the effort to avoid using them in an arbitrary, self-serving or paternalistic fashion. It would be wonderful if the call for leadership never cropped up, given the fearful chance for abuse, and everything instead would just go according to established procedure. Yet we know that this is mere wishful thinking. A leader fills a very real need: on one hand, a need for vision, an objective or a strategy, and on the other, for drive, energy and motivation. At certain moments, the alternative to not having a leader is downright chaos, organizational paralysis and dissolution. The organization has no choice but to rely on a leader, and the leader, in turn, has none other to depend on but himself, his physical, mental and moral powers.

Leadership is one of the most observed yet least understood human phenomena (Bennis and Nanus 1978: 4). Practically each generation has come up with its own definition of leadership, with varying points of emphasis. In the 1990s, perhaps the most widely accepted definition was that of Joseph Rost, for whom 'Leadership is an influence relationship among leaders and followers who intend real changes that reflect their mutual purposes' (Rost 1993: 102). Rost's definition hits the mark in at least three main aspects of leadership. Firstly, in its recognition that leadership is a reciprocal relationship – basically, a partnership – between a leader and his followers: a leader cannot accomplish anything without his followers. Secondly, it is also right in establishing that leadership goals have to be thought of or set together by the leader and his followers. And lastly, as a consequence of the previous point, it is correct to imply that only a voluntary followership would be deemed appropriate or acceptable to true leadership.

However, at the margin of Rost's merits, the real issue here at stake is not how well leadership is defined, but how well leadership is practiced, as Joanne Ciulla opportunely remarked (Ciulla 1998: 13). The point of our inquiry on leadership is how to achieve good leadership, in its double sense of morally good and technically good or effective. (In leadership, as in virtue, it's the practice and not the theory that counts.) Therefore, a *sine qua non* condition for a good leader is that he be, at the same time, morally upright and professionally competent or effective. Accordingly, in the measure that we figure out what sort of person – especially from the viewpoint of ethical qualities – should lead, to that same extent we advance in our understanding of the nature of leadership. This conjunction between technical competence and moral excellence is what Ciulla refers to when she affirms that 'ethics lies at the very heart of leadership' (Ciulla 1998: xv, 18).

Former US President Harry Truman once gave the following litmus test of leadership: 'the ability to get other people to do what they don't want to do, and like it' (Solomon 1998: 91). Earlier we said that the need for leadership is most keenly felt when an organization realizes that it has to move on, yet finds no rules nor indications on how to proceed. As a result of this puzzlement and inaction, that organization's members may at the same time also feel depressed or deeply discouraged. The leader then comes to provide the necessary vision and energy. This task is easy when group members agree with the leader, or when they pose little or no resistance to the overall orientation of the move. But this is hardly ever the case. It takes special leadership skills to get other people to do what they initially would not want to do, while at the same time respecting their freedom. A further proof of leadership lies in getting people to actually like and enjoy what at first they had not even thought or imagined they would be doing. How does one go about this?

In principle, there are a variety of pathways to leadership. Machiavelli posed the well-known alternative of leading – and being followed – either out of love or out of fear. Fear, like love, is indeed a very strong motivator; but unlike love, fear prevents people from feeling good about their work. They focus on avoiding punishment, rather than on getting work done and doing it well. Besides love and fear, there are other routes to leadership such as wealth, position, intelligence and skill. What all of these have in common is that they are diverse forms of power, different capacities to effect change in someone or something. It is usually at this juncture when the issue arises of whether these qualities are innate in the leader or, on the contrary, they are something that the leader has developed or acquired. The best response, perhaps, consists in saying that unless proven otherwise, everyone has, at the very least, the potential to become a leader, or to behave as one in some special circumstance. Unfortunately, however, very few ever take the trouble of developing such a potential.

What seems clear at this point is that the followership that leadership demands cannot come about merely as the result of external pressure, force, coercion or intimidation; it simply cannot be decreed. It is an adherence that has to spring naturally, as it were, from within the minds and hearts of people, in response to their having felt recognized, respected and valued by their leader. Rather than a mechanical reaction to a superior force, leadership is 'a complex moral relationship between people based on trust, obligation, commitment, emotion, and a shared vision of the good' (Ciulla 1998: xv).

Above all, leadership consists in exerting a moral influence over one's followers. Others express this influence in terms of moral authority (Casson 2000: 6). The beneficial moral influence of the leader over his followers is the source of his authority; it is the instance that legitimizes his power. This moral influence, in turn, could be understood in a two-fold manner. Firstly, from the viewpoint of the followers, it comes in support of the findings of nearly every survey, that moral attributes such as honesty, integrity, credibility and trustworthiness in general are the qualities most desired in leaders (Kouzes and Posner 1993: 255). Secondly, from the perspective of the leaders themselves, it confirms the intuition that, inasmuch as all their decisions have a moral dimension, leaders shape the ethical choices of their followers, either enhancing or inhibiting their personal growth and flourishing. James MacGregor Burns saw this point very clearly: leadership is a two-way transformative and intrinsically moral relationship between a leader and his followers (Burns 1978). The two parties involved in a leadership relation – the leader and the followers – morally transform and elevate each other through their interaction. Thus, ethical leadership becomes the primary conduit through which not only persons, but also the organizations for which these persons work, become ethical. Leadership nurtures personal ethics, allowing it to grow and configure an auspicious organizational culture.

Building upon the model that leadership is essentially a reciprocal, morally uplifting relationship between leaders and followers, the notions of stewardship and servant-leadership have emerged. The first, stewardship, represents a pivotal shift in leadership thinking, insofar as it acknowledges a leader's deep moral accountability to the organization and its workers (Block 1993). In accordance with the idea of stewardship, a leader cannot behave despotically and go about his tasks in the organization as if he were its sole proprietor, answerable to no one but himself, with respect to its purposes and procedures. Instead, a steward-leader should recognize the power of workers to make decisions regarding their own jobs, as well as their capacity to influence the organization's goals, systems and structures. Rather than control workers, a steward-leader should empower them to the point that they become leaders themselves, albeit in a more limited scope.

Servant-leadership is an even more revolutionary trend than stewardship, for it turns traditional leadership thinking, with its emphasis on a high-profile figure and his stellar interventions, upside down. A servant-leader should not only recognize the interests of others in the organization; he is also duty-bound to transcend his own self-interest to better serve the others' needs (Greenleaf 1977). His obligation is to provide those under his care with a chance to grow and develop as persons; he ought to furnish them with opportunities to gain, both materially and morally, through the work that they do in the organization. In other words, the integral fulfillment of others in the organization is the servant-leader's principal aim and the criterion with which his own self-fulfillment is to be judged and measured.

Many construe ethical leadership as an emotional relationship fundamentally based on charisma; the quality of being 'touched by grace'. Charisma is that mysterious, rare and extraordinary power possessed by certain people who are successful in influencing others. Being a nonrational characteristic, charisma is extremely difficult to define, and at most, it lends itself to a series of vague descriptions. Generally, charisma has to do with a leader's message, with how he says it, with the whole gamut of emotions (hopes, fears, enthusiasm and so on) that he evokes or is able to infuse in his audience. Charm, intelligence and a minimum semblance of sincerity also contribute to the overall perception of charisma. Nonetheless, in the words of Robert Solomon, 'charisma doesn't refer to any character trait or "quality" in particular, but is rather a general way of referring to a person who seems to be a dynamic and effective leader. And as a term of analysis in leadership studies, I think that it is more of a distraction than a point of understanding' (Solomon 1998: 98).

In place of charisma, Solomon proposes the emotional relationship of trust as the basis of ethical leadership (Solomon 1998: 101, 105). An ethical leader is one who establishes and sustains a framework of reciprocal trust, firstly, between himself and his followers and, by extension, among his followers themselves. Without this atmosphere of trust, no dialogue, no understanding, no cooperation, no commerce, no community would be possible. For this reason, despite all the cynicism and suspicion acquired through unfortunate experiences, human beings in general still tend to have an open and trusting attitude towards others. This open-mindedness is the necessary starting point for future dealings. The more successful subsequent transactions are, the better the parties involved get to know each other, and the deeper the trust relationship between them grows. The social cohesion that arises from the growth of trust, as we already know, lowers transaction costs, facilitates entrepreneurial initiatives and boosts economic competitiveness (Casson 2000: 17–18). Now then, the source of trust, on which ethical leadership is founded, is none other than moral capital or virtue.

All along what we have been looking at as we examined the art of leadership is what was known in the classical world as rhetoric. In the words of Aristotle, 'Let rhetoric be [defined as] an ability, in each [particular] case, to see the available means of persuasion' (*Rhetoric*, henceforth, Rh, 1355b). Having excluded force as a legitimate means of influence, the remaining instrument available to the potential leader is reason. The word is nothing else but the vehicle for reason. First and foremost, a leader has to persuade his audience to act. Yet words are such that in order to move the listeners, reflection and understanding on the part of the receivers are required. Words are effective only in the case of free and rational agents who are appropriately addressed as such. Furthermore, words alone do not move, but rather they require the complicity of feelings and emotions. That is why Aristotle directed his treatise on rhetoric or civic discourse to the citizens of the fledgling Athenian democracy, to those who have the right and the duty to discuss the public good in their condition as equals before the law. It would not have made sense to teach the rules of rhetoric in communicating with slaves or irrational animals. Unlike citizens, they do not participate in deliberation about the public good nor in tasks of government.

Today as in Aristotle's time, there are people who seem to have a knack, a natural gift, for communication and persuasion. Others, through no fault of their own, seem to be almost completely bereft of it. However be the case, both types of persons could always hone their rhetorical skills by studying the principles of speech and composition, by observing and imitating successful speakers and writers, and by constant practice. Aristotle was well aware of the controversy surrounding the art of rhetoric and its teaching. Socrates, first, and Plato, like him, both thought that rhetoric as practiced by Gorgias, Isocrates and the Sophists amounted to nothing more than mere flattery, the use of empty words and misleading arguments to one's own advantage, a brazen appeal to emotions without regard to knowledge of the truth. Partly in reaction, Plato described his ideal rhetorician in the dialogue *Phaedrus* as a virtuous person with a firm knowledge of the subject under discussion; one who has mastered the logical techniques of exposition and who understands the mind of his audience well enough, to the point that he becomes capable of leading them to the experience of the truth. For Plato, therefore, the only valid form of rhetoric was one that wedded persuasive skills with personal virtue and love of truth. In no other instance would language abilities, by themselves, be enough.

Aristotle, for his part, held that rhetoric as a communication art was morally neutral. It could be used for good or for ill, and to that extent it was independent of both truth and virtue. This was largely the spirit with which he wrote his treatise. He was careful, however, not to separate rhetoric from ethics completely; rather, he insisted on its subordination to the architectonic subject of politics (NE 1094b). As Aristotle cogently argued, the study of rhetoric is useful – almost necessary – for three main reasons (Rh 1355a–b). Firstly, because without rhetoric, the truth can be easily defeated in debate, for true knowledge alone may not be enough to persuade certain audiences who rely on uncontrasted feelings and opinions. Secondly, rhetoric helps the speaker understand the real state of an issue by giving him a chance to consider both sides, thus enabling him to refute an opponent with less difficulty. And thirdly, rhetoric permits one to defend himself without recourse to physical violence as in cases of false accusation, for example.

According to Aristotle, there are three instruments available to the speaker or potential leader in order to persuade his public or his followers: the speech or argument itself (*logos*), the character (*ethos*) of the speaker and the emotional disposition (*pathos*) of the listeners or audience (Rh 1356a).

Speech or argument persuades in the measure that it shows the truth, or at least, a semblance of truth, in a particular case. As we have already seen, the truth or the appearance of truth, although necessary, may nevertheless prove insufficient in convincing others because certain audiences may not be able to follow complicated reasonings and are wont to rely on common beliefs or untested intuitions in their decisions. This should not be taken to mean that true reasoning has to be abandoned; rather one should just realize its limitations, due to circumstances foreign to reasoning itself.

Persuasion could also come about when the public is led by the speech to experience the appropriate emotions; these emotions, in turn, become the sources or triggers of choice and action. Those who hold a purely technical view of rhetoric focus exclusively on the role of the listeners' emotions. Nevertheless, aside from the listener's emotion or state of mind, it is also relevant to consider in regard to whom a particular emotion is directed and for what reason. Aristotle strikes a balance by recognizing, on one hand, the role of emotions in human judgment and by making it clear, on the other, that emotions are not the deciding factor in persuasion. Insofar as human judgment is affected by emotions, it is not an entirely rational act, but neither should the influence of emotions be exaggerated to the detriment of reason.

The character of the speaker is what Aristotle considers to be the controlling factor in persuasion: 'we believe fair-minded people to a greater extent and more quickly [than we do others] on all subjects in general and completely so in cases where there is not exact knowledge but room for doubt' (Rh 1356a). Listeners are convinced mainly by the image of trustworthiness that a speaker or potential leader projects. Now then, what better way to assure an image of trustworthiness than by being trustworthy as a matter of fact?

Regarding the personal qualities that a speaker or an aspiring leader should possess to be credible before an audience, Aristotle lists three: practical wisdom (*phronesis*), virtue (*arete*) and good will (*eunoia*) (Rh 1378a). By so doing, he goes farther than most leadership scholars who simply cite trust as the basis of the relationship without going further. In fact, Aristotle traces a speaker or a leader's trustworthiness to the confluence of the three aforementioned qualities. Practical wisdom permits one to form correct opinions over concrete, contingent issues; virtue prods him to express his views justly and fairly; and good will ensures that he give the best advice for the benefit of his listeners. A person who displays these characteristics – constitutive not only of trustworthiness or credibility, but also of moral capital – necessarily becomes persuasive to his listeners. Because of this, most likely, he'll also be successful and effective as a leader.

The qualities of a persuasive speaker – as we have seen, identical to those of a good leader – could then be employed in the service of any of the following purposes (Rh 1358b): in a deliberative mode, to exhort or to dissuade from a certain future action, by showing its potential advantage or harm; in a judicial mode, to approve what is just or to condemn what is unjust in past actions; or in a demonstrative mode, to point out what is honourable or shameful in a thing or a person, without calling for any immediate action. Whatever end the leader pursues in communicating with his followers substantially coincides with any one of the above-mentioned purposes. With respect to future actions, he may want to exhort or dissuade them, on the basis of potential advantage or harm; with regard to past actions, he may want to move them to uphold innocence or

to condemn guilt; and with regard to present examples, he may want to distinguish what is honest from what is not. A convincing speaker and leader would
be able to accomplish this through the personality that he projects, in the first
place; although certainly, he would also have to count on the clarity and
tightness of his arguments and on the sympathetic feelings or emotions that he
manages to elicit among his listeners.

IV.   IN BRIEF

- As we learn from the Enron experience, no amount of human, intellectual, or social capital could make up for the lack of moral capital among
  workers for the long-term success of a business enterprise. Without moral
  capital, all other forms of capital could easily turn from the source of a
  firm's advantage to the cause of its downfall. They are a double-edged
  sword that could be used equally for the good as for the bad.
- Ideally, moral capital relates to human, intellectual and social capital by
  encapsulating them, like the biggest piece in a nest of tables or in a
  collection of Russian dolls. However, if in the beginning one only had
  his moral capital to count on, it should nevertheless be easier for him to
  acquire the human, intellectual and social capital that he lacks, rather than
  proceeding the other way around.
- Moral capital is excellence of character, or the practice of virtues appropriate for a human being within a sociocultural context. Integrity is a
  useful synonym. Virtues behave as capital insofar as they are productive
  capacities that grow through proper investment of time, effort, and other
  resources. Unlike other forms of capital that focus on just one aspect (for
  example wealth, health, intelligence or social connections), virtues perfect
  the human being as a whole; that is, as a person in all dimensions.
- In the Aristotelian tradition, virtue or human excellence is discovered
  through appropriate inquiry into what human beings are (their nature)
  and what human beings are for (their final end). On account of their
  nature, human beings are social and rational animals. On account of their
  final end, human beings seek happiness, a flourishing, shared existence
  within a polity.
- In the Platonic tradition – Socratic irony notwithstanding – virtue may
  be explained in the following terms: it is a form of knowledge; it is
  unitary; it requires special learning (and correlatively, special teaching)
  because it could only be acquired through practice; and in practicing it,
  one can do no wrong (therefore, evil could only be the result of ignorance
  on the part of the agent).

- Moral capital or virtue arises from the positive feedback among three operational levels that constitute the human being: actions, habits and character. A virtuous character comes from possessing virtuous habits and virtuous habits come from the performance of virtuous actions. The reverse is also true: virtuous habits issue into virtuous actions and a virtuous character predisposes one to acquire virtuous habits.
- Given the impossibility of completely foreseeing how human endeavors develop, the need for leadership becomes inescapable. There always comes a point at which someone has to make a decision without having clear rules to rely on. Fundamentally, a leader provides an organization with a vision and a strength of will to effect and direct change.
- The most successful definitions of leadership emphasize its being a reciprocal relationship – that is, one that requires voluntary followership, a partnership of sorts – in which goals are set in common (Rost). However, theoretical, definitional issues are only secondary in importance to the practical matter of good leadership. A good leader is one who is morally upright and professionally effective at the same time (Ciulla).
- The supreme test of leadership consists in overcoming resistance or opposition from one's potential followers. In the final analysis, the alternative posed is between force (or fear) and persuasion (something more akin to love). The second option determines moral leadership: a two-way transformative and morally uplifting relationship between a leader and his followers (Burns). Stewardship (Block) and servant-leadership (Greenleaf) may be taken as different kinds of moral leadership.
- Moral leadership is based on the trustworthiness of the leader rather than on his charisma (Solomon). Trustworthiness is a token for moral capital or virtue of character. The focus on virtue of character as the most powerful means of persuasion furnishes the link between modern leadership studies and classical rhetoric, understood as the art of persuasion.
- Although rhetoric as a communication art is morally neutral, Aristotle took pains to subordinate it to politics and ethics in his overall structure of the sciences. By so doing he distanced himself equally from Socrates and Plato, for whom no independent skill of rhetoric was possible, as well as from Gorgias, Isocrates and the Sophists, for whom rhetoric was completely divorced from ethics and politics.
- Aristotelian rhetoric lists three means available to the speaker – or leader – in persuading his audience: speech or the argument itself (*logos*), the character a speaker projects (*ethos*) and the emotional dispositions of the listeners (*pathos*). Among these, character is the controlling element of persuasion. Aristotle also enumerates three character traits or personal qualities that a speaker or an aspiring leader should possess, to give a

semblance of trustworthiness before potential followers: practical wisdom (*phronesis*), virtue (*arete*) and good will (*eunoia*).
• Parallelisms could be made between the purposes of a persuasive speaker and the objectives that a moral leader may pursue: to exhort or to dissuade from future action by the use of the deliberative mode; to approve or to condemn past action through the judicial mode; or simply, to indicate what is honorable or shameful in a person or a thing at present, by way of the demonstrative mode.

REFERENCES

Aristotle (1985), *Nicomachean Ethics*, trans. Terence Irwin, Indianapolis, IN: Hackett Publishing.
Aristotle (1991), *Aristotle on Rhetoric: A Theory of Civic Discourse*, trans. George A. Kennedy, Oxford: Oxford University Press.
Barboza, D. and J. Schwartz (2002), 'The wizard behind Enron's deals', *The New York Times*, 6 February.
Bennis, Warren and Burt Nanus (1978), *Leaders: The Strategies for Taking Charge*, New York: Harper & Row.
Block, Peter (1993), *Stewardship: Choosing Service Over Self-Interest*, San Francisco: Berret-Koehler Publishers.
Burns, James MacGregor (1978), *Leadership*, New York: Harper & Row.
Casson, Mark (2000), *Enterprise and Leadership: Studies on Firms, Markets and Networks*, Cheltenham, UK and Northampton, MA, USA: Edward Elgar.
Ciulla, Joanne B. (1998), 'Leadership ethics: mapping the territory', in Joanne B. Ciulla (ed.), *Ethics, The Heart of Leadership*, Westport, CN: Praeger.
Eichenwald, K. and D.B. Henriques (2002), 'Web of details did Enron in as warnings went unheeded', *The New York Times*, 10 February.
Glater, J.D. and M. Brick (2002), 'Ex-official says Enron employees shredded papers', *The New York Times*, 22 January.
Greenleaf, Robert K. (1977), *Servant Leadership: A Journey into the Nature of Legitimate Power and Greatness*, Mahwah, NJ: Paulist Press.
Herbert, B. (2002), 'Silencing the alarm', *The New York Times*, 14 January.
Keller, B. (2002), 'Enron for dummies', *The New York Times*, 26 January.
Knowledge at Wharton (2001), 'Oh, the games Enron played', 22 November.
Kouzes, James M. and Barry Z. Posner (1993), *Credibility: How Leaders Gain and Lose It, Why People Demand It*, San Francisco: Jossey-Bass.
Labaton, S. and R. Oppel, Jr (2002), 'Testimony of Enron executives is contradictory', *The New York Times*, 8 February.
New York Times, The (2001), 'Did Ken Lay understand what was happening at Enron?', 16 November.
Nicomachean Ethics (see Aristotle).
Norris, F. (2002), 'Chief used stock to repay loan, lawyer says', *The New York Times*, 15 January.
Oppel, R., Jr (2001), 'Former head of Enron denies wrongdoing', *The New York Times*, 22 December.

Oppel, R., Jr (2002a), 'Auditor received warning on Enron five months ago', *The New York Times*, 17 January.

Oppel, R., Jr (2002b), 'Wide effort seen in shredding data on Enron's audits', *The New York Times*, 24 January.

Oppel, R., Jr (2002c), 'Ex-chief of Enron will not testify before congress', *The New York Times*, 11 February.

Oppel, R., Jr and K. Eichenwald (2002), 'Arthur Andersen fires an executive for Enron orders', *The New York Times*, 16 January.

Oppel, R., Jr and S. Labaton (2002), 'Enron hearings open, focusing on destroyed papers', *The New York Times*, 25 January.

Oppel, R., Jr and A.R. Sorkin (2001), 'Enron files largest U.S. claim for bankruptcy', *The New York Times*, 3 December.

Phaedrus (see Plato).

Plato (1953), *The Dialogues of Plato*, trans. by B. Jowett, vols. I–IV, Oxford: Clarendon Press.

Protagoras (see Plato).

Rhetoric (see Aristotle).

Rost, Joseph (1993), *Leadership for the Twenty-First Century*, Westport, CN: Praeger.

Schwartz, J. (2002), 'Darth Vader. Machiavelli. Skilling set intense pace', *The New York Times*, 7 February.

Solomon, Robert C. (1998), 'Ethical leadership, emotions, and trust: beyond "charisma"', in Joanne B. Ciulla (ed.), *Ethics, The Heart of Leadership*, Westport, CN: Praeger.

van Natta, D., Jr. and A. Berenson (2002), 'Enron's chairman received warning about accounting', *The New York Times*, 15 January.

Walker, S. (2002), 'Enron: stakeholder – not just shareholder – relations at its worst', *Stakeholder Power*, 30 January.

Weber, J., D. Little, D. Henry and L. Lavelle (2001), 'Arthur Andersen. How bad will it get?', *Business Week*, 24 December.

Yardley, J. (2002), 'Influence lost, ex-Enron chief faces congress', *The New York Times*, 3 February.

Yardley, J. and J. Schwartz (2002), 'Calling inquiries a distraction, Enron chief quits under pressure', *The New York Times*, 24 January.

Zellner, W. (2001), 'Skilling: the man who knew ... how much?', *Business Week*, 10 December.

3. Actions, moral capital's basic currency

The key to developing moral capital consists in taking advantage of the dynamics among three operational levels found in the human being, namely, the level of actions, the level of habits and the level of character. Among these levels, actions are the elementary building blocks and may be considered the basic currency of moral capital. This means that nothing in a human agent acquires moral significance unless it issues into actions or comes as a consequence of actions. Until then, it could only be regarded as something that happens to an individual; not something that he does nor something for which he is responsible. Certainly these happenings or events could be judged as good (for example, when one wins the lottery) or bad (when the same person loses the winning ticket to thieves), but we never interpret them as reflecting the ethical quality of the individual to whom they occur. In this chapter we shall look into the elements and conditions of actions – the things that make these acts human – as well as the criteria according to which actions are judged ethically valuable or good.

We shall likewise examine – by way of extended accounts of business experiences – how particular actions on the part of company leaders determine their personal future and that of their firm. We shall show not only how personal and corporate fates are linked, but also how favorable economic consequences somehow derive from sound, ethical decisions. This should not be taken to mean, however, that economic consequences justify ethical decisions, for moral choices sometimes bring along with them unavoidable loss and suffering. Strictly speaking, ethical choices or actions should be their own reason for being. Nevertheless, there is no harm in knowing that these same decisions could result in economically advantageous situations besides. This would definitely contribute to their persuasive power, serving as an additional incentive to do good, and further strengthening the case for moral leadership.

I. THE FORD–FIRESTONE FINGER-POINTING EXERCISE

The Ford Explorer was the US's best selling sport utility vehicle (SUV) in the 1990s. Together with other Ford SUV models – the Expedition, the Lincoln Navigator, and the Excursion – they accounted for a fifth of the company's sales and the bulk of its profits, with margins ranging from $10,000 to $18,000 per unit. No wonder, then, that the Ford factory in Wayne, Michigan, that churned out Expeditions and Navigators was the most profitable in any industry the world over, generating $3 billion a year in pre-tax profits (Bradsher 2000b).

SUVs, however, also had an ominous side to them. They unquenchably guzzled fuel, getting a mere 10 to 13 miles to the gallon, depending on whether it was city or country driving. At the same time, they emitted up to 5.5 times more smog-causing fumes than cars. Even worse was the safety threat they posed, to their occupants as well as to those of other vehicles (Bradsher 2000a). SUVs had a greater tendency to roll over and had fewer crumple zones than cars. Furthermore, they were found to be three times deadlier than cars to other drivers in head-on collisions, tending to ride-over the other automobile's front seats. When it came to side crashes, SUV records weren't any better. Their higher hoods were wont to inflict greater damage to the other vehicle and more serious injury to passengers. Since 1997, several studies had established a positive link between SUV designs and motorist deaths, yet, for at least three more years, SUV makers consistently denied any truth in such claims. Only in March 2000 did SUV manufacturers finally acknowledge the grave risks their vehicles presented, and adopt pertinent safety measures for the first time.

On 9 August 2000, after investigating dozens of complaints and 21 fatal accidents involving SUVs, particularly the Ford Explorer, Bridgestone/Firestone announced the recall of some 6.5 million tires, belonging to the ATX, ATX II and Wilderness models (Deutsch 2000). Memories of a government-ordered recall that nearly drove it bankrupt haunted the tire company, formerly known as Firestone Tire and Rubber, before it was bought by the Bridgestone Corporation of Japan in 1988. In 1978 Firestone was fined $500,000 by federal regulators and forced to retrieve more than 14 million defective 500-series tires. This time around, Firestone withstood only about a week's worth of horror stories before reacting to public demands. It put up a hotline for motorists and offered to replace all affected tires, no questions asked. Initially, Firestone had given itself an 18-month period for the recall, beginning with the southern and western states, since tire problems seemed to grow worse in hot weather driving. But lawyers and safety advocates later on prevailed on the company to step up the pace and widen the scope of replacements. In its damage control efforts, Firestone was able to trace the root of the problem to its Decatur, Illinois plant, particularly with the tires manufactured there between 1994 and 1996. During those years, the factory was experiencing intense labor disputes and was operated largely by non-union replacement workers (Bradsher 2000c).

The first disagreements between Ford and Firestone on the issue of optimum tire pressure surfaced immediately after the recall. Firestone recommended that tires be inflated at 30 lbs/in^2, whereas Ford suggested that anywhere between 26 and 30 lbs/in^2 would be all right (Deutsch 2000). Tire makers normally recommended higher pressure because this lessened the surface area in contact with the road, thus decreasing risks of tread separation, blowout and other forms of wear or failure due to heat. Automakers, on the other hand, routinely suggested lower pressure, because softer tires gave smoother rides. The enhanced comfort was very noticeable in the case of SUVs, since these were equipped with stiff truck suspensions. On 15 August 2000, the US Federal Government released data showing that nearly all of the deaths linked to Firestone tires occured when the SUVs – the majority of which were Ford Explorers – rolled over after experiencing tire failure (Bradsher 2000d).

A few days earlier, however, Ford released documents showing that Firestone first became aware of the tire flaws way back in 1997, through numerous injury and property damage complaints (Bradsher 2000c). Yet, apparently, the tire company chose to keep quiet. In late July 2000, Ford carried out its own analysis of the data provided by Firestone, focusing on the problematic ATX, ATX II and Wilderness tires with which it fitted its SUVs. Ford discovered that while there were just one to six per million tread separation claims for Wilderness tires produced in plants other than Decatur, the claims for Wilderness tires from Decatur rose to more than 50 per million in 1996 and 1997. Similarly, the claims for ATX tires from Decatur between 1994 and 1996 ballooned to the range of 350 to 650 per million, whereas the figure for the same tires produced elsewhere hardly approached 100 claims per million. There was also talk of how disgruntled workers from the Decatur plant manually pierced blisters in the flawed tires then sent them back to the warehouse for sale, instead of scrapping them. For their part, Firestone representatives hastened to discredit these stories, standing firmly by their replacement workers and factory procedures.

Less than a week after Ford aired its claims against Firestone, a group of lawyers representing crash victims made public a Ford memo indicating that it had in the past considered using tires with higher pressure for the Explorer (Bradsher 2000e). In the end, Ford decided against these tires, because they would have increased the risks of the vehicle's turning turtle, and instead, the automaker settled for the ones that Firestone was currently recalling. The lawyers made the charge that the Explorer's design was inherently flawed, since the vehicle was prone to tipping over. Ford officials, on the other hand, strongly defended the stability of the Explorer, asserting that it even had a 20 to 24 per cent lower death rate than other mid-sized SUVs in crashes. Ford engineers also said that the decision against higher pressure tires was not due to rollover concerns. Rather, what the automaker sought was to improve maneuverability and gain better control of cornering forces.

Meanwhile, the only sign of cooperation between the two embattled companies was the Ford announcement on 21 August 2000 that it would close three Explorer plants for two weeks to reduce output (Bradsher 2000f). This measure would make an extra 70,000 Firestone tires available for replacement.

Industry analysts found this resolution quite heroic on the part of Ford, since it was already short on Explorers and had been struggling to keep up with market demand for years. Ford executives maintained that they were simply putting customer safety and satisfaction above profit concerns. Legal experts, nonetheless, surmised that the motor company was actually trying to limit its liability exposure.

Towards the end of August 2000, federal regulators demanded that Ford disclose whatever previous knowledge it had of tire and SUV problems outside the US (Labaton 2000a). Seemingly, Ford had been receiving complaints about Firestone tires on its Explorers for a long time, first in Venezuela in 1998, then in Saudi Arabia in 1999, and during the first quarter of 2000 in Thailand. Nevertheless, the motor company did not inform US regulators until the Firestone tire recall at the beginning of August 2000.

During the US Congressional hearings in September 2000, it became evident that both Ford and Firestone had substantial information on tire failure and vehicle rollovers for the past two years, yet they equally kept silent about it. Instead, the two companies continued to sell their products to the American market and elsewhere without issuing any form of warning.

In some respects, Firestone had been more forthcoming, with its Chairman and CEO Masatoshi Ono pronouncing the following words in one of the sessions at Capitol Hill: 'I come before you to apologize to you, the American people and especially to the families who have lost loved ones in these terrible rollover accidents' (Bradsher and Wald 2000). Investigators had unearthed a Firestone document, dated 19 January 2000, where its financial managers calculated that 64 per cent of the total $2.88 million in claims for tread separation in 1999 originated from tires produced in a single plant, Decatur, Illinois, out of the ten that the company operated in North America. Previously, Firestone alleged that it had not noticed any problem with its tires until early August 2000, when the results of the Ford analysis came out.

Another memo, this time from Ford, dated March 1999, revealed that Firestone was reluctant to send letters to tire owners in Saudi Arabia for replacements. The tire company feared that it would be banned from the Saudi market as a result, and that later on, it would be forced to inform the US Department of Transportation of the recall program. However, the author of the memo, a Ford executive named Chuck Seilnacht, admitted in the same document that a colleague at Ford had shared Firestone's concerns. Finally, Ford – unlike Firestone – sent a letter to Saudi consumers telling them to have a change of tires. The automaker shouldered the replacement costs entirely by itself, since Firestone contended that the tire failures were due to customer misuse and refused to pay. But just the same, neither did Ford inform American officials of the incidents in Saudi Arabia, despite having carried out the recall program.

Parallel investigations in Venezuela yielded the same silences and denials, identical accusations and counteraccusations between Ford and Firestone (Reuters 2000, Bradsher 2000g). According to Ford's Venezuela manager, Firestone had assured Ford in 1999 that there were no problems with its tires, even as the tire company compiled information about manufacturing defects. Local Firestone officials, for their part, refused to accept blame, and insisted that the tires were made to the specifications of the motor company. At any rate, Firestone Venezuela contended that the tire failures were isolated cases caused by customer abuse and poor maintenance. In August 2000, the Venezuelan Consumer Protection Agency reported that inadequate suspensions on Ford Explorers together with weak Firestone Wilderness AT tires led to high-speed blowouts causing at least 46 deaths in that country.

In stark contrast to the apologies of Bridgestone/Firestone Chairman Ono, the testimony of Jaques Nasser, Ford's CEO, had always been a self-exculpatory: 'This is a tire issue, not a vehicle issue' (Bradsher and Wald 2000). However, this was a line increasingly difficult to hold in the wake of mounting evidence. US Department of Transportation statistics showed that from 1995 to 1998, fatal crashes involving Explorers were nearly three times as likely to cite tires as a contributing factor compared to other SUVs; although admittedly drawing such an inference from the database was not an easy task (Wald and Barbanel 2000). A finer analysis of the data would have also revealed that between 1996 and 1997, when Ford plants alternatively fitted Explorers with Firestone and Goodyear tires, there was only one fatal accident involving Goodyear tires against nine involving Firestone tires. When asked why Ford did not take action in the US, once it had replaced Firestone tires in Saudi Arabia, Malaysia and Venezuela, Nasser retorted that its review of databases indicated – wrongly, as it later turned out – that it wasn't a problem in the States. In the same vein, Nasser affirmed that the cases overseas were mere anecdotal data, not something worth reporting to US agencies. The most that Ford would concede was that the Firestone tire defects blamed for scores of injuries and deaths, mainly in Ford Explorers, eluded detection because they occurred infrequently. Later, however, these defects certainly proved deadlier than other more common vehicle problems (Wald and Bradsher 2000).

During the hearings, John Lampe, Firestone's executive vice president, sought to focus the public's attention on the design of the Explorer itself (Wald 2000a). Of the 16,000 Explorer rollovers known at that time, tire failure was the cause of only a very small fraction, less than 10 per cent, Lampe asserted in his testimony.

A problem about which Ford was aware – despite its claims to the contrary – and yet did not inform regulators or consumers, was one involving its 'thick film ignition' system (Labaton and Bergman 2000). In the 1980s and 1990s, Ford car owners often complained that their vehicles would unexpectedly stall on highways or while making left turns across oncoming traffic. Company officials repeatedly assured that there was no way to find out what could be causing the problem. But all along, Ford engineers, safety officials and even board members knew that its computerized ignition system was shutting the engine down whenever it grew too hot.

As early as April 1982 Ford engineers had already raised concerns regarding the overheating of the ignition module. In January 1984, a warranty analysis disclosed that the ignition system – which was supposed to last the vehicle's lifetime – in fact failed at a rate of 56 per cent after five years, or after covering a distance of 50,000 miles. In July 1985, the company organized a task force to study why the ignition module failed even within the warranty period in hot climates, or after warranty expiration in temperate ones. In the meantime, Ford continued to tell government agencies that there was 'no common pattern or cause' in the stalling complaints. In October 1986, on the same day that regulators closed investigations because Ford had assured them that there was nothing to warrant a recall, the company board discussed the elevated costs – more than $200 million – of fixing the module. In November of that year a report was supposedly submitted to Harold A. Poling, then Ford's chairman, although he denied ever having received it. By that moment, the potential cost of an across the board fix would have already surpassed the $429 million mark and, for this reason, it was no longer feasible. Ford then decided in favor of a limited notification and replacement program, knowing fully well that the alternative for motorists was a 'quit on the road'. In July 1988, a memo from the electrical and electronic division strongly urged the 'thick film ignition' system be discounted in future models because it was 'not consistent with company quality goals'. Not until the 1996 models – that is, after nine long years of stonewalling – did Ford actually stop using these ignition systems (Labaton and Bergman 2000).

On 13 April 2001 a California judge ordered Ford to replace defective ignition devices on an estimated two million cars statewide, at a cost of around $300 million (The Associated Press 2001). Similar cases were pending in other states and could coalesce into a class-action suit affecting some 20 million vehicles all over the US. At a cost of $150 per vehicle, the replacement program could cost Ford a total of $3 billion, although only around 60 per cent of the damaged vehicles are normally reached. The decision, however, came too late, at least for the victims of fatal crashes and serious injuries, several of whom had already reached informal settlements with Ford. A study presented by the plaintiffs – and cited by the judge's decision – alleged that drivers of the 22 million Ford cars equipped with the defective ignition device faced 9 per cent increased chances of figuring in a fatal crash (Labaton 2000b).

Going back to the tire and rollover problems, if proven that Ford and Firestone were aware of them and yet did nothing, federal regulators at that time could impose fines of up to $925,000 on both companies, aside from mandating a recall of the defective products. The two companies and their executives could also be held liable and face criminal charges for injuries and deaths, from the time they learned of the product defects onwards.

On 11 October 2000 the US Congress passed a bill that raised civil and criminal penalties for failing to report defects in cars and tires. The legislation also required automakers to notify US regulators of vehicle part replacements they conduct in other countries for safety reasons (Wald 2000b). That same day, Masatochi Ono, the chairman and CEO of Bridgestone/Firestone, tendered his resignation and was replaced by John Lampe, until then the executive vice president of the American subsidiary.

It was not until December 2000 that Firestone engineers finally offered an explanation for the slew of accidents involving their tires (Bradsher 2000h). They blamed an unfortunate mix of tire and vehicle design, tire manufacturing errors and customer abuse for the mishaps. They likewise asserted that by allowing the Explorer's weight to swell in the mid-1990s, Ford further cut into an already slender safety margin in the tires' load-bearing capacities. From the Firestone engineers' perspective, drivers too could have shared part of the fault, to the extent that they kept tires underinflated or fixed flats incorrectly.

Ford took a bit more time to respond. And when it did, four months later, the automaker attributed the accidents mainly to Firestone's poor design and manufacture of tires, aggravated by improper consumer maintenance (Bradsher 2001a). Ford firmly rejected the idea that the Explorer's design made it more vulnerable to tire blowouts than other midsize SUVs. Similarly, the automaker contended that since SUVs had to be able to perform heavy duty tasks, like towing trailers, they needed the extra weight.

The dispute between Ford and Firestone reached its boiling point in May 2001, when the tire company announced that it would stop selling tires to the automaker, thus severing a century-old corporate relationship (Bradsher 2001b). The two companies' respective founders, Henry Ford and Harvey S. Firestone, were already friends even before the establishment of either firm. Moreover, one of Henry Ford's grandsons married a granddaughter of Harvey S. Firestone, and to that union was born William C. Ford – current chairman of Ford Motor Corporation – as the only son. Firestone's decision was in fact a pre-emptive strike, because the following day Ford made public its intention to replace 13 million Firestone Wilderness AT tires with other brands, like Goodyear or Michelin. The recall program was estimated to cost Ford $3 billion.

Jacques Nasser, Ford's president and CEO, curtly declared at a news conference, 'We simply do not have enough confidence in the future of these tires' keeping our customers safe.' A statement to which John Lampe, Firestone's president and CEO, responded, 'Our tires are safe ... When we have a problem, we admit it and we fix it. The real issue here is the safety of the

Explorer.' Shortly after the exchange of salvoes, Firestone asked the US Trans-portation Department to open an investigation of the Ford Explorer, claiming that its design made it prone to rollover crashes whenever tires failed. It was the first time that a parts supplier sought a federal investigation of an automaker (Bradsher 2001c).

But it wasn't only Ford and Firestone that had lost confidence in each other. William C. Ford, Ford's chairman, also seemed to have lost faith in Jacques Nasser, his CEO. First came a corporate reshuffling in June 2001, in which Ford, the chairman, gained important executive powers, and Nasser was made to share responsibilities with some other senior executives. Supposedly, the reason was to allow Nasser to pay better attention to vehicle quality issues. Nonetheless, the power-sharing arrangement between the two men didn't seem to work, or at least didn't seem to work for very long. By the end of October 2001, Nasser was out of the executive suite and Ford assumed full control of the corporation, the first family member in a generation to do so (Burt 2001).

By November 2001, the US Highway Traffic Safety Administration had set the total count of the combined Ford–Firestone victims at 271 deaths and 700 serious injuries (Mayer and Johnson 2001). Both Ford and Firestone had tried to reach out-of-court settlements in the hundreds of lawsuits involving tread separations and vehicle rollovers. Aside from apologies, these agreements typically included disbursements in the tens of millions of dollars: as purport-edly was the case of Donna Bailey, a woman from Texas who became quadriplegic after her Explorer rolled over due to tread separation. Those elevated sums still seemed a reasonable price for both companies to pay, however, if only to avoid rending public trials and thus be able to put the scandal behind them as quickly as possible (Winerip 2001). The Bailey case was an exceptionally strong one from the plaintiff's perspective. The police report indicated that the accident occurred on a flat pavement, with no signs of driving error, and that the victim was found hanging by her seat belt inside the overturned vehicle.

That same month, November 2001, Firestone partly made good its apologies by agreeing to pay \$41.5 million to the different states. By so doing, it averted charges of deceptive and unfair trade for selling tires that were later recalled (Hakim 2001, Mayer and Johnson 2001). Additionally, the tire company set aside a \$10 million fund to reimburse consumers for replacing tires with other brands. So far, the case as a whole had already cost Bridgestone/Firestone more than \$1 billion, a large chunk of which was earmarked for settling claims in over 400 private lawsuits.

Aside from the dead and the injured, one could also include among the casualties the thousands of workers laid off due to the weakened financial situation of the companies (Barboza 2001). First to go were about 450 Firestone employees in October 2000, followed by 1,100 more in November 2000. Then came an additional 1,500 as the blighted Decatur plant closed down in June 2001. A great number of those employees were union workers, with more than 20 years of experience on the job.

Senator Ernest F. Hollings from South Carolina once likened the Ford–Firestone hearings to 'tying two cats by the tail and throwing them over the clothesline and letting them claw at each other' (Wald 2000a). It was a vivid description not only of the proceedings, but also of the two companies' overall attitudes. Both Ford and Firestone seemed to be more concerned with denying their own responsibility for the accidents than with giving plausible explanations of why these had ever occurred. Each one desperately sought to cover up its own mistakes and oversights, and pin the blame on the other. Yet neither hesitated in letting consumers and regulators carry their part of the fault. The hundreds of out of court settlements that both companies deftly engineered – with apologies, yes, but with no admissions of guilt – were just another form of whitewashing, albeit a very expensive one. They were rather costly ways of silencing or sound-proofing scandals, yet ingenious and, to a degree, effective.

Every effort was taken to avoid straight answers to the crucial questions of what did each company know and when. Because together with that knowledge, acquired at a given moment, came the responsibility over particular actions and their consequences.

Firestone had been aware of the tire problems since 1997, judging by the property damage and injury complaints it had been compiling. With its experience in Venezuela, Ford, too, was aware of the tire risks, and it could have been alerted to the effect of the Explorer's design on those risks, at least since 1998. Certainly, Ford's decision to carry out a tire recall on its own, in Venezuela, Saudi Arabia and Malaysia, without Firestone's support or cooperation, was very commendable. But why did neither company inform consumers and regulators in other countries, not the least in the US, of the serious dangers to which they were exposed? Did cost–benefit analyses once more get the better of them?

What is most troubling here was the pattern, first of silences, then of denials and, when pushed against the wall, of counteraccusations in the behavior of the two companies and their management teams. Apparently, Ford had not learned its lesson well enough in the Pinto episode a few decades ago, as it had to come up with this deplorable sequel starring the Explorer, with the thick film ignition system as a side attraction. Something similar could be said of Firestone, with regard to the defective 500-series tires it sold in the 1970s, and to the Wilderness, ATX and ATX II models that it marketed as of late. In both Ford and Firestone, and among the executives they had at the helm, there had been an excess of zeal in finding fault with others, and perhaps a dearth of courage in assuming responsibility for their own actions.

II. MY BROTHER'S KEEPER: HOWARD LUTNICK OF CANTOR FITZGERALD

Cantor Fitzgerald, L.P. is a financial brokerage firm dealing mainly with American Treasury bonds, where it eventually came to hold a 90 per cent share of the market. It was founded in 1945 by Bernie Cantor, a former hot dog vendor at the Yankee Stadium, who went on to become the world's largest collector of Rodin sculptures. Cantor Fitzgerald's other businesses included portfolio trading, investment banking, financial spread betting, market advice, energy brokerage, CO_2 emissions trading and, since 1999, electronic trading technology, as parent of eSpeed, Inc. The company eSpeed is an interactive electronic marketplace for both financial and non-financial B2B commerce. Its global private network provides the infrastructure through which financial instruments worth over $200 billion are transacted daily. For the past few years, Cantor had been migrating its core bond-trading business among institutional clients from expensive, human traders to eSpeed's less-expensive electronic trading system (Henriques 2001b). Until 11 September 2001, both Cantor and eSpeed were headquartered at One World Trade Center (North Tower), New York City, with around a thousand employees occupying floors 101, 103, 104 and 105.

Howard Lutnick was Bernie Cantor's protégé and took over the firm when the latter fell seriously ill in 1996. Perhaps he was so quick and eager to fill in Cantor's shoes that he provoked the ire of his mentor's wife, Iris, engaging her in a bitter courtroom battle for company control (Henriques 2001a). Eventually, upon Iris's instructions, Lutnick was blocked from attending Bernie Cantor's funeral. Since then, some brushes with market regulators plus a couple of other business disputes aggressively pursued in court have contributed in creating a ruthless, hard as nails and prickly as barbed-wire image for Lutnick. Shortly before the tragedy, he had fired almost 300 bond traders after reassuring them that their jobs were secure (Gordon 2001). Apparently, these workers were unable to adapt their skills to the Internet trading system the company had developed.

That fateful September morning when the Twin Towers were attacked, Lutnick was taking his five-year-old son, Kyle, to his first day at kindergarten school. That saved him from certain death. His brother, Gary, together with 658 other Cantor and eSpeed employees were not as lucky and perished. No other firm lost so many of its staff in that tragedy.

On the following day, 12 September 2001, Lutnick issued a statement wherein he clearly set his priorities as Cantor and eSpeed Chairman (Cantor 2001a). The first was to learn of the whereabouts of Cantor employees and provide for the welfare of their families, and the second to continue with the work of their lost colleagues, convinced that this was the best memorial in their honor. His determination and commitment to these two goals have been unswerving since then, despite suspicion and misunderstanding from within the firms and without.

From that moment onwards, Lutnick began addressing the survivors' and the victims' families as his own. In a statement a week after the disaster in which he eulogized some members of senior management, Lutnick wrote:

> eSpeed has always been more than a team, or a vision, or even a company. At its heart eSpeed is a family. As a family, we mourn the losses of our siblings, our best friends – our partners. We cannot imagine work or life without them nor their vast array of qualities and characteristics that enhanced our lives ... All of our survivors are now bound together in a manner never seen before in business. We are a large family that has lost its brothers and sisters ... Godspeed to eSpeed – I love you (Cantor 2001e).

This was among the first of between 1,300 and 1,400 handwritten notes that Lutnick penned in the succeeding months directed to families of lost employees (Henriques 2002).

Lutnick's concern went well beyond words and sought to reach the overall well-being of surviving families. Throughout the week after the attacks, Cantor offered counseling and crisis-support services for its employees, families and friends at a local Manhattan hotel: 'We are fully committed to providing our employees and their loved ones with the tools to cope with this unprecedented tragedy. We are all feeling the devastation of this incredible loss and will join together to cope at this this terrible time', its chairman said (Cantor 2001b). Support groups and company-sponsored professional grief counseling as well as therapeutic retreats and camps were organized, with topics ranging from 'Managing Your Emotions, Time, Finances' to 'Believing and Trusting God'. Also included in these gatherings were courses, for example, on entrepreneurship and debt management for adults, and for youngsters, workshops on household repairs, floral arrangements and crafts. To attend to people's spiritual needs, a memorial service honoring fallen colleagues was celebrated, and the firm had even booked complimentary hotel rooms for those who were coming to New York from afar (Cantor 2001f).

But this show of care, even of familial affection, would all have come to naught, had the issue of the material and financial well-being of the surviving families been left unattended. After all, for most people, the main reason for coming to work – to Cantor, eSpeed or elsewhere – was to earn a living for themselves and their dependent families. How did Lutnick address these matters?

On 15 September 2001, Cantor promptly dropped its missing employees – almost 70 per cent of the total – from the payroll (Henriques 2001a). This brought down an avalanche of criticism from angry Cantor families, who thought that such a measure did not match Lutnick's tearful media image. It was certainly true that the employees were no longer working, but still, other firms kept missing workers on the payroll until families managed to get some safety net in place. Why couldn't Cantor do the same? Aside from being insensitive, wasn't this policy a bit too draconian? Was Lutnick sincere in his public mourning or was it just for show? Was he being plainly hypocritical? The hard fact was that neither Lutnick nor Cantor was under any legal obligation to do otherwise. And everybody knew it.

Rather than charge at the complaints at full force – thus adding fire to the flame – Cantor representatives tried their best to understand these reactions within context, that is, as emotional outbursts of people overwhelmed by their bereavement. They said that some relatives could just have been mistaken, or simply have not given the firm enough time to keep its promises. As someone speaking for the company commented: 'This was the most difficult by far of all the business decisions. But to have done otherwise would made it harder to restore the business that is so important to the long-term welfare of these families' (Henriques 2001a). Meanwhile, what did Lutnick do?

First of all, he persuaded the American Red Cross to give grants to families to enable them to meet living expenses for three months. A caseworker was also assigned to assist each family. Secondly, he instructed Cantor's insurance company to expedite payment of the $100,000 life policy due to each employee, without requiring the presentation of a formal death certificate. And thirdly, he promised that the company would maintain its fully paid health insurance for all families for a period of 12 months.

Typically, a major portion of a Cantor employee's income comes through the year-end bonus, the amount of which varies according to the firm's profitability and the individual worker's performance and contribution. Unfortunately, the records necessary for calculating those bonuses were destroyed, and at first there were no guarantees they could be reconstructed. However, the will on the part of the firm to meet those obligations on scheduled time was always unflinching. By 10 October 2001, Cantor had made public its resolution to expedite the distribution of bonuses in the following terms (Cantor 2001i): estates of employees in non-revenue producing departments would receive the full cash bonus paid in 2000, plus all accrued, unused 2001 vacation pay by 22 October; estates of employees in revenue producing departments would receive their bonuses and commissions based on restored records of client transactions by 22 November, Thanksgiving Day; and all the other employees would be getting their bonuses and commissions by December, in advance of normal company policy. Even employees who started working for the firm as recently as 10 September 2001, or those who had never reached the bonus plateau in the past – most probably, the people most in need – in the end received a minimum bonus of $5,000.

In the weeks after the tragedy, there were some qualms among relatives of missing Cantor partners regarding the fate of the obligatory partnership investments (Henriques 2001a). They feared that given the damage that the firm had sustained, the value at which those investments could be redeemed would be unfairly low. But the remaining partners – under Lutnick's leadership – had already taken a more than adequate decision to allay those fears. They had voted to allocate 25 per cent of year-end profits to the families of lost employees.

In another communiqué issued on 10 October, Cantor renewed its pledge to allocate 25 per cent of its profits for the next five years for the support of the families of its lost employees (Cantor 2001h). This amount would have otherwise been distributed among the partners. Instead, it would be used in part to pay for 10 years' worth of health care for the surviving families, at an estimated cost of $70 million, with the remainder being equally distributed – even beyond five years, if necessary – until every family received at least $100,000 in cash. In addition, non-supplemental life insurance policies were to be paid, at a rate of twice an employee's salary, tax-free, to a maximum of $100,000. On that occasion, for and on behalf of the partners, Lutnick remarked: 'While nothing can replace the loss of a loved one, we want to do everything we can to help ease the short-term financial burden on the families of our lost employees. It is because of the commitment and exceptional efforts of our surviving staff, working around the clock to rebuild our businesses, that we are in the position to make our previous statements a reality' (Cantor 2001i).

As with any other family, small children and their educational needs were the object of special concern on the part of the firm. For this purpose, initially, the Cantor Fitzgerald Relief Fund was put up, with a $1 million personal donation from Lutnick as seed money (Cantor 2001k). Before the events of 11 September, Lutnick – who owns a third of Cantor and 1.5 million shares of eSpeed – had a personal fortune calculated between $300 million and $1 billion (Gordon 2001). Since then, the fund had received more than 20,000 donations from all over the world reaching a total of $8.7 million. As the 2001 holiday season approached, the fund set for itself a new goal: to match all contributions received between then and the end of the year up to an amount of $5 million. Nearly 1,300 children – including those of Cantor suppliers and contractors who died in the attacks – were to benefit from the fund monies, receiving checks within the range of $1,500 to $5,000, for their educational needs. Specially poignant were the cases of 36 Cantor women, pregnant at the time of the attacks. They suddenly became widows and gave birth to already fatherless children.

Lutnick's leadership was not confined to what was going on at Cantor. On 27 November 2001, Lutnick made the following proposals to the US Department of Justice (DOJ) for the administration of the 11 September 2001 Victim Compensation Fund (Cantor 2001j): First of all, victims' estates should not have their compensation from the fund reduced by the amount of contributions they had already received from employees, charities and other private entities. Secondly, the Department of Justice should finalize rules as quickly as possible, to provide victims with the information they needed to decide whether or not to file a claim. This recommendation was particularly relevant because the fund itself was designed as a way for victims to receive compensation without resorting to lawsuits. Thirdly, there should be a chart with specific dollar amounts so that a victim's estate could choose to file a simple 'EZ' form and receive compensation immediately. However, should claimants wish to file more extensive damages, they should be allowed to do so and not be bound by the figures on the chart, so long as they proved their losses within the time frame of the statute. And fourthly, awards should not be artificially capped based on the class or status of the victim, to ensure that they were consistent with what would otherwise be recovered through trial. Commenting on the submission, Lutnick said: 'We continue to be committed to helping our families in any way that we can and we have worked hard, on their behalf, to pro-actively submit these recommendations to the DOJ' (Cantor 2001j).

What about Lutnick's other avowed goal of getting Cantor back to business as soon as possible? Two days after the tragedy, on 13 September 2001, Cantor confirmed that its trading systems were fully operational in time for the re-opening of the US Treasury market (Cantor 2001c). Thanks to its multiple sites in the US and overseas, the firm managed to continue operating in both the European and Asian bond and equity markets. In this regard Lutnick wrote: 'There is no adversity our survivors cannot overcome. Our survivors reopened this company 47 hours after the attack. I cannot be more proud to be associated with this group of people' (Cantor 2001e). And still, on another occasion, Lutnick added:

> The lengths to which our employees across the globe worked to ensure eSpeed system maintained its global connectivity speak volumes about each of our employees' depth of character. With so much pain from the loss of their business family, they dedicated themselves to back eSpeed in honor of those we lost. The accomplishements of our staff stand as a testament to their love of those friends we have lost (Cantor 2001g).

In fact, the only exceptional measure the company undertook was to request a temporary halt in the trading of eSpeed stock on the Nasdaq market on 17 September 2001 (Cantor 2001d). This was, of course, fully conscionable, due to the heavy loss of life – including half of senior management – that Cantor and eSpeed had sustained. Nevertheless, as Lutnick energetically affirmed as he reflected on the events:

> it is impossible, impossible, to destroy the spirit of our eSpeed family and together we are forging ahead. The unity and togetherness of our eSpeed family are unprece-

dented in the business world. We will remain the market leader with the foremost electronic trading platform in the world and in doing so honor the integrity of those employees, executives, family and friends we have lost (Cantor 2001g).

On 5 October 2001, after an interruption of 18 days, trading of eSpeed stock resumed, with the board reaffirming its decision for a $40 million stock repurchase program. Thus, in the words of Lutnick:

> those investors who can comprehend the enormity of what this Company has already rebounded from and those investors who have an inkling of our passion for this business will know that eSpeed will never forget, never settle, never give up. It is our promise that this Company will stand as a testament to those we have lost and a badge of honor to those who have survived. In our view, eSpeed will become, along with Cantor Fitzgerald, an American business miracle (Cantor 2001g).

Barely three months after Lutnick pronounced those words, the general turn of events seemed bent on proving him right. Since Cantor is a private partnership, it is not required to disclose profits. Nonetheless, as Lutnick assured his Cantor family, regarding its fourth quarter performance: 'We will be highly profitable – not barely profitable, but highly profitable' (Henriques 2002). As for eSpeed, Lutnick also forecasted on 20 November 2001, the Tuesday before Thanksgiving, that it would be profitable for the first time in the fourth quarter of 2001, with earnings from a penny to a nickel per share. In consequence, eSpeed stock soared by more than 20 per cent, almost reaching its pre-September 11 level (Gordon 2001).

Apart from the $40 million property insurance and the $25 million business interruption coverage that Cantor and eSpeed each carried, a host of other factors serendipitously came together in Lutnick's favor. In first place was the rebounding stock market in the fourth quarter of 2001, plus the fact that some 75 per cent of Cantor's top revenue producers worked outside of its doomed New York headquarters. A dash of schadenfreude also came by way of Enron's demise, since Enron Online was one of TradeSpark's main competitors. (TradeSpark is the electronic energy trading service jointly owned by Cantor, eSpeed and five other large American energy companies.) TradeSpark is powered by eSpeed's technology and pays eSpeed a commission for each transaction carried out.

In the end, however, what became clear in everybody's mind was that bank accounts were a lot easier to replenish than people. Since then, each and every one of the survivors could rightly be considered a living miracle. The tragedy forced business executives who focus almost exclusively on the financial bottom line to challenge such conventional wisdom and reset their priorities. It taught them that profits defer to the physical and emotional well-being of their employees, and that the management of business is above all a management of people, in ways that had become far more personal and intimate than before.

A month after the terrorist attacks on the World Trade Center veteran analyst Douglas Atkin gauged their repercussions in the following terms:

> It's had a huge impact on the Wall Street culture. This has been a culture where, to get ahead, it's been, you must work weekends, you must work 18 hours a day or 20 hours a day. It took an event such as September 11 to jolt Wall Street in general and the people who work in Wall Street in particular, to really refocus on what their priorities are. I see it, just going around to the different trading desks or going to the different fund management firms (*The New York Times* 2001).

It's an apt description of what Howard Lutnick has personally gone through. Despite the tremendous change that they had wrought on his life, the attacks were something that just happened to him, events over which he had no control. An entirely different matter were his reactions, during moments of great physical, emotional and moral upheaval. There were two instances wherein his true mettle and moral leadership were critically tested: when he stopped paying salaries to the missing employees on 15 September, and when he unveiled the compensation package the company would be granting to surviving Cantor families on 10 October. These two events provoked diametrically opposed reactions: Will the real Howard Lutnick please stand up?

In the first one he was cast in the role of the cruel archvillain, a modern day Shylock, Scrooge or Fagin, who suffered no qualms of conscience in cutting off widows and orphans from their mite or denying paychecks to the dead. He insisted that he had no choice but to do it, for it was the only way to staunch the bleeding – at the rate of more than $500,000 a day – in a company that was barely operational (Gordon 2001). Likewise, it was an unequivocal sign to bankers and investors that despite the outpouring of emotion, he still had sangfroid and maintained a clear head. He was driven and motivated more than anyone to keep his business alive. He had a plan and he had the guts to put that plan into action.

In the second one Lutnick played the role of the provident Good Samaritan, his brother's keeper, who announced a detailed financial plan for the surviving families, so munificent and magnanimous that it was hard to believe. Of course there was no obligation for him to go to such lengths, except, perhaps, for a deeply held personal conviction, regarding life's – and money's – true and greater purpose. Everything now rested on how well he would keep his promises.

III.   CONSTRUCTING HARRY

Human actions are the basic currency of moral capital, the elementary building blocks with which an agent's – and by extension, a firm's – moral life is constituted. As Woody Allen would put it, they are the bricks used in constructing Harry. In the same way that an edifice cannot be built with bricks alone, neither are actions by themselves sufficient to construct an individual's moral person, or that of an organization, for that matter. Although actions, like words, are themselves endowed with meaning, they still need a context, something like a sentence, in order to express complete thought. Actions, which arise from one's inclinations and tendencies, gain significance to the degree that they develop into permanent habits. These habits, in turn, configure an individual's character, and thereon, one's life. Only when we take into account this structured and dynamic relationship that actions hold with other operational levels do we obtain a clear picture of the moral existence – individual or corporate – that they reflect.

That moral capital relies mainly on actions means, in first place, that thoughts or ideas are not enough, no matter how indispensable they may be. Leadership, or the accrual of moral capital for oneself and one's organization, is not a theory but an art, a practice. Like Aristotelian statecraft and rhetoric, its end is action not mere knowledge. Its task is to equip us with know-how, rather than with a bare 'knowledge that so and so...'. Leadership establishes what must be done and, conversely, what must be avoided.

Moreover, leadership always pursues a goal in the light of the highest good or happiness to which human beings aspire. Any worthwhile leadership goal is itself a means to ultimately achieving happiness. In a sense, leadership may be construed plainly as enabling followers to fulfill their proper function, knowing this to be the way they achieve their own good and contribute to the collective good of all. However, despite the multitude and diversity of tasks, there seems to be one in which all of us by nature engage. That is our 'proper human function', the activity towards which all human beings necessarily tend. From this no one, much less a business leader, could excuse himself.

From Aristotle's inquiries we know that it consists in 'some sort of life of action of the [part of the] soul that has reason'; but not in a 'life' understood just as a capacity or potency, rather, in using or exercising it, in 'life as activity, since this seems to be called life to a fuller extent' (NE 1098a). That moral capital is comprised of actions means, in the second place, that merely having a capacity for action – or for a life according to reason – by itself will not do. The actual exercise of such a capacity is required. For this same reason we say that a person who is asleep is not fully alive, although indeed, he has the capacity to be so. Instead, we only call someone fully alive when he is wide awake and wholly engaged – exercising reason – in some serious, meaningful human action.

The specifically human function lies in a certain kind of life. This kind of life is an activity of the soul which – unlike nutrition, growth or sense-perception – expresses reason. Human excellence or virtue, therefore, resides in fulfilling this function in accordance with reason finely and well. As Aristotle unequivocally remarks, 'the human good turns out to be the soul's activity that expresses

virtue' (NE 1098a). Happiness, or that complete and over-arching human flourishing at which leadership of whatever kind ultimately aims, involves 'living
well and doing well in action' (ibid.): not just for a few isolated moments, nor
for a limited span of time, but throughout an entire lifetime. Such permanence
or sustained duration is another trait sought in action that builds up moral capital,
or analogously, in that kind of life that is imbued by thought.

Moral capital is built upon actions, on the exercise of actions, and not on the
mere possession of capacities for action. Actions do not all qualify, however,
only those which respond to the description of a 'proper human function'. A
proper human function is what is carried out in accordance with reason. Virtue
consists primarily in the proper human function being done finely and well.
Such an activity, by its very nature, directs us towards happiness, our supreme
good and final end. A necessary requirement for this happiness-generating
activity is its permanence, that it be realized through a sustained duration. All
worthwhile leadership endeavors are set against this backdrop of action and
the proper human function of virtue and happiness.

That actions are the basic elements of the moral life also means, in a very real
sense, that our whole life transpires in the performance of different actions, one
after another: sleeping, waking up; eating and drinking; playing the piano or
painting a portrait; valuing a company's assets, purchasing stocks; designing a
strategy, presenting that plan to the board; firing a CEO, hiring another, and so
on. How do we account for the moral significance of all these actions?

Before anything, we must distinguish between involuntary acts and voluntary
human actions. Involuntary acts occur by force of nature and affect a human
being's physical, biological or psychological dimensions. The deaths of the
Cantor Fitzgerald employees as the planes crashed and the Tower toppled down
were involuntary from their perspective. They were victims, not agents; they
suffered the tragedy rather than actively causing it.

An external, non-rational force is the real cause and origin of involuntary
actions: 'What comes about by force or because of ignorance seems to be involuntary. What is forced has an external origin, the sort of origin in which the
agent or victim contributes nothing – if, e.g., a wind or human beings who
control him were to carry him off' (NE 1110a). The deaths of the Cantor
workers in the World Trade disaster were violently forced, and therefore, involuntary. In the Ford–Firestone case, before the injuries and deaths from tire
blow-outs and vehicle rollovers were reported, ignorance could have also been
claimed by both the automaker and the tire company, thus making their actions
involuntary and their responsibility diminished.

Voluntary human actions, on the other hand, are what we reasonably find to
be objects of praise, if they are good, or of blame, if they are evil. Unlike involuntary acts, human actions proceed from a principle internal to the agent, such
as his own appetite, feeling, desire or will. Furthermore, they are always accom-

panied by knowledge of purpose, and of the means that attain it. The agent performs these actions intentionally and deliberately. Hence, Aristotle's definition: 'what is voluntary seems to be what has its origin in the agent himself when he knows the particulars that the action consists in' (NE 1111a). Examples of voluntary actions were Howard Lutnick's decision to stop paying salaries to the missing Cantor employees a few days after the tragedy, or his determination, a month later, to offer victims' families generous compensation packages. Neither one of these were physically forced upon him. On the contrary, both policies came about as consequences of carefully thought about and deliberated decisions.

As a descriptor, the term 'voluntary' may be appended not only to an action, but also to a choice or desire, a decision, and the external effects that ensue from an action. From the viewpoint of Ford and Firestone, their choice or desire to manufacture vehicles and tires, respectively – instead of ovens and doughnuts, for example – was voluntary. So was their decision to produce those vehicles and tires according to a specific design. Inasmuch as the choice and the decision surrounding the vehicles and tires were voluntary, the external effects that arose from their use – that is, the blow-outs and the rollovers – may also be called, to an extent, voluntary. For each and every one of these phenomena, choices, decisions and the external effects of actions, we rightly hold the agents responsible. Herein lies the moral importance of voluntary human actions: their ability to fully compromise agents, so much so that they become objects of value judgements in their character and person.

Although all human actions have the capacity to implicate their agent, some are nonetheless more revealing than others of an agent's moral worth. This depends on the degree of voluntariness that a particular human act displays, which in turn results from the knowledge and the consent involved in the performance of the act.

Choosing a lifetime partner or deciding on a profession usually requires full awareness of the mind and a solid determination of the will. They are examples of what may be called 'perfectly voluntary actions'. However, not all activities demand an equally intense concentration of mental energies. One may write a short note while attending a phone call, or one may hesitatingly visit the dentist because he still vividly recalls the pain in his last visit. Despite the lack of knowledge or advertence, in the first case, due to distraction, or the defect in consent because of the fear of pain in the second, both situations still describe voluntary actions, albeit 'imperfectly voluntary' ones.

It took Ford and Firestone managers some time before gathering substantial evidence regarding possible defects or dangers in their products. Selling SUVs and tires while proof about risks was still inconclusive could have made for an imperfectly involuntary action. On one hand was the fear for injuries and deaths their products could cause, and on the other was the need to respond to demands for these products and for profits. Similarly Howard Lutnick, when he decided to drop missing employees from the payroll, almost certainly engaged in an imperfectly voluntary act, because of the very strong and contradictory emotions to which he was subject. Like most people, his heart would have prodded him to help the surviving Cantor families, but his mind would also have warned him of the serious jeopardy in which he would be putting the firm.

Voluntariness could refer to an action considered in itself or as the cause of another. Aristotle brings this distinction to bear in the situation of someone who throws his possessions overboard in face of an impending shipwreck (cf. NE 1110a). No one in his right mind would ever throw his possessions to the sea just like that; such an action would never qualify as voluntary in itself. However, for the sake of saving one's life – the chances of which would be greatly increased if the ship's cargo were lessened – it would be reasonable at that moment to get rid of any excess baggage. Although that action may not be voluntary in itself, it would nevertheless be voluntary as the cause of the other.

This distinction between a voluntary action in itself and a voluntary action in its cause is highly relevant in the case of the tires and the SUVs. Certainly, neither Ford nor Firestone would have desired any of the accidents to occur; and in part, the mishaps could have been caused by hot weather, poor roads or bad driving. Yet, as manufacturers, they could be held liable for the possible defects their products had, and for the harm and damage they could have caused.

The roots or sources of the morality of actions are three-fold: the object of the action itself; the end or intention with which the agent carries the action out; and the circumstances in which the action is performed. There is likewise an established order in which these criteria are to be considered, in judging the ethical quality of a voluntary human act.

The first criterion refers to the object of the action itself. It applies to what the agent does as a humanly meaningful whole, and not simply to the series of physical movements he may go through. With regard to the Ford and Firestone managers, the problem was not that they kept silent while simply doing their jobs, selling SUVs and tires, respectively. They refused to inform the public even when they already had substantial proof of the risks to life and limb that their products posed. And with respect to Howard Lutnick, a month after the attacks, the issue was not just the offer of a compensation package, but the care and thoughtfulness with which that package had been designed.

The object is what principally determines whether an action is good or evil. Certain actions are prohibited without exception by virtue of their object, such as lying, theft, murder or torture. As Aristotle observed: 'there are some things we cannot be compelled to do, and rather than do them we should suffer the most terrible consequences and accept death' (NE 1110a). These belong to the class of the absolute moral prohibitions; those that admit no exceptions.

After the object, the agent's intention is the next criterion to be examined in order to find out the moral quality of an action. The crucial question is whether that intention is properly oriented towards an agent's final end. Should Ford's and Firestone's desire for profits be allowed to outweigh the negative risks their products presented? Should profit be put over and above safety and service? Will this decision accurately reflect company policy?

At times, an action that is choiceworthy by virtue of its object becomes ethically flawed due to the intention with which it is carried out. This could have been Howard Lutnick's case, if the tears he had shed in public were just for show, and there was no sincere desire to help Cantor survivors. However, after announcing his company's compensation plan, Lutnick veered away from the media spotlight and instead chose to meet his Cantor families privately. Aside from being choiceworthy or good on account of its object, an action also has to be performed with a noble end or intention.

After the object and the end or intention come the circumstances as a determinant of the moral quality of actions. Seemingly favorable circumstances cannot change the moral quality of an action from evil to good. No act of torture could ever be justified by any intention, no matter how lofty. Not even if the fate of a hundred people depended on it, should torture be legitimized as a means to acquire some vital piece of information. However, unfavorable circumstances could sometimes effect the opposite change, rendering an otherwise good action morally censurable. In principle, there shouldn't be anything wrong with the generous compensation package Lutnick had arranged, except, perhaps, in the hypothetical case that it put the firm's economic viability in peril. This would truly be a negative circumstance that would change the act's moral quality. For not only would the firm be unable to keep its promises, but it could even cease to exist, thereby losing all opportunity to do good in the future.

The moral goodness of a human act requires the integrity of all these; the object, the agent's intention or end, and the circumstances. A defect or flaw in any of the three would be sufficient to render a voluntary human act evil. Apart from being useless or even harmful, such an action would also be wasteful or depreciatory from the viewpoint of moral capital; it would devalue a person's and an organization's moral worth.

IV.   IN BRIEF

- Actions are moral capital's 'basic currency' because nothing acquires moral significance unless it issues into action or comes as a result of it.
- In order to build up moral capital, a mere capacity for action is not enough; that capacity has to be exercised. Neither does any kind of action qualify in building up moral capital; it has to be a 'proper human function' – that

is, one in accordance with reason – performed finely and well. Virtuous action is what constitutes moral capital.

- Virtuous action brings an agent closer to his supreme good or final end. We call the attainment of this supreme good or final end 'happiness'. Leadership consists in nurturing virtuous action in one's followers by performing virtuous actions oneself; that is, by giving good example. Genuine leadership is always carried out with a view to the 'proper human function', virtue and happiness.
- A precondition for virtuous action is that it be voluntary: that it proceed from an internal principle (appetite, feeling, desire or will) in the agent with knowledge of purpose. What originates from an external force or is done in ignorance is involuntary. Aside from actions; desires, decisions and the external effects actions produce could also be considered voluntary. Only voluntary actions are proper objects of praise or blame. Voluntary actions reveal the moral worth of their agents.
- Knowledge, or awareness of mind, and consent of the will affect the voluntariness of actions. Voluntariness could refer to an action considered in itself or to an action as the cause of another.
- To determine the moral worth of voluntary actions, one should examine, in descending order, the following criteria: the object of the action itself; the intention with which the agent carries the action out; and the circumstances in which the action is performed. The integrity of the three is required for an action to be morally good, and any defect among them makes an action evil.
- Good actions build up an individual agent's or firm's moral capital, while evil actions make the individual agent's or firm's moral capital lose value.
- We learn from the Ford–Firestone case that responsibility over one's actions and their consequences derives from what one knows at the time of making and carrying out a decision.
- Howard Lutnick's example at Cantor Fitzgerald teaches us that in moments of great emotional upheaval, reason, rather than feeling, is a better guide for action. Furthermore, to follow reason does not entail eliminating feeling; it simply means not allowing oneself to be overcome by it. There is also a 'reasonableness' to be achieved, for caring to be truly effective.

REFERENCES

Aristotle (1985), *Nicomachean Ethics*, trans. by Terence Irwin, Indianapolis, IN: Hackett Publishing.
The Associated Press (2001), 'Ford ordered to fix defect in 2 million cars', *The New York Times*, 14 April.

Barboza, D. (2001), 'Bridgestone/Firestone to close tire plant at center of huge recall', *The New York Times*, 28 June.

Bradsher, K. (2000a), 'Carmakers modifying SUV's to reduce risk to others', *The New York Times*, 20 March.

Bradsher, K. (2000b), 'Ford is conceding SUV drawbacks', *The New York Times*, 12 May.

Bradsher, K. (2000c), 'Ford says Firestone was aware of flaw in its tires by 1997', *The New York Times*, 14 August.

Bradsher, K. (2000d), 'Tire deaths are linked to rollovers', *The New York Times*, 16 August.

Bradsher, K. (2000e), 'Ford chose tires now being recalled to reduce risk of rollovers, document shows', *The New York Times*, 20 August.

Bradsher, K. (2000f), 'Ford reduces output to help recall of tires', *The New York Times*, 22 August.

Bradsher, K. (2000g), '2 Firestone studies in 1999 pointed to tire problems', *The New York Times*, 10 October.

Bradsher, K. (2000h), 'Firestone engineers offer a list of causes for faulty tires', *The New York Times*, 19 December.

Bradsher, K. (2001a), 'Ford concludes tires at fault in rollovers', *The New York Times*, 20 April.

Bradsher, K. (2001b), 'Firestone to stop sales to Ford', *The New York Times*, 22 May.

Bradsher, K. (2001c), 'Firestone asks U.S. to study Ford Explorer', *The New York Times*, 1 June.

Bradsher, K. and M. Wald (2000), 'More indications that hazards of tires were long known', *The New York Times*, 7 September.

Burt, T. (2001), 'Jac the knife falls foul of family pressures', *Financial Times*, 28 November.

Cantor (2001a), 'Howard Lutnick, Chairman of Cantor Fitzgerald and eSpeed, comments on World Trade Center tragedy', www.cantorusa.com, 12 September.

Cantor (2001b), 'Cantor Fitzgerald to offer counseling, crisis-intervention services', www.cantorusa.com, 12 September.

Cantor (2001c), 'Statement from Cantor Fitzgerald and eSpeed', www.cantorusa.com, 13 September.

Cantor (2001d), 'Trading in eSpeed class a common stock temporarily halted', www.cantorusa.com, 17 September.

Cantor (2001e), 'Statement from Howard W. Lutnick, Chairman and CEO of eSpeed, Inc.', www.cantorusa.com, 20 September.

Cantor (2001f), 'Cantor Fitzgerald to hold memorial service', www.cantorusa.com, 25 September.

Cantor (2001g), 'eSpeed's Chairman Howard W. Lutnick discusses the company's business', www.cantorusa.com, 4 October.

Cantor (2001h), 'Cantor Fitzgerald L.P. announces details of support for families of employees lost in the World Trade Center attack', www.cantorusa.com, 10 October.

Cantor (2001i), 'Cantor Fitzgerald and eSpeed to expedite bonus distributions for families of employees lost in the World Trade Center Tragedy', www.cantorusa.com, 10 October.

Cantor (2001j), 'Cantor Fitzgerald L.P. submits public comment to U.S. Department of Justice', www.cantorusa.com, 27 November.

Cantor (2001k), 'Cantor Fitzgerald CEO Howard Lutnick and Cantor Partners announce new $5 million matching fund for Cantor Fitzgerald Relief Fund', www.cantorusa.com, 2 December.

Deutsch, C. (2000), 'Recall of Firestone tire is viewed as a first step toward damage control', *The New York Times*, 10 August.

Gordon, M. (2001), 'Howard Lutnick's second life', *New York Magazine*, 10 December.

Hakim, D. (2001), 'Firestone said to reach tire settlement', *The New York Times*, 8 November.

Henriques, D. (2001a), 'Some families doubt sincerity of Cantor', *The New York Times*, 26 September.

Henriques, D. (2001b), 'Cantor survivors are rebuilding and remembering', *The New York Times*, 2 November.

Henriques, D. (2002), 'Horrible year ends on up note at Cantor', *The New York Times*, 3 January.

Labaton, S. (2000a), 'Regulators investigate Ford's handling of defective tires abroad', *The New York Times*, 31 August.

Labaton, S. (2000b), 'Judge orders Ford to make huge recall', *The New York Times*, 12 October.

Labaton, S. and L. Bergman (2000), 'Documents indicate Ford knew of defect but failed to report it', *The New York Times*, 12 September.

Mayer, C. and C. Johnson (2001), 'Firestone, States reach settlement', *Washington Post*, 8 November.

New York Times, The (2001), 'Round table: the new challenges for Wall Street', *The New York Times*, 14 October.

Nicomachean Ethics (NE) (see Aristotle).

Reuters (2000), 'Ford says Firestone hid defects', *The New York Times*, 5 October.

Wald, M. (2000a), 'Rancor grows between Ford and Firestone', *The New York Times*, 13 September.

Wald, M. (2000b), 'House passes bill on tire and car defects', *The New York Times*, 11 October.

Wald, M. and J. Barbanel (2000), 'Link between tires and crashes went undetected in federal data', *The New York Times*, 8 September.

Wald, M. and K. Bradsher (2000), 'Ford says problems with tires were too infrequent to detect', *The New York Times*, 9 September.

Winerip, M. (2001), 'Ford and Firestone settle suit over explorer crash', *The New York Times*, 9 January.

4.   Habits, moral capital's compound interest

The ethical value of an action derives from the knowledge and consent with which it is performed. An act acquires human significance and counts as moral capital only to the extent that it involves both the intelligence and the will of an agent. An individual assumes responsibility for actions carried out according to a plan or intention he has defined as well as for actions carried out by others at his bidding. Something analogous occurs within a corporation or any other organization.

At times it may be difficult to determine the degree of knowledge and consent that accompany an act. We know that in principle, actions just don't occur by themselves; rather, they are the fruit of deliberate efforts on the part of identifiable human agents. However, it is possible that in a concrete instance an action comes about as the result of accident or chance. For example, although typing a document on a computer is a human act that entails both understanding and will, one's fingers may slip on the keyboard and produce an error, such as a misspelled word. Normally, we tend to take such mistakes lightly. Yet when a mistake is repeated often we begin to have second thoughts. We tell ourselves that it probably wasn't an occasional slip of the finger, but an ingrained cognitive error on the part of the typist. The frequency with which an action is carried out, therefore, bears a significance of its own. It could dispel doubts as to whether a specific act – like a misspelled word – occurred by chance, or on the contrary, it was the result of the agent's desire, intention and erroneous knowledge. The repetition of an action is an observable sign that establishes and reinforces not only an agent's knowledge, will and intention, but also our belief regarding that agent's knowledge, will and intention. Repetition affects the voluntariness of an act, and transitively, the responsibility of its agent.

Habits develop from the repetition of voluntary human actions. They indicate many other things besides the firmness of an agent's mind and will with regard to a particular act. They explain an ease or flourish in the performance of an act and they modify the amount of responsibility attributed to an agent for it. For this reason, habits comprise a second level, superior to that of actions, in the constitution and dynamics of moral capital.

In the realm of business and economics, everyone more or less knows what 'interest' stands for. It is the return an investor receives for the original amount or 'principal' he has disbursed; it is what a bank or borrower pays a depositor or saver for an amount invested or loaned. But aside from 'simple interest', there is also another thing called 'compound interest'. Briefly, it is the interest paid on interest. Returning to our previous example, compound interest is what the bank pays the depositor or owner of a savings account whenever interest is credited on a daily basis. In that case, interest is earned not only on the principal, but also on the credited interest. Now then, if actions, which make up the basic currency of moral capital, constitute the principal in an account, habits correspond to their compound interest. Habits are the payoff in terms of moral capital for the repetition of voluntary human actions.

In this chapter we shall see how habits develop through the conscious and willful repetition of actions by an agent. As we know, protocols or standard operating procedures are the equivalent of habits in a corporate agent. Habits, in the case of individual actors, and standard operating procedures, in the case of corporate ones, have a unique way of increasing or decreasing moral capital. Later in the chapter we shall also be discussing work, since it is ordinarily understood as a regular habit rather than just an isolated, one-shot activity. The story of Microsoft's epic antitrust battle with the US federal government and a score of states shall serve as the backdrop for our study.

I. MICROSOFT'S MANTRA – EXTEND, EMBRACE AND EXTINGUISH

On 21 August 1995, in a Washington DC courtroom presided by Judge Thomas Penfield Jackson, the US government – represented first by the Federal Trade Commission and later by the Department of Justice – signed a 'consent decree', a court-approved anti-trust agreement with Microsoft Corporation (Brinkley and Lohr 2001: 3). This act was supposed to bring to an end the more than five years that the federal government had spent investigating what it considered to be Microsoft's abusive practices in the software market. The six-page document contained – in attention to government's claims – a provision that prohibited Microsoft from tying the sale of any one of its products to another. But it also established, upon Microsoft's insistence, that such a prohibition should not be construed as to prevent the company from developing integrated products. With these contradictory stipulations in mind, it was easy to imagine that the consent decree was a mere truce between the warring parties. It only served to set the stage for future battles.

Even before the terms of the agreement were finalized, there were already signs that Microsoft was never really committed to them. In a meeting with top executives of the computer chip manufacturer Intel in Santa Clara, CA on 11 July 1995, Microsoft's founding chairman Bill Gates remarked: 'This antitrust thing will blow over... We haven't changed our business practices at all' (Brinkley and Lohr 2001: 83). Although Microsoft may have consented to the letter of the decree changing the way it licensed its industry-standard Windows operating system (OS), it had no intention of fundamentally modifying its business conduct as the spirit of the document required. That same year, Joel Klein, the chief of the antitrust division of the US Justice Department, received a complaint from the internet service provider America Online (AOL), alleging that Microsoft was violating court orders by bundling Windows with Microsoft Network (MSN), its new online service (Brinkley and Lohr 2001: 4). Months later, in June 1996, authorities again received protests from the PC (personal computer) maker Compaq. Microsoft had threatened to cancel Compaq's Windows license because of its plans to ship computers with the Netscape Navigator browser, instead of Microsoft's Internet Explorer (Brinkley and Lohr 2001: 5).

By the following year, government and Microsoft were again on the warpath, with Klein filing a suit on 20 October 1997. His grievance was that Microsoft was forcing PC makers to take its browser, the Internet Explorer, as a condition for obtaining a Windows license. Given the extremely rapid pace of the digital economy, Klein was of the opinion that antitrust authorities had to intervene early, if ever they were to intervene at all, and he wanted the court to step in before Microsoft released the new version of Windows with the Explorer (Brinkley and Lohr 2001: 8–9).

Upon Klein's petition, Judge Jackson ordered Microsoft to offer PC manu-facturers a version of Windows that did not include the Internet Explorer. The most that Microsoft could offer, however, was an alternative between an obsolete version of Windows and another that did not work properly. The company staunchly defended that the Internet Explorer browser was now an integrated, inseparable component of Windows OS. As an interim measure, Microsoft agreed to provide a Windows version with the Internet Explorer icon hidden and the program partly disabled, while awaiting a decision from the appeals court (Brinkley and Lohr 2001: 9).

On 18 May 1998, the 'last rites' or final attempt at an agreement before for-malizing a lawsuit were held between the government and Microsoft (Brinkley and Lohr 2001: 11–12). Previous contacts between Klein and Gates had fostered hopes that Microsoft would allow PC makers to alter the Windows opening screen, giving freedom of choice among competing products on the desktop. Yet in the end the talks failed, due to Microsoft's protests at what it considered to be the government's unreasonable demand for it to renounce its intellectual property rights over the 'look and feel' of Windows. The government, for its part, thought that Microsoft had obstinately held on to a mistaken notion of design freedom that included the ability to integrate anything it wanted into Windows. That was plainly intolerable.

A milestone was passed on 23 June 1998 when the Appeals Court overturned Judge Jackson's decision ordering Microsoft to take Internet Explorer out of Windows. The new ruling affirmed that Microsoft had every right to integrate new products into Windows, as long as it could make a 'plausible claim' of business efficiency or consumer benefit (Brinkley and Lohr 2001: 13). This setback however did not deter the Justice Department from pursuing its case, an effort in which it was joined by 19 states plus the District of Columbia as plaintiffs. The appeals court decision simply drew the lines along which major arguments in the antitrust proceedings were to develop, that is, the issues of 'business efficiency' and 'consumer benefit'. The government had to prove a habit or pattern of behavior in Microsoft that consisted in bullying industry partners and rivals, thus hobbling any potential challenge to its de facto monopoly and harming consumers by stifling innovation and overcharging.

The most relevant legal doctrine in this case was, undoubtedly, the Sherman Act of 1890. It was a piece of social legislation meant to prevent economic exploitation that comes as a result of the accumulation of power. Its key provisions were found in Section 1: 'Every contract, combination in the form of trust or otherwise, or conspiracy, in restraint of trade or commerce among the several States, or with foreign nations, is declared to be illegal' and Section 2: 'Every person who shall monopolize, or attempt to monopolize, or combine or conspire with any other person or persons, to monopolize any part of the trade or commerce among the several States ... shall be deemed guilty of a felony' (Brinkley and Lohr 2001: 17).

Probably the most influential documents in the US government's accusations were a 1995 white paper written by Gates, *The Internet Tidal Wave*, together with two e-mails from James Alchin, a senior Microsoft scientist who was in charge of developing Windows (Brinkley and Lohr 2001: 7–8). Gates in his essay identified Netscape, with its Navigator browser, as the new formidable competitor on the Internet, because it altered the rules of web-based computing and commoditized underlying operating systems. In other words, Netscape's Navigator browser threatened the Windows OS dominance by positing itself as the new platform for Internet computing. The Navigator posed the threat of rendering Windows irrelevant. Alchin, for his part, candidly wrote in e-mails addressed to a fellow Microsoft executive between late December 1997 and early January 1998: 'I do not believe we can win on our current path. Even if we get Internet Explorer totally competitive with Navigator, why should we be chosen? They have 80 per cent market share. My conclusion is we have to leverage Windows more. We need something more: Windows integration.'

On 19 October 1998 the trial of US v. Microsoft finally began. David Boies, the lead lawyer for the Justice Department, opened with Gates' taped deposition (Brinkley and Lohr 2001: 21–5). Microsoft chairman Gates, when asked about the main charges leveled against his company, responded that he knew very little, if anything at all. His only source of information, supposedly, was a *Wall Street Journal* article, and according to him, he became utterly surprised upon reading its contents. When queried regarding a meeting in which Microsoft apparently offered its chief competitor, Netscape, a deal to divide the browser market between them, Gates said that he was never involved in such negotiations. Immediately after, Boies produced over a dozen memos and e-mails written by Gates in the last three years. These clearly indicated that Gates knew about the allegations and that he had in fact masterminded them. This was a serious blow to Gates' credibility at the the the witness stand, a theme to which the plaintiffs would often return. All that John Warden, Microsoft's chief legal counsel, could muster in Gates' defense was that no matter how aggressive, such messages did not break the law. 'The antitrust laws are not a code of civility in business', said Warden.

Between 20 October 1998 and 12 January 1999, some twelve witnesses took the stand on the part of government. The coincidences among their testimonies on Microsoft's stubbornly abusive behavior were indeed striking.

First to appear was James Barksdale, the president of Netscape (Brinkley and Lohr 2001: 38–49). Microsoft contended that its browser, Internet Explorer, was a feature of its operating system, Windows, rather than a stand-alone program. Barksdale however argued that Internet Explorer was not a part of Windows, and that it was simply called into play whenever browser functions were needed. In reality, what Microsoft sought was to extend its control of the OS market (Windows) to the browser market (Internet Explorer). By embracing the browser market, Microsoft could effectively extinguish any competition or innovation at its source. Barksdale related how, in the spring of 1996, Compaq was forced to reverse its decision to use Netscape upon receiving Microsoft's threat to cancel the Windows 95 license if Internet Explorer were not installed on its computers instead.

Barksdale also narrated what transpired in a meeting with Microsoft executives on 21 June 1995: 'In all my years in business, I have never heard nor experienced such an explicit proposal to divide markets. I have never been in a meeting ... in which a competitor had so blatantly implied that we would either stop competing with it or the competitor would kill us.' His account largely concurred with other pieces of evidence. Gates, in a memo addressed to Paul Maritz, a Microsoft executive, expressed his worry over having to compete with Netscape, 'but in the meantime, we can help them [Netscape]. We can pay them some money' (Brinkley and Lohr 2001: 23). An e-mail from Gates to other Microsoft managers in 1995 expressed similar ideas: 'I think there is a very powerful deal we can make with Netscape. I would really like this to happen!' (Brinkley and Lohr 2001: 24).

Microsoft's lawyer Warden countered by suggesting that the purported deal to divide the browser market was Netscape's idea, not his client's. To this end he submitted an e-mail dated 29 December 1994 written by James Clark, chairman and co-founder of Netscape, addressed to Dan Rosen of Microsoft: 'We never planned to compete with you. ... We want to make this company a success, but not at Microsoft's expense. We'd like to work with you. Working together could be in your self-interest as well as ours. Depending on the interest level, you might take an equity position in Netscape, with the ability to expand this position later.' Warden's attempt to discredit Barksdale's testimony however boomeranged, since Clark himself concluded his note by saying, 'No one in my organization knows about this message.' This meant that Clark's initiative was entirely his own and did not in any way represent company policy.

Compaq was not alone in being badgered by Microsoft to use Internet Explorer as default browser. Barksdale had also received a letter from Fred Anderson, Jr, chief financial officer of Apple Computers, in this regard. Anderson explained that Microsoft had threatened to stop developing its word processor, Microsoft Word, and its spreadsheet, Excel, for Macintosh computers, if Apple did not accede to its demands (Brinkley and Lohr 2001: 53).

Next to take the witness stand was David Colburn, senior vice president of America Online (AOL), the US' largest internet service provider (Brinkley and Lohr 2001: 53–61). Colburn recounted how his company first entered into an exclusionary distribution contract with Microsoft in March 1996. Microsoft gave AOL a prominent link in the Windows desktop in exchange for ensuring that Internet Explorer was on 85 per cent of the browsers that AOL sent to subscribers. This deal was particularly important because Windows already carried a Microsoft Network (MSN) icon, the online service Microsoft had created to compete with AOL. A promotional agreement in October 1996 further established that Microsoft would pay AOL $0.25 for every subscriber who converted to Internet Explorer, aside from a $600,000 bonus for doing so promptly. Colburn added, 'Microsoft had no limitations on what it could spend to gain market share for Internet Explorer'.

Then came Dr Avadis Tevanian, Jr from Apple, the manufacturer of Macintosh computers (Brinkley and Lohr 2001: 61–70). At a time when Apple's QuickTime program was the industry standard for audio, video and animated graphics files, the company suffered intense pressure from Microsoft to abandon the multimedia software market. When Apple refused, Microsoft tinkered with Windows OS – used by 85 to 90 per cent of all PCs – so that QuickTime no longer worked smoothly with computers running on Windows. Tevanian recalled how a Microsoft executive unambiguously stated his company's strategy: 'We're going to compete fiercely on multimedia playback, and we won't let anybody play back in Windows.'

As a computer engineer, Tevanian's witness was particularly valuable in undermining Microsoft's assertion that Internet Explorer was a fully integrated and inseparable part of Windows, in such a way that removing Internet Explorer meant breaking Windows. Tevanian argued that browser integration into the OS, instead of just bundling the two programs, simply resulted in greater confusion and overheads. For him, integration brought no benefit, perhaps it only brought harm. Basing himself on Apple's experience, Tevanian said that it was possible to remove the Cyberdog browser from the Mac OS without compromising the OS in any way. (This was, of course, the complete opposite of what Microsoft had all along maintained.) In Tevanian's view, Apple could better serve customers' needs by bundling – instead of integrating – browsers with operating systems.

Another government witness was Intel vice-president Steven McGeady (Brinkley and Lohr 2001: 80–86). In 1995 Intel was developing its 'native signal processing' (NSP) software, intended to enhance the performance of multimedia applications. Initially, PC makers were enthusiastic with NSP, although Microsoft did not like it because it inhered in the operating space of Windows. In the end, both Intel and PC makers had to give in and toe Microsoft's line, since NSP would practically be useless without Windows compatibility. Additional conflicts arose when Intel prepared programs to support Java, the internet programming language of Sun Microsystems. Theoretically, Java could overshadow Windows' dominance as computing migrated from isolated PCs to the web.

John Soyring, an IBM executive in charge of developing the OS/2 operating system, was also presented as government witness (Brinkley and Lohr 2001: 90–95). Way back in 1981, IBM gave Microsoft its big break; first, by choosing MS-DOS as the operating system for its personal computers, and second, by allowing Microsoft to license MS-DOS to other PC makers. A decade later, however, Microsoft failed to reciprocate IBM's largesse. Instead, Microsoft imposed contract restrictions on software developers, effectively preventing OS/2, IBM's operating system, from competing with Windows. Software engineers need certain programming tools to write applications that would be compatible with a given operating system. Microsoft, however, expressly forbade software designers from using their tools in writing applications for operating systems other than Windows. Therefore, if a software developer wanted to create an application – like a word processing program, for example – for computers running on OS/2, Microsoft's restriction forced him to re-create the application almost entirely from scratch. This lack of support made it extremely difficult to justify the cost of developing applications that were compatible with the OS/2 operating system. As a result, Windows had practically driven OS/2 out of the market, leaving it with a paltry 6 per cent share.

A couple of weeks later Dr John Gosling, vice president of Sun Microsystems and chief scientist of the Java internet programming language, took his turn at the witness stand (Brinkley and Lohr 2001: 102–10). Gosling created Java in 1991 for the specific purpose of freeing programmers from platform-specific software. At that time, Sun began to work closely with Netscape, using the Navigator browser to distribute Java. The goal was to make applications run on any computer in the future, regardless of the operating system. Hence, the Java motto, 'Write once, run anywhere.' The end result was what Bill Gates had feared the most: the 'commoditization' of operating systems – such as Microsoft's Windows – by an Internet programming language, such as Sun's Java. This outcome was virtually the same as the substitution of operating systems by browsers, such as the Netscape Navigator, in Internet computing.

After obtaining a Java license from Sun in 1995, Microsoft wrote its own version of Java, which was incompatible with the original. According to Gosling, in September 1997, Microsoft introduced an upgrade of its browser, Internet Explorer 4.0, linked to Windows OS in such a way that it undermined Java's cross-platform technology. What Microsoft did to Java was similar to polluting the English language with jargon that nobody else understood, Gosling explained. Speaking on behalf of software designers, Gosling expressed his resentment at the way Microsoft hampered innovation through abusive practices and predatory behavior: 'Microsoft has this basic strategy they call "embrace and extend" which some people call "disgrace and distend" ... But it's all about making it easy so that people can get on to the Microsoft platform. And then they screw around with it so that going the other direction is really hard' (Brinkley and Lohr 2001: 103).

David Farber and Edward Felten, computer experts from the University of Pennsylvania and Princeton, respectively, were likewise called upon to testify for the government (Brinkley and Lohr 2001: 110–19). Crucial to Microsoft's defense was the claim that integrating Internet Explorer with Windows improved the efficiency of both products. Farber attacked this argument head-on: 'there are no technical barriers that prevent Microsoft from developing and selling its Windows operating system as a stand-alone product separate from its browser software. ... There are no technical efficiencies for users achieved by combining Microsoft's browser software sold as Windows 98 that could not be achieved by writing two programs in a manner that could later be loaded and "integrated" [by manufacturers or consumers themselves]' (Brinkley and Lohr 2001: 111).

Felten's intervention was particularly devastating to Microsoft's stand, since he demonstrated that it was possible to disable and remove Internet Explorer from Windows without interfering with the latter's functions. This was the complete opposite of what Microsoft had all along maintained. Felten, with his prototype removal program, showed that Windows 98 still booted properly and remained stable under ordinary use, even without Internet Explorer. In fact, in September 1998 Felten provided Microsoft with a copy of the removal program. But then, in a manner reminiscent of what it had done with Java, Microsoft 'modified' – 'sabotaged', would be more accurate – the updated versions of its software, rendering them incompatible with programs altered by Felten's prototype.

A sign of monopolistic abuse is an overriding ability to dictate prices to the market. An internal Microsoft document revealed that between 1990 and 1996 Windows licensing fees rose from $19.03 to $49.40, representing a five-fold increase in its share of a PC's total price (Brinkley and Lohr 2001: 123). This was despite a clear downward trend in the prices of PC parts, as Joachim Kempin, a senior Microsoft manager, himself acknowledged in an e-mail to Bill Gates on 16 December 1997: 'While we have increased our prices over the last 10 years, other component prices have come down and continue to come down' (Brinkley and Lohr 2001: 124). At first, Microsoft tried to justify price increases by alluding to the new features added to Windows. But then William Harris, the CEO of Intuit, the software company responsible for such programs as Quicken or TurboTax, offered a spiked response in his testimony (Brinkley and Lohr 2001: 125). Harris said that all software vendors – Intuit and Microsoft included – add functionalities to their programs over the years, as part of business development. But while the price of other software programs like Quicken declined, the price of Microsoft Windows constantly rose.

The government, towards the end of its presentation, cited cases in which Microsoft used strong-arm tactics against companies, as soon as these grew cozy with competitors (Brinkley and Lohr 2001: 120). Disney was threatened with the removal of its logo and link from the Windows channel bar, for example, when it tightened its relationship with Netscape. Not even the 'Big Blue', IBM, was exempt from such harassment. Joachim Kempin, a Microsoft manager, annoyed by IBM's growing ties with Lotus, a rival in business software, circulated an e-mail in March 1994 saying that the company should organize a 'hit team to attack IBM as a large account, whereby the OEM [original equipment manufacturer] relationship should be used to apply some pressure' (Brinkley and Lohr 2001: 120).

In September 1999 Judge Jackson manifested his intention to deliver his verdict in two installments in order to urge both sides to settle. On 6 November 1998, Jackson made public his 'findings of fact' or conclusions regarding factual issues (Brinkley and Lohr 2001: 263–7). Jackson established that Microsoft had abused its monopoly power, simultaneously hampering innovation, thwarting competition and harming consumers. To facilitate settlement, Jackson had appointed a mediator in the person of Richard Posner, chief circuit court judge in Chicago. But all efforts were in vain.

Finally, Jackson had little choice but to issue a draconian ruling on 4 April 2000. In violation of the Sherman Antitrust Act, 'Microsoft maintained its monopoly power by anticompetitive means and attempted to monopolize the Web browser market unlawfully tying its Web browser to its operating system' (Brinkley and Lohr 2001: 292). In one point, however, Jackson ruled in Microsoft's favor. The company's marketing contracts promoting Internet Explorer cleared the legal standard. At this juncture the case entered the phase of determining remedies.

Judge Jackson was at first reluctant to impose a drastic structural remedy, feeling more inclined towards lighter conduct remedies. Yet he confessed to having been astounded by remarks made by Gates and Ballmer – the chairman and president of Microsoft, respectively – insisting that they had done no wrong and brazenly proclaiming to the four winds that they would not change the company's business practices. Expecting signs of contrition from Microsoft and getting a show of defiance instead, Jackson retorted: 'I'm in the midst of a growing realization that, with what looks like Microsoft intransigence, a break-up is inevitable' (Brinkley and Lohr 2001: 316). So he decided on 8 June 2000.

On the same day that he ordered the breakup of Microsoft into two separate companies – one with the Windows operating system and another with the remaining computer programs and Internet business – and mandated a long list of conduct remedies, Jackson afforded a peek into his motives for such a severe decision. First was Microsoft's continued claims to innocence; second, its unwillingness to alter business practices significantly to conform to law; and third, the fact that Microsoft 'has proved untrustworthy in the past' (Brinkley and Lohr 2001: 319).

Jackson's thoughts on Microsoft's recidivist ways later on proved to be prophetic. In October 2000, Microsoft purchased 25 per cent of Corel, the Canadian software firm that made WordPerfect, until then perhaps the only remaining competitor to Microsoft Word (*The Economist* 2000). WordPerfect, once the market leader in word processing programs, had thus completely succumbed to Microsoft's mortal embrace. In December 2000 Microsoft announced that it was abandoning its PC-centric world view and unveiled plans for a pure Internet era; its core '.Net' strategy, however, sounded eerily familiar (Markoff 2000). Through the .Net operating system, Microsoft would transform itself from a software vendor into a supplier of a myriad of on-line services including digital wallets, software subscriptions and even e-commerce portals. Among the .Net's components would be the XBox video game player; the Ultimate TV, a cable and satellite TV that builds on the WebTV Internet TV service; the Windows Media Player for multimedia functions; the MSN Messenger for instant messaging; the Reader electronic publishing software;

the SQL Server 2000 for databases; the Pocket PC for hand-held computing; a Windows-based cellular phone service and of course, new tailor-fitted versions of the Windows XP operating system. Need we have further proof of the breadth of Microsoft's embrace?

Since then, the Microsoft antitrust case seems to have developed a life of its own, with a history too tedious to follow in all of its ramifications. It went from the Federal District Court to the Appeals Court, and after a failed attempt to be heard at the Supreme Court it returned to the Federal District Court once more, but this time around with Judge Thomas Penfield Jackson recused and Judge Colleen Kollar-Kotelly presiding. Half of the original plaintiff states have settled, half still pursue their case. Meanwhile, class action lawsuits have mushroomed in at least 10 states.

Certainly, Judge Jackson's original penalties may never be applied, yet the mere fact of the trial and the scrutiny it has invited of Microsoft's practices have already caused a serious dent in the company's once shining armor. Regardless of whether the government were ultimately to lose or to settle, Microsoft would have already been fundamentally changed by this experience, its voracious and predatory appetites tamed and curbed.

II.   HABITS: HIGHER, FASTER, STRONGER

Habits are the 'compound interest' of moral capital; they are what make one's level of moral capital grow higher, faster and stronger. Just like regular practice and exercise for athletes, habits enable individual and corporate agents to perform more actions and to perform them better, with greater naturalness, pleasure or ease. Agents not only do better, but they also become better; their doing determines what they become. This is because habits and customs – standard operating procedures or protocols, in the case of organizations – produce 'automatic mechanisms', allowing agents to direct thoughts and energies to other novel concerns.

Habits are not only a help, they are a necessity for human life. Human life cannot be reduced simply to a series of actions performed by an agent. Other integrating factors are needed, aside from an agent's memory and the continuity of time. Every voluntary human act – no matter how insignificant or isolated – leaves a lasting trace or mark; something always remains in the agent, even after an act is completely finished. This inexorable by-product of human action is what we call habit: a stable disposition or manner of being, doing, acting or behaving in a subject.

Human beings are creatures of habit because they are bereft of instincts. Our capacity to develop customs or habits makes up for our natural lack of instincts. Any other animal at birth behaves as if it were the first of its kind, relying solely on its instincts or innate tendencies for survival. In place of instincts, we humans depend on an acquired culture or tradition, usually transmitted from one individual to another through families and communities, to keep ourselves alive and flourishing. This culture is ultimately composed of habits, acquired common practices or customary ways of behaving and doing things. Without habits and culture our existence on earth would hardly qualify as human.

Certain conditions have to be met before habits appear. Basically, habits require time and freedom on the part of the agent. These conditions could only be satisfied properly by human beings.

Time means a certain permanence or duration in being. More precisely, time signifies a capacity for change, such that an agent could distinguish between a 'before' and an 'after' with respect to some kind of movement. Time measures change. However, this change or motion should not be too radical or absolute, so as to destroy an agent's identity. In order to acquire habits, an agent should not only be capable of change – and thus be subject to time – but should also be able to withstand change without loss of his identity.

In explaining the virtues as habits, Aristotle first insists on differentiating them from natural conditions. Habits are acquired and their acquisition – an agent's habituation – involves time. Time is necessary not only in producing a change in the agent, but also in developing the habits themselves, since as a rule habits grow gradually through the repetition of acts. Natural conditions, on the other hand, are not acquired but innate; and no amount of time, habituation, repetition, exercise or practice could ever change their state. Natural conditions are timeless, in the sense of unchanging or permanent.

This does not mean, however, that virtues are completely independent of natural conditions. For as Aristotle painstakingly teaches, 'the virtues arise in us neither by nature nor against nature, ... we are by nature able to acquire them, and reach our complete perfection through habit' (NE 1103a). We are capable of acquiring habits because it is a demand of our human nature. And although our nature orients us towards the acquisition of virtues and habits, human nature alone – that is, without the concurrence of individual choice and action – is insufficient for virtues and habits to develop. Temporality or the capacity for change manifests itself in a special way in human beings through our distinctive ability to adapt ourselves to our environment and to learn. In developing proper habits we improve and achieve perfection as agents and human beings.

Apart from time, the other necessary condition for habits to develop is freedom. That is why the formation of good habits – or proper habituation and education – is a primary task of legislators: 'the legislator makes the citizens good by habituating them, and this is the wish of every legislator; if he fails to do it well he misses his goal. [The right] habituation is what makes the difference between a good political system and a bad one' (NE 1103b).

It makes no sense to legislate on natural phenomena because these occur as a matter of necessity: a stone always falls to the ground, in the same way that a flame always rises in the air. Rather, we legislate on what is contingent, on what could be otherwise, on that whose determination depends on us or is within our power.

Freedom is said to exist on three different levels. The first is physical freedom which consists in an openness of one's nature and a capacity for movement. A human being is deprived of this freedom when bound or held captive. Although such a person normally has the physical capacity to move around, neverthe-less, he is unable to do so, because he is prevented by a superior and contrary external force. His physical powers are, to an extent, rendered useless. Next comes psychological freedom or freedom of choice. This means that whenever a person chooses, the determining factor in his choice is none other than himself, that is, his sovereign will. No amount of external pressure, physical, psycho-logical or of any other sort, would ever be sufficient to bend his will towards a certain direction, so long as he internally resisted. The moral principle of the 'inviolability of conscience' derives from this level of freedom, the freedom of choice. Another important consequence of psychological freedom is that one completely identifies himself with his moral choices, assuming full responsi-bility for them.

The third and last level of freedom belongs to moral freedom. Unlike the first two levels of freedom which are givens, forming part of the natural condition of human beings, moral freedom only comes about as the result of a laborious conquest. Physical freedom and psychological freedom are 'negative freedoms'; freedoms from contrary physical forces and psychological deter-minants respectively. Moral freedom, on the other hand, is a 'positive freedom', a freedom for something superior and greater than one's natural condition. Moral freedom is achieved when one develops virtues or good habits.

If physical freedom corresponds to a certain 'power', and psychological freedom, to a 'power to choose', moral freedom builds up on both as a 'power to choose the good'; that is, a 'power to choose that which perfects one's nature and being'. Thanks to the virtues or good habits that constitute moral freedom, we are able to widen the scope of our 'natural freedoms', increasing and inten-sifying them. That is, we are able to perform more good actions and perform them better, not only from the objective viewpoint of the actions themselves, but also from our own subjective viewpoint (in terms of 'moral skill', pleasure or satisfaction).

What habits could we detect from Microsoft's corporate behavior over the decade of the 1990s? First is the pattern of integrating products to exploit the market dominance of one of its components, which happens to be the de facto industry standard. Microsoft has repeatedly engaged in such actions, despite their having been declared illegal, or at least, objectionable from the perspective of fair competition. This occured with Windows OS, whose licensing was practically tied to the Microsoft Office suite, containing programs as Word or Excel, with Windows multimedia player, and of course, with Internet Explorer web browser. More recently, the same strategy was employed in the development and marketing of the .Net initiative, which brought together a variety of on-line services, including instant messaging. None of these events happened by accident or chance. Rather, they all formed part of a deliberate corporate plan, aptly summarized in the phrase 'embrace, extend and extinguish'.

Another Microsoft vice or corporate bad habit consists in stifling innovation whenever it comes from other companies. Microsoft perceived Sun's internet programming language, Java, as a threat, and consequently tried to force it out of the market, because it was compatible with any platform and was not subservient to Windows OS. Microsoft applied the same tactics to Intel's NSP software, designed to improve multimedia applications, because it occupied part of Windows' digital space. For more than a decade – as an e-mail from a senior manager attested – Microsoft also engaged in the habit of raising prices abusively. As a result, Window's share of the total price of a PC quintupled. This ran counter to the software industry trend, notwithstanding price adjustments for new programs features. All of these behaviors took place reiteratively during prolonged periods, thus increasing Microsoft's responsibility over them.

On a more personal note, Microsoft chairman, Bill Gates, and his second-in-command, Steve Ballmer, both displayed the unfortunate custom of never admitting mistakes, not even after these had already been proven in the courts. Not once did Gates or Ballmer go past the stage of denial regarding errors. Instead, they always insisted on their innocence and tried to portray themselves as victims of an unholy alliance between the government and their competitors. According to Gates and Ballmer, since Microsoft did no wrong, they personally had no reason to repent nor motives to amend their business practices. Such insistence was taken to be a sign of defiance that ended up consuming the patience of Judge Jackson.

We know that for habits to arise, it is not sufficient that actions be done repeatedly for extended periods. It is also necessary that these actions be performed freely. What about Microsoft's allegation that it could not have done otherwise regarding the charge of illegal integration? Apparently, for the company, that was what product development was all about: integrating programs into Windows OS and subsequent versions. However, as several expert witnesses demonstrated, it was possible – indeed, preferable, from the consumer's viewpoint – to 'deconstruct' Windows, selling the operating system separately from the Internet Explorer browser and other applications.

One may ask, what about Microsoft's freedom to do with Windows as it pleases? What of Microsoft's legitimate intellectual property rights? No doubt this issue requires serious thought, for it draws from the very base of existing economic, legal and political institutions. Yet any argument that Microsoft tries to build upon this foundation cannot help but be discredited by its past conduct; for example, by the way it copied the 'look and feel' of Apple Macintosh's operating system. Or more recently, by the manner in which Microsoft sabotaged versions of Sun's Java or Felten's prototype removal program to suit its purposes. One could only demand as much respect as it is willing to show towards the property rights of others.

After this peek into the nature of habits as related to the necessary conditions of time and freedom, we are now in a better position to understand the dynamics of habits. Following Aristotle, our starting point once again becomes the contrast between habits and nature:

> if something arises in us by nature, we first have the capacity for it, and later display the activity ... Virtues, by contrast, we acquire, just as we acquire crafts, by having previously activated them. For we learn a craft by producing the same product that we must produce when we have learned it, become builders, e.g., by building and harpists by playing the harp; so also, then, we become just by doing just actions, temperate by doing temperate actions, brave by doing brave actions (NE 1103a–b).

A purely sequential mode of thinking is not appropriate to understand how habits develop, because unlike in nature, where the capacity precedes the activity, in habits, the activity itself creates the capacity. In other words, the creation of the capacity and the exercise of the activity require each other; they occur simultaneously and are mutually reinforcing. Habits comprise a perfectly integrated feedback loop in human beings, capable of increasing their own potential. A habit is produced when a human being – by his own choice, although relying on his nature – performs a free act, and that free act, once finished, nevertheless still leaves a trace, a modification, that the agent retains or keeps. That modification is a stable disposition to further action in a specific manner, towards a certain goal or direction. This modification is called habit, for it vests human nature – the principle of operation or action – with a new, improved and reinforced tendency. Habits constitute a 'second nature'.

Perhaps it would be best to continue with the craft analogy to further explain the acquisition, growth and perfection of habits. In order to play the guitar, one also needs, aside from the guitar itself, certain physical faculties like human arms, hands, fingers, an ear for music, a capacity to read a musical score, and so on. But all of these things are worthless if one decides not to exert the effort of learning. Of course there are all sorts of external influences that could affect one's decision-making, but in the end, for the decision to be truly effective, it would have to be of one's own choosing. The first time you pick up the guitar and strum a few chords, chances are that the result would be a horrific noise that hardly qualifies as music. This would be so no matter how simple the musical piece played. The tips of your fingers, even your whole hand, could get sore while trying to press on the strings, reach for the chords and coordinate these movements with the strumming. It could not be an enjoyable experience at all.

However, if you were to persevere and continue practicing, the sounds would come out each time with a little less pain and effort than the last. You then begin to make beautiful music – more or less harmonious, depending on your native talent – on the guitar. You could try more complicated scores and even improvise, jazzing up pieces, perhaps, and leaving your personal mark on the music. Then you could really enjoy yourself, for the music – aside from being objectively beautiful – also comes out effortlessly, naturally, as it were. It could only be a matter of time before the guitar player turns into a virtuoso. By then, not only would you have acquired the craft of guitar playing, but you would have also perfected it. In this sense, the dynamics of the art of guitar playing are similar to the development of any other moral virtue or good habit. Both of them enable their possessor to do more things and do them with greater perfection, objectively and subjectively. In neither case does theory alone suffice; practice and habituation are of the essence. Note further how the different levels of freedom intervene, in the development of a craft as in the development of moral virtue.

After these reflections on the dynamics of habits, we now understand how and why the corporate vices attributed to Microsoft – preeminently, the serial abuse of its monopolistic position – became so deeply ingrained in its culture. At first, these decisions could have been difficult to make, but after a time engaged in these practices, the main difficulty had become for the company to abandon this mode of conduct. These practices had created an almost over-whelming tendency in Microsoft to constantly extend its tentacles farther, squeeze tighter and snuff out competition faster, all as a part of normal corporate strategy. Time – not to mention legal experience – just made it a lot easier. Microsoft had learned that lawyers could be used to stall proceedings through appeals, while keeping the corporate steamroller charging at full speed. In light of these circumstances, Judge Jackson's order for a structural break-up – instead of mere admonitions for better behavior – appeared less drastic and more realistic as a remedy.

Insofar as they participate in the nature of habits, of craft expertise and its deficiency, virtues and vices indistinctly arise from the repetition of actions. This is what is meant by the phrase 'just as in the case of a craft, the sources and means that develop each virtue also ruin it' (NE 1103b). Not any sort of action will do, however, 'for building well makes good builders, building badly, bad ones' (NE 1103b). Only the right sort of actions produce craft expertise, in the same way that only good actions produce virtues or good habits. For example, when faced with the same terrifying situation, those who have acquired the habit of courage react bravely and confidently, while those who have acquired the habit of cowardice, fearfully. 'The same is true of situations involving appetites and anger; for one or another sort of conduct in these situations makes some people temperate and gentle, others intemperate and irascible' (NE 1103b).

Therefore, the right sort of habituation produces virtues or good habits, whereas the wrong sort, vices or bad habits. But how are we to distinguish the right from the wrong sort of habituation? How are we to differentiate virtues from vices?

First and foremost, in order to acquire proper habituation, 'actions should express correct reason' (NE 1103b). The individual actions whose repetition constitute a habit should be done in accordance with reason; not in theory or in the abstract alone, but as what is reasonable or opportune in each particular case, as expert doctors or navigators decide, for example, in actual practice. Business decisions are, of course, of this nature.

Secondly, the right sort of habituation equally shuns actions in excess and in defect:

> Too much or too little eating or drinking ruins health, while the proportionate amount produces, increases and preserves it. The same is true, then, of temperance, bravery and the other virtues. For if, e.g., someone avoids and is afraid of everything, standing firm against nothing, he becomes cowardly, but if he is afraid of nothing at all and goes to face everything, he becomes rash. Similarly, if he gratifies himself with every pleasure and refrains from none, he becomes intemperate, but if he avoids them all, as boors do, he becomes some sort of insensible person. Temperance and bravery, then are ruined by excess and deficiency but preserved by the mean (NE 1104a).

Most business decisions are directed towards striking a balance between acquis-itiveness or greed and earning sufficient profits to maintain and improve operations.

Thirdly, proper habituation comes from an individual's experiencing pleasure or pain in the appropriate kind of action. 'For if someone who abstains from bodily pleasures enjoys the abstinence itself, then he is temperate, but if he is grieved by it, he is intemperate. Again, if he stands firm against terrifying situations and enjoys it, or at least does not find it painful, then he is brave, and if he finds it painful, he is cowardly' (NE 1104b). In success as well as in failure, there is a certain 'graciousness' to be lived in business.

In summary, therefore, with respect to habit, 'virtue is a state that decides, [consisting] in a mean, the mean relative to us, which is defined by reference to reason, i.e., to the reason by reference to which the intelligent person would define it. It is a mean between two vices, one of excess and one of deficiency' (NE 1107a). This explains why there is no single cut and dried formula for good business and why each firm has to chart its own course to succeed.

An apparent contradiction surfaces, after these explanations about the nature and the necessary conditions for virtue. Contrary to what we initially held, it may not be possible to acquire virtue, and virtue may instead be a natural state, for in order to become just – for example – one must first do just actions. Yet just actions could only be done by one who is already just! This circular reasoning leads us to think that either one is already – that is, by nature – just, and therefore, could perform just actions, or one is not, and being incapable of just actions, no amount of habituation would ever make him just.

The clarifications which Aristotle offers, apart from undoing this seeming paradox, likewise serve to establish the limits of the craft analogy. In the crafts, it is possible to produce something that conforms to a certain expertise only in appearance. In fact, the object may have been produced 'by chance or by following someone else's instructions' (NE 1105a); that is, without the proper accompanying knowledge. Furthermore, 'the products of a craft determine by their own character whether they have been produced well; and so it suffices that they are in the right state when they have been produced' (NE 1105b). There is an objective goodness, therefore, in craft products, that allows their identification as such, without need of further reference to the creator.

This is not the case, however, with the virtues:

> for actions expressing virtue to be done temperately or justly [and hence well] it does not suffice that they are themselves in the right state. Rather, the agent must also be in the right state when he does them. First he must know [that he is doing virtuous actions]; second, he must decide on them, and decide on them for themselves; and third, he must also do them from a firm and unchanging state (NE 1105a).

There is no such thing as an objectively virtuous action in itself considered, that is, independently of the person who performs it. A virtuous act could never be separated from the virtuous habit that emerges, nor ultimately, from the virtuous person who possesses the habit. For an action to be virtuous it has to be performed as a virtuous person would do it, and this entails three conditions: knowledge or advertence that one is doing a virtuous act; the will or decision to do the virtuous act for itself, not for any other; and lastly, the presence of a habit – that 'firm and unchanging state' – from which the virtuous act proceeds.

The insistence not only on the external, objective, conditions surrounding a virtuous act, but also on its internal, subjective, conditions is indeed very important. Virtue cannot be confined to what is merely apparent, or to what is only superficially good. As we may recall, 'every virtue causes its possessors to be in a good state and to perform their functions well' (NE 1106a). Virtue demands integrity, a complete, thorough and integral goodness. Therefore, rather than any form of partial goodness or excellence, 'the virtue of a human being will likewise be the state that makes a human being good and makes him perform his function well' (NE 1106a).

Albeit in contrast, we could say that Microsoft's habitual anticompetitive practices were not in accordance with 'right reason' as established by the regulators and the courts. The company repeatedly went beyond the limits of just and fair competition – thus sinning in excess – abusing its dominant position in the market. And it even seemed to take perverse pleasure in its unlawful actions, locking customers in, locking competitors out, keeping innovation at bay and raising prices. The most that the courts' negative rulings obtained were temporary slowdowns, or bits and pieces of purely external compliance, without any true internal change of corporate heart.

III. WORKING CAPITAL

If virtues fulfill a constitutive, integrating and perfecting role with regard to human beings, then they must be the right lens under which to consider the reality of work. Work certainly consists in a purposive and free human act, although not all purposive and free human acts qualify as work. Rather, work is normally reserved to designate productive actions exclusively. Productive actions are those which focus on concrete, individual objects, with a view to changing or transforming them. They differ from pure theory or abstract thought, which simply aims at uncovering or reflecting what is universal and necessary in reality. While the conclusions of productive knowledge are prescriptive, that is, they ordain how things ought to be done, those of theoretical knowledge are descriptive, they just express or manifest things as they are.

Work, as we said, is a form of production, and production itself may be divided into two sorts: making or doing. Each time a human being produces, or causes something to be, from previously existing means and materials, two different products always come out as a result. The first is an objective product, usually something capable of independent existence from the human agent, or at least, something that manifests itself externally and is observable by others. The second is a subjective product that inheres in the agent himself and is inseparable from him; it need not show itself directly to the outside, although it would always have its indirect consequences. Depending on where one places the emphasis, production could be considered as mainly of either kind: making, if on the objective product, and doing, if on the subjective product.

Examples of making would be the practice of the crafts and of the fine arts. What is important in making is the external object itself, considered a work of art or a prime example of a craft, with the skill of the artist or artisan taking second place. Many kinds of work – understood as regular and stable, rather than as isolated or intermittent activities – belong to this category. A lot of ink has run trying to figure out the difference between craftsmanship, or the work of an artisan, and the work of an artist or exponent of the fine arts. One of the better solutions consists in establishing that the rule or norm for craftsmanship is external to production itself, whereas in the fine arts, it is internal. In the crafts, the procedure or steps to be taken in the production process could, in principle, be externally captured and verbally expressed in the form of instructions or guidelines. In theory, anyone following a craft rule-book could be guaranteed of the product or results, as long as he kept to the letter of the instructions. In the case of the fine arts, however, no such valid manual or set of instructions exists. Instead, the rule or norm seems to be particular or idiosyncratic to each work of art, and the principal task of the artist consists in discovering it, as he comes in contact with the raw materials. The distinction between the crafts and the fine arts explains why objects belonging to the former could be mass produced, while those belonging to the latter are necessarily unique or one of a kind.

The other kind of production that centers on the subjective product is what we normally call doing. It denotes an activity that is more immanent or reflexive than transient or transitive: it begins with the agent and ends in himself, instead of in an external object. The human being is, at the same time, the agent and the patient of the production process. In a very real sense, therefore, we are dealing here with a process of 'self-production', where man is maker (*homo faber*) of himself. The main end product or result of doing is not an independent artifact, but rather, an operative moral habit. And in the measure that what one acquires are virtues, the process of self-production is, at the same time, a process of self-perfection. Finally, while making is guided either by the habit of craftsmanship or that of a fine art, doing is guided above all by the habit of prudence, practical reasoning or practical wisdom.

After distinguishing the two kinds of production, making and doing, and after explaining the habits that accompany each of them, craftsmanship and art for making, prudence for doing, it is convenient to clarify the relationships between each pair. As stressed earlier, making and doing are two inseparable dimensions present in any form of productive human activity. It just so happens that in certain kinds of production, a greater emphasis is placed on the external product (making), while in others, on the internal product (doing). Conscious of the inseparability of the two, for purposes of moral capital formation, one should endeavor to safeguard the primacy of the internal product over the external product. That is, subject the practice of both craftsmanship and the fine arts – all forms of productive work, for that matter – to the guidance of the moral virtue of prudence.

Being a regular and stable productive activity, we understand work as a habit and generator of habits. It is in and through the exercise of work that our good actions; the basic currency of moral capital, become virtues or good habits; the compound interest of moral capital. Considering that work normally occupies the greatest part of our useful, waking hours, its significance extends far beyond the limits of any other ordinary habit. No other habit plays such a large role in the constitution of the self or the agent's identity as work.

There are many ways in which human beings refer to the sociological reality of work; as an occupation, an employment, a career or a profession. Although these terms designate the same objective reality, they are not synonymous, they do not mean the same thing. Rather, they point to different dimensions or different ways of viewing one and the same multifaceted reality, work. In order to discover how work could best contribute to the formation and growth of moral capital, it would be worthwhile to explore its full range of meanings.

Occupation is the physical category with which we refer to work. It signifies work as the activity in which we spend most of our useful or productive time. For the vast majority of human beings, work as occupation is a given, nothing to fret or worry about. It would only be problematic in special cases, for those who are too young, too old or too sick, and are thus unable to engage in any concrete activity for long periods. These people find difficulty in filling their time, to the point of having to sign up for occupational therapy, perhaps. Being enormously wealthy could also present one with similar problems, since there would be no need to be tied down by any activity in order to earn one's keep. As occupation, work is a terminus or an end in itself, whose value is measured in the time or duration that one spends engaged in it. A human being relates to his work, understood as occupation, as a 'place' he occupies or in which he 'stays'.

Employment, on the other hand, is a formal, economic category that we use in referring to work. It denotes a job, a stable, regular and even legally regulated activity for which one receives income or money. For this reason, despite having a well-defined occupation, housewives, students and apprentices, for example, are not considered employed. Employment is work as a means of livelihood, for oneself and for all those under one's care. In this regard, employment is not valued in terms of the time spent in it, but in the money or income it generates. Money, of course, gives one access to anything and everything that bears a price. Normally we say that a person has a job or employment; although unfortunately, in some cases, it seems to be the other way around. That is, a person is 'possessed' by his job, whenever he is held captive or trapped by the financial rewards that a job brings. In other words, whenever money is the prime motive or exclusive reason for working.

By career, we highlight the psychologically satisfying dimension of work. A career traces a worker's progress through several jobs or occupations in the course of a lifetime. It is work viewed as a means for self-fulfillment. The more or the higher the goals that one reaches within a shorter period of time, the more successful one is in one's career. The value of a career, therefore, depends on the success, honors or fame that one achieves; and this, in turn, is contingent upon the standards that any given organization or society has set for itself and its members. Success in work considered as a career consists in 'making it' or clearing an established standard. In this respect, it is very revealing that Vincent

Van Gogh, career-wise, as a painter, was a remarkable failure. He was neither understood nor appreciated by his contemporaries; he was unable to sell any single painting during his lifetime. Little did he – or anyone, for that matter – suspect, that a century after his death, his paintings would draw princely sums in auctions and his exhibits attract record-breaking crowds.

Finally, when we refer to work as a profession, we underscore its social dimension. As a profession, the work that one does defines his identity. It answers the fundamental questions about who he is and what is his place or function in the web of personal relationships that constitutes society. A profession is work viewed with a communitarian orientation; it is a public declaration of one's office or commitments towards his fellow men. Traditionally, such would be the case of public school teachers or family doctors, for example, in small provincial towns. They perceive their work, above all, as a means of service, as the response to a transcendent mission, vocation or calling. Work as a profession becomes synonymous with their purpose in life or the reason for their existence. Hence, the value of a profession is measured in terms of the diligence with which persons respond to their calling or the faithfulness with which they keep their commitments. For a worker, a profession is his being; a profession is all-encompassing.

These various concepts and meanings associated with work require that a hierarchy or an order be established among them. Certainly, work as occupation should not rank the highest, for it ignores the particularly human, self-perfecting capacity of work. Neither should work as employment, although in times of need it would be understandable that material rewards take precedence. Otherwise, putting one's job before everything else would be symptomatic of the vice of avarice or greed. Such an outlook necessarily brings frustration and deception, for the money that one seeks is not an end in itself but only a means. Similarly, a person who judges his career as the most important aspect of his work is, in truth, someone to be feared. In strict logic, he will not stop and will even destroy any obstacle that comes in the way of his self-affirmation. The remaining option, therefore, is the consideration of work as a profession. A profession expresses the highest value of work. It alone could properly accommodate the other concepts or meanings that we attach to work, leaving each one in its own place. Only within the context of a profession could the other dimensions of work – occupation, employment and career – be harmoniously integrated in a flourishing human life. By considering work as a profession, one earns the highest interest rate for his moral capital.

Analogously, in the case of Microsoft as a corporate agent, we could say that it has clearly put 'making' before 'doing', allowing its technological expertise to go berserk while turning its back to fair market conditions and consumer welfare. In its conduct, Microsoft has relegated any profession of service to the last place, busying itself instead with keeping a dominant market position (the equivalent of an individual's occupation or employment) and maintaining its corporate pride (what would be an individual's career) afloat at all costs.

IV   IN BRIEF

- Habits, which arise from the repetition of voluntary human actions, reinforce an agent's will and intention with regard to those actions and modify his responsibility for them. Protocols or standard operating procedures are the equivalent of habits for corporate agents. Habits and protocols function like the compound interest of moral capital, allowing their respective subject's level of moral capital to grow higher, faster and stronger.

- In cases before US courts, Microsoft was accused of the 'corporate vice' or 'pattern of bad behavior' of illegally extending its monopoly from operating systems (Windows) to other software markets, embracing them and effectively extinguishing in them any form of competition. Similarly, Microsoft was charged with harming consumers by repeatedly stifling software innovation and dictating inflated prices to the market over the years. For all of its faults, however, Microsoft stubbornly insisted that it did no wrong, that it could not do otherwise in the course of developing its products, and that there was no reason for it to make amends. Microsoft's permanently defiant attitude prodded Judge Jackson to order the break-up of the company, instead of mandating lighter, conduct remedies.

- Time and freedom are the necessary conditions that enable a subject to acquire habits. An individual must be capable of change, but without losing his identity, and his actions must be determined by his own intelligence and will, rather than by instincts. Freedom in human beings may be found in three levels: physical freedom, psychological freedom and moral freedom. Habits perfect moral freedom, in particular, because they enable an agent to perform more actions and to perform them better, both objectively and subjectively.

- Habits display a peculiar dynamism in their acquisition, growth and perfection. The performance of an activity itself creates the capacity for it, in the form of a habit. A habit grows through the repetition of actions: practice makes perfect. A good habit or virtue is one that expresses correct reason, one that equally avoids excess and defect, and one that allows its subject to experience pleasure and pain appropriately.

- Moral habits differ from craft knowledge in that their actions cannot be truly virtuous without reference to the agent's knowledge, will, and 'firm and unchanging state' or disposition.

- A human agent primarily increases his moral capital through a productive habit called work. Work has two inseparable dimensions: an objective one, with emphasis on the external product or 'making', and a subjective one, with emphasis on the internal product or 'doing'. For purposes of moral capital development, a greater importance must be put on the subjective aspect of work than on its objective aspect. Through work, the *homo faber* becomes the product of his own doing and making.
- The sociological reality of work has acquired multiple meanings: occupation, employment, career and profession. Apart from their own particular significance, each of these terms expresses a way in which the individual relates to his work and values it. Profession is proposed as the deepest understanding of work, that which expresses its supreme value. It is what best accommodates the other dimensions of work, integrating them into a full life for the purpose of moral capital development.

REFERENCES

Aristotle (1985), *Nicomachean Ethics*, trans. Terence Irwin, Indianapolis, IN: Hackett Publishing.
Brinkley, Joel and Steve Lohr (2001), *U.S. v. Microsoft. The inside story of the landmark case*, New York: McGraw-Hill.
Economist, The (2000), 'Microsoft creates another perfect rival', 7 October.
Markoff, J. (2000), 'Microsoft shifts to new vistas', *The New York Times*, 18 December.
Nicomachean Ethics (see Aristotle).

5. Character, moral capital's investment bond

We learned from the preceding chapter that moral capital grows primarily through the development of habits, which function in a manner akin to compound interest in financial capital. Habits, because of their permanence, represent a level of moral capital superior to that of actions. Habits are what remain in the form of acquired inclinations or predispositions after voluntary actions have been completed by a human agent. Habits indicate a higher degree – indeed, the perfection – of personal freedom insofar as they enable an agent to perform more actions of a certain kind and perform them better. This is true both objectively, from the viewpoint of the action itself, and subjectively, from the perspective of the agent. Thanks to habits, the results of an agent's actions improve, and so does the agent, who then performs those actions with greater naturalness, pleasure and ease. Habits therefore create a positive feedback on an agent's skills, reason and will, reinforcing their inclination towards a particular action or class of actions. Through habits our actions influence what we become, and ultimately, who we come to be.

Habits, however, are not the last word in moral capital development and formation. Beyond them we find the level corresponding to character. A person's character enjoys even greater permanence than habits; although in a sense, character is constituted by the different habits – each with its corresponding degree of development – that he has acquired. Again, as often is the case with matters concerning human beings, the whole is greater than the sum of its parts. Although character is, for the large part, made up of habits, it is more difficult to change or modify one's character than it is to change or modify one's habits.

A person's character provides a more accurate expression of his reason and will than his habits taken individually or separately. Not only is character more stable, but it also is more firmly rooted in a person's being. It takes longer and more repetition of a particular act for it to configure a person's character than for it to evolve into a habit. If a person's knowledge and choices best reflect his being, character gives a more complete picture of such a being than habits, which are normally limited to single traits. Knowing a person's character, we would be better able to predict his actions or reactions to different stimuli, than if we just knew of some concrete habit or habits he possessed. Greater voluntariness, advertence and consequently, moral responsibility are involved in matters pertaining to one's character than in those belonging to single habits.

In the same way that a habit unifies the many different although related acts that a person performs, character integrates the diversity of habits that a person possesses into a whole. As we may recall, there are a multitude of habits perfecting each one of a person's indeterminate 'faculties' or operating principles, and every single one of these habits, in turn, is subject to a certain degree of perfection or development. In effect, a person could be not only temperate or brave, but he could also be braver than he is temperate. Character accounts for the various habits that a person possesses as well as for the degree of perfection in which he has developed every one of them. Needless to say, a certain habit becomes more or less effective depending on the other habits a person has cultivated, and the intensity or strength with which he has cultivated each one of them. In any particular person's character, a given habit or group of habits reinforces the influence of some, while diminishing the effect of others. For example, it would be easier for a person who is prudent and wise to be brave, just or temperate. And contrariwise, it would be more difficult for one who is immoderate to be brave, just or prudent. Character lends a unique, personal touch to the host of habits any individual person possesses.

How is personal character related to corporate culture? Since Plato's (1981) *Republic*, a constant theme of social and organizational theory is the parallelism between human beings and society: man is society in miniature whereas society is a human being writ large. A human person may be understood as structured into several levels. At the very core are basic inclinations, tendencies or capacities, only some of which effectively issue into actions. These actions generate habits and these habits, in turn, configure an individual's character.

Similarly, a business firm – which is a particular form of society or organization – may be conceived of as composed of many different layers. At its base are a number of core competencies or strengths, a set of fundamental activities in which an organization is admittedly proficient. Then, supported by these strengths, come a variety of selected goods and services that the firm produces and offers to the market. In the production of these goods and services every firm develops its own standard operating procedures, protocols or techniques. The combination of these proprietary processes characterizes that firm's culture. Far from being a mere collection of pins, slogans and uniforms, therefore, a company's culture ultimately connects with its core competencies, its own portfolio of products and the processes involved in the delivery of these products to the market.

Each of the levels that constitutes a human being has its corresponding layer in an organization or firm. In place of a person's inclinations, tendencies or capacities are the core competencies of an organization. The different actions that an individual carries out have their equivalent in the variety of products that a firm offers. In the same way that in a human being the repetition of actions gives rise to habits, in the case of an organization the continued production of goods and services gives origin to unique methods and procedures. And finally, what character is for a human being, that is culture for an organization or firm: in fact, the same Greek term, *ethos*, is used to refer to both character and culture.

What role does a person's character – or an organization's culture – play with respect to moral capital formation? Following the financial metaphor, we could say that character or culture is like a bond in moral capital. Bonds are financial instruments that governments or corporations use in order to raise funds. An investor defers consumption and purchases a bond in the hope of receiving an income for a set number of years. Only after this period does he expect to recover the principal or original amount loaned. Bonds have a fixed life or date of maturity on which they are to be paid in full, a fixed yearly interest rate normally superior to that of ordinary savings accounts and deposits, and a fixed redemption value.

Bonds are commonly graded according to the triple criteria of risk, rate of return and liquidity. Despite their long lifetimes – which could extend from one to thirty years depending on issuers – bonds are generally considered low risk or safe, thus being the instrument of choice among conservative or defensive investors. Proportional to a bond's risk is its rate of return, interest or income. 'Junk bonds' or the high risk debt of companies in a precarious state promise exceptionally high yields, when compared to low risk sovereign bonds, such as US Treasuries. Also affecting a bond's rate of return is its accompanying tax liability. Liquidity indicates the readiness of a bond's convertibility to cash, with trading oftentimes carried out in secondary markets. Ideally, therefore, investors would be seeking bonds that have low risks, high rates of return, a tax exempt status and high liquidity. In the real world, that would be tantamount to chasing the will-o'-the-wisp.

What is mere wishful thinking in financial markets becomes real and true to life when it comes to moral capital, thanks to the peculiar development of character and culture. Just like bonds, character and culture are the result of long term investments, usually of several years' worth of continued efforts on the part of agents. Once established, however, they no longer change easily, nor are they ordinarily susceptible to loss. They entail the barest minimum of risk. That is because character and culture embody the conscious and willful determination of one's freedom and reason in a motley set of deep-rooted and enduring habits. Unlike bonds, however, character and culture could enjoy high rates of return, income or interest, together with low risk. A person's habits, once securely entrenched in character, do not only enable him to perform ever more and better actions, but they also predispose him to acquire other habits similar to those he already has, and likewise increase their perfection.

Apart from being 'sold at a premium' – that is, heavily discounted in terms of effort as to their face value – the rates of return of investments in moral capital through character and culture grow exponentially. And as long as virtues or good habits are cultivated, and the character or culture developed is the appropriate one, no penalty or 'tax liability' is applied. Remember that a distinctive feature of moral capital is that no harm could ever arise from it. As for 'liquidity', moral capital bonds in character and culture also enjoy great advantages, since they readily give rise to the desired appropriate habits and actions upon their holder's decision.

In the succeeding pages we shall further develop the metaphor of character and culture as 'investment bonds in moral capital' by analyzing the background story of the Hewlett Packard (HP) and Compaq merger. We shall focus, in particular, on the proxy battle between Carleton (Carly) S. Fiorina, HP president and chair, and Walter B. Hewlett, an HP board director and son of one of its co-founders. This fight was largely based on the conflicting characters or personalities of the two protagonists, and their clashing interpretations of the HP culture, the so-called 'HP way'. We shall then explain the different elements that constitute an individual's character, distinguish between innate and acquired character, and give some guidelines in determining a particular character's worth or value in terms of moral capital. All through the chapter we shall expound on the relationship between personal character and organizational or corporate culture, since both play a crucial role in moral capital formation and development.

I. THE PARTING OF THE HP WAY

Late in the evening of 3 September 2001, Hewlett-Packard (HP) announced that it was acquiring Compaq Computer for $25 billion in an all stock deal (Ross Sorkin and Norris 2001). The combined entity would have a revenue of $87 billion, only slightly less than International Business Machines (IBM), the world's largest computer company, with which it would be competing across the entire product line. Aside from keeping the top slot in printers, the merged company would also be number one in PCs – outranking Dell – and data storage; second in the server business, after Sun Microsystems; and third in the market of information consultancies and services, where IBM was king (Burrows and Park 2002). Its employees would number around 145,000 worldwide, from among which at least 15,000 would have to be laid off in order to meet cost-saving goals of $2.5 billion. A hefty $675 million break-up fee payable by HP to Compaq was likewise agreed upon.

This announcement immediately focused the spotlight on Carly S. Fiorina, who would occupy the post of chairman and CEO of the new company.

(Michael D. Capellas, Compaq's chairman and CEO, would become its president.) Fiorina was then president, chairman and CEO of HP. Her two year record at HP had been far from stellar, reporting an 89% profit slump and important job losses for the second quarter of 2001 (BBC 2001). Having missed corporate earnings targets, she was forced to return $625,000 from her total compensation package; although with more than $2 million a year in salary, she still remained one of the best paid female executives in the world. With the effects of the Asian Crisis still lingering and the global slump especially acute in the computer sector, perhaps Fiorina was simply unlucky. But at the same time, doubts regarding her competence or fit with HP culture somehow could not be dispelled. A few people even thought that the merger was a desperate attempt for Fiorina to redeem herself, after having failed to take over Price-WaterhouseCooper's consulting arm. She needed to do something quick if she wanted to keep her job (Burrows 2002).

Wall Street reaction to the merger was unmistakably adverse, seeing it more as an admission of weakness than a pooling of strengths by the two companies (Norris and Ross Sorkin 2001). HP's shares sank to their lowest level in three years, 72 per cent down from their peak in the summer of 2000, while Compaq's stocks plunged by 10 per cent to a five year low, 78 per cent down from an early 1999 record. Normally, the stock price of a company about to be acquired like Compaq would experience a spectacular rise as soon as the news broke out. But despite the 18.9 per cent premium that HP was offering for every Compaq share, its price nevertheless tanked. As a result, almost $6 billion worth of shareholder value was wiped out. By contrast, the shares of their main competitors, such as Dell, Sun and IBM, posted significant gains in the trading.

Investors feared that there was no synergy at all between HP and Compaq, that Compaq was too much like HP minus its printer business, that is, just another PC company (Schonfeld 2001). In essence, the HP–Compaq combination would simply result in a larger PC maker, right at the time when the PC hardware market was maturing and profit margins were diminishing to the point of irrelevance. According to the sales pitch of Fiorina and Capellas, the merger of their companies would be able to capture the benefits of scale in PC manufacturing better; in effect, 'out-Delling' lean and mean, just-in-time champion Dell. The joint vision of the two CEOs for the future of the merged company consisted more in selling servers, like Sun, and 'services' – not only advice, but also setting up, organizing and maintaining networks – like IBM, rather than just supplying PCs (Richtel 2001). Needless to say, any one of these industry leaders – Dell, Sun or IBM – was already a formidable opponent even for a combined HP–Compaq to challenge. How much more, then, all three of them at the same time?

Memories of how Compaq botched its $9.6 billion takeover of Digital Equipment in January 1998 similarly haunted the scene (*The Economist* 2001a).

This time around, with the overlapping product portfolios of HP and Compaq, not to mention their odd mix of corporate cultures, why would the acquistion turn out differently? On 16 October 2001, Matrix Asset Advisors, which held more than 531,000 HP and 826,000 Compaq shares, became the first major investor to urge both companies to abandon the merger (*Bloomberg News* 2001). Since the 3 September 2001 announcement, HP shares had already fallen by a full 22 per cent and Compaq shares by 20 per cent.

Then Walter B. Hewlett entered the stage. A son of William Hewlett, HP's co-founder, and the only family member sitting on the HP board, he said he would be voting against the takeover proposal. 'The combination would dramatically increase Hewlett-Packard's exposure to the unattractive PC business and dilute current stockholders' interests in Hewlett-Packard's profitable printer business,' he explained (Ross Sorkin 2001). Together, Walter B. Hewlett and the Hewlett family controlled around 8 per cent of HP.

Later in the day, David W. Packard, son of David Packard, the company's other co-founder, said that he too would be opposing the deal. David W. Packard's vote represented 1.3 per cent of HP. 'The announced logic of this merger plan depends on massive employee layoffs' – and after acknowledging that the founders had never guaranteed absolute job security to anyone, Packard nonetheless added – 'I also know that Bill and Dave never developed a premeditated business strategy that treated HP employees as expendable. While change is necessary and inevitable, it does not follow that every innovation is an improvement' (Lohr 2001a). HP shares jumped by 17.3 per cent, signifying investor cheer at the prospect of the deal being called off, while Compaq shares dropped by another 5.5 per cent.

A month later, the David and Lucile Packard Foundation – controlling 10.4 per cent of HP shares – also decided that it would be voting against the merger. 'After thorough study and analysis the board has preliminarily decided, on balance, that the best interests of the foundation would be better served by Hewlett-Packard not proceeding with the proposed transaction,' its chairman, Susan Packard Orr, explained (Lohr and Gaither 2001b). In a speech she delivered a few years earlier she had quoted her father as once saying, 'Hewlett-Packard does not exist to make a profit, it exists to make a contribution' (Lohr 2001c). Once more HP's shares rose and Compaq's fell upon receiving news of this development.

This series of moves by the founding families, purported guardians of the HP way, clearly pitted them against the direction set by Carly Fiorina, her management team and board. Fiorina's 'reinvention' of the HP way was plainly not to the founding families' liking; on the contrary, it seemed to have stirred their wrath. As David W. Packard commented: 'For some time I have been skeptical about management's confidence that it can aggressively "reinvent" HP culture overnight – a culture that developed over many years and was thoroughly tested under all kinds of business conditions' (Reuters 2001). HP management, for its part, dismissed these reactions as 'emotional', provoked by the radical changes the company was then undergoing. But who should have a better claim to being the founders' oracle, their biological descendants or their corporate successors?

First, let's have a look at Carly Fiorina (Burrows and Elstrom 1999). Her father had worked as a law professor and judge, her mother, as an artist-painter. The family moved homes so often that Carly herself had been through five different high schools, including one in Ghana. After graduating from Stanford with a BA in Medieval History and Philosophy, she enrolled at the UCLA Law School to follow in her father's footsteps. However, by the first semester she realized that she and law were not made for each other. Although it distressed her to have to tell her father she was leaving UCLA, the decision at the same time gave her a newfound sense of freedom. It seemed as if now she could do with her life as she truly pleased. In time she would earn a master's degree in business administration from the Robert H. Smith School of the University of Maryland at College Park and a master's of science from the Sloan School at MIT.

Carly Fiorina then went through a series of dead-end jobs, working as a receptionist and an English teacher in Italy, until she landed at a post as a sales representative for AT&T. There, she steadily climbed up the corporate ladder in the sales and marketing departments for a period of nearly 20 years. In 1996 she successfully directed the Lucent Technologies spin-off from AT&T and in 1998 she became president of Lucent's $19 billion global service provider business.

On 19 July 1999 Carly Fiorina was appointed CEO of Hewlett-Packard (Burrows and Elstrom 1999). She was then 44 years old and became the first female CEO of a Dow Jones 30 company. Being an outsider to HP – the original Silicon Valley start-up then on its 60th year – was partly an advantage, because she had to strike a balance between its dependable but stodgy engineering culture and the demands for lightning-speed innovation in the Internet age. The search committee composed of Sam Gin, Vodafone AirTouch chairman, Lewis Platt, HP CEO, and Richard Hackborn, HP chairman, was unanimous in singling out Fiorina's strengths: 'the ability to conceptualize and communicate sweeping strategies, the operations savvy to deliver on quarterly financial goals, the power to bring urgency to an organization, and the management skills to drive a nascent Net vision throughout the company' (Burrows and Elstrom 1999).

Upon joining HP, Fiorina's main challenge was to create a corporate strategy attune to the Internet age (Burrows 1999). After a three-year lag behind rivals as IBM and Sun, HP had just unveiled its 'E-services' initiative, pulling together different technologies that allowed clients to add new functionalities to their machines on the fly. HP also needed a jolt in innovation. Since 1984, when its inkjet printer first came out, HP had been experiencing a drought of new, ground-breaking products. When an HP scientist presented a Web browser prototype in 1993 – two years before the Netscape Navigator – Platt, who was then CEO, missed the cue and allowed the project to die an ignominious death. HP management just couldn't figure out how the browser could help sell more computers. Its department heads were reluctant to invest in new ideas lest they fall short of quarterly goals. Likewise, HP was struggling with serious organization and marketing problems. More than 130 product groups functioning with balkanized autonomy seriously disconcerted customers. The Internet obviously demanded a more seamless approach. Neither could the human dimension of HP's problems be missed. Although in 1999 its turnover rate was a mere third of the Silicon Valley average, there were worries that it was not keeping the right people. Top talent with a taste for risk was leaving, while the ones who stayed behind were primarily those attracted to HP's safe, paternalistic employment practices. Pressure was mounting for options to be given and a performance-based pay to be used instead of simply distributing small profit-sharing checks. In fact, Fiorina's compensation package consisted almost entirely of stock options. In short, Carly Fiorina seemed to be the charismatic and dynamic leader that Lewis Platt wasn't and that HP at that juncture of its corporate history needed. But was her character in keeping with the HP way?

The HP way was the spirit that infused the tiny shop that Bill Hewlett and Dave Packard began in 1938, in a Palo Alto, CA, garage, with a little more than $500 in their pockets (Markoff 2001). Since then, HP had grown into the model for thousands of Silicon Valley startups in electronic instrumentation, semiconductors and personal computing. Steven Jobs, Apple's founding chairman, began his career with a summer job at HP's frequency counter division, when he was fresh out of eighth grade.

Equally endowed with technical and business genius, Bill and Dave created an informal, egalitarian culture where brilliant engineers could make significant contributions in the field of electronics. They produced the first desktop and pocket scientific calculators, among other noteworthy products. Their slogan consisted in integrity, teamwork and innovation. They were consummate practitioners of the art of management by walking around. They eschewed hierarchy, sitting at the middle rather than at the head of tables during meetings, and implementing the open plan office, where workers were separated by low-rise dividers into cubicles without doors. Decision making was highly decentralized. Both Bill and Dave emphasized respect and a progressive attention to employees' needs, offering catastrophic medical coverage and flexible work hours. They too displayed a solid commitment to local communities and were actively engaged in philanthropy. Together they contributed more than $300 million to Stanford University, their alma mater. Although they had amassed fortunes that ran into the billions, they did not live jet-set lives, and instead tried to keep their wealth in the proper perspective for their families.

In the opinion of the Hewlett and Packard heirs, it was precisely the HP way that was at stake in the planned merger with Compaq. In this Fiorina agreed with them, but of course she had a different version of the HP way in mind. For her, what was once the company's greatest strength had unfortunately turned into its greatest weakness (Foley and Scott 2001). Furthermore, despite Fiorina's efforts to deny it, there was a dark cloud of personal misunderstandings between her and the founding families, looming over the controversial corporate decision:

> Most of the media, especially here in the Bay Area, is positioning the merger with Compaq and the recent actions by Walter Hewlett and David Packard as a fight between the past and the future – between the Hewlett-Packard of our co-founders and the future that we're trying so hard to position ourselves to achieve. I absolutely refuse to accept this line of reasoning ... There is no conflict in honoring our past while at the same time determining that we must change to secure our future. I do not desire to tear down the foundation of Hewlett-Packard. In fact, we must continue to build upon that foundation (Fiorina 2001).

Let us now turn to the heirs and their vision of the HP legacy.

Walter B. Hewlett, Bill Hewlett's eldest son, was once derided by the HP board in a letter to shareholders as a clueless 'heir ... a musician and an academic ... who has never worked at the company or been involved in its management' (*The Economist* 2002a). Indeed Walter B. Hewlett, with his advanced degrees in music, engineering and operations research, was a professor of music at Stanford (Lohr 2001c). He also had to his credit the authorship of the software program 'MuseData', which represented musical scores in symbols. Similarly, David W. Packard was a former classics professor at Harvard who at the same time possessed an engineering degree. His expertise was in computational linguistics. His business experience included having founded Ibycus, a company that developed computer systems for data storage and retrieval in languages such as Latin, Greek, Coptic and Hebrew. In turn, his sibling, Susan Packard Orr, worked as the CEO of a software company called Technology Resources Assistance Center, specializing in management programs for non-profit groups (Lohr and Gaither 2001a).

As the lone family member sitting on the HP board, Walter Hewlett commissioned a study of the merger deal from Friedman, Fleisher & Lowe, an investment firm in San Francisco (Lohr and Gaither 2001a). The report arrived at two main conclusions. Firstly, big mergers rarely succeed in the rapid-moving technology sector due to the disruption created by disparate operations and cultures. These efforts tend to entangle and distract the new company to the benefit of its rivals. Moreover – according to Walter Hewlett – getting big by acquiring a rival is just not the HP way; instead, the company should seek to expand through innovation and organic growth (*The Economist* 2002a). Secondly, HP shareholders would lose from merging with Compaq because proceeds from its crown jewel, the highly profitable printing business, would be diluted in a collection of troubled, low margin concerns, as expanded PC manufacturing. 'With this transaction, we get what we don't want, and we jeopardize the things we already have', Walter Hewlett complained (*The Economist* 2001b). He later added that pressing ahead with the merger would only serve to 'misdirect time and energy, waste money, suffer further degradation of employee morale and continue to confuse customers' (Lohr 2001f).

Shortly after voicing his opposition, Walter Hewlett revealed that the only sure winners if the deal pushed through would be the senior executives of the combined company (Lohr 2001b). They would be receiving bonus payments totaling more than $55 million if they stayed on until September 2003. However, both Carly Fiorina and Michael Capellas chose not to participate in the executive retention program, renouncing to potential bonuses of $8 and $14.4 million respectively. As the proxy voting approached, Walter Hewlett further asserted that the HP board had even considered paying Carly Fiorina and Michael Capellas the combined sum of $115 million in salary, bonuses and stock options (Lohr 2002a). These charges of greed in executive compensation were specially damning in face of the thousands of ordinary employees whose jobs would be lost. This drew a stark contrast with the experience during a business downturn in 1970, when Bill Hewlett and Dave Packard reacted by asking employees to work only nine days every two weeks, thus effectively taking a 10 per cent pay cut. For Bill and Dave, this plan was preferable to implementing a 10 per cent layoff in the labor force (Poletti 2001). The HP board promptly denied Walter Hewlett's allegations. In turn, it accused Walter Hewlett of 'disseminating misinformation about nonexistent employment terms ... Simply put, Walter Hewlett is again attempting to mislead investors ..., it is plainly deceptive. It is unfortunate that he is willing to blatantly breach his fiduciary duties as an HP director', the board added (Lohr 2002a).

In support of Walter Hewlett's portrayal as some sort of 'clueless heir', Carly Fiorina and the HP board liked to point out his absence in the July 2001 meeting when the merger was discussed (*The Economist* 2001b). Purportedly, the reason was that he was playing with the Bohemian Club Symphony Orchestra, composed of rich businessmen, politicians and influential artists. David Packard, for his part, was also readily disregarded for his views as an 'emotional philanthropist' oblivious to the business (*The Economist* 2001c). The opinions of the remaining family members in the opposition were similarly brushed aside because their priority was 'to preserve wealth rather than to create it'. Unlike many investors, the old rich inherently disliked risk, despite the opportunities it brought along.

The big question to Walter Hewlett's credibility, however, arose from his change of votes in the merger issue, from a yes to a no in scarcely a few weeks (Gaither 2001). How come the turnaround? According to Walter Hewlett, when he first learned of the initiative in May 2001, he already felt inclined not to support it. However, a few days before the final vote he was told that the transaction would – in principle – require the board's unanimous approval. This position was modified afterwards. Walter Hewlett was then told by HP's legal counsel, Larry Sonsini, that the merger would go ahead just the same, with or without his endorsement. The only difference would be that HP might have to renegotiate a higher price with Compaq for Hewlett's dissenting vote. Therefore, in order not to increase the price of acquisition, Walter Hewlett agreed to vote in favor of the deal. But he also said – and Sonsini assured him of this possibility – that even if he had approved the merger as director, he could in the future vote against it as a shareholder.

Despite the disqualifications, family members are generally recognized as the most faithful caretakers of the values and standards that make family firms successful. In the opinion of Timothy Habbershon, director of the Wharton Enterprising Families Initiative:

> Families have an allegiance that is stronger than most shareholders, so families feel the obligation to fix things. Obviously, values can constrain as well as energize, but a family ownership group is the steward of values, vision and legacy of a company. Families tend to be in a business for the long haul. Markets are in it for the short term, as are managers (*Knowledge at Wharton* 2001).

As a young boy, Walter Hewlett was regularly brought to work by his father, Bill Hewlett, to whom he was very close (Burrows 2002). Like his four other siblings, he opted to carry on with his parents' homespun ways, shunning ostentation. Regarding business experience, apart from sitting on the HP board since 1987, he also happened to be the chairman of Vermont Telephone Co., a 21,000 line local outfit he founded with a Stanford chum in 1994. But not even that was enough for Fiorina, who insisted that Walter Hewlett was incapable of coming up with any alternative plan for HP, aside from annoying press releases. 'Walter Hewlett is a good man. But remember, it is he who is asking investors to accept his business judgment over that of HP's board and management team. We believe comparative business experience is germane', Fiorina had once commented (Burrows 2002).

For Carly Fiorina and her team, the heirs' position amounted to nothing more than a well-intentioned but misguided effort to preserve the legacy of HP's past (Lohr 2001c). Walter Hewlett and companions were simply displaying uncalled for stubbornness and self-righteousness. Fiorina, for her part, was recruited to lead HP's board precisely because of her qualities as a young, articulate, charismatic, iron-willed and dynamic outsider who could reinvigorate the company's lethargic and inbred corporate culture.

Richard Hackborn, the former chairman and longstanding HP icon, stood by Fiorina from the beginning until the very end. 'There's no way in my view that the company can stay the same – let alone go back – and be the kind of company that I personally think Bill and Dave would be proud of', he said (The Associated Press 2001). As Fiorina's adviser and mentor, Hackborn approved of her plan citing two main reasons (Lohr 2001e). Firstly, combining with Compaq would give greater size and efficiency to HP's PC business. Secondly, the merged company would have a lead in the huge, lucrative market of corporate servers, thanks to the new Itanium chip HP was developing together with Intel and Compaq's expertise with PC-based servers and data storage systems. In keeping with his views, Hackborn made public his resignation from the board of the Hewlett Family Foundation – of which Walter Hewlett was chairman – on 13 December 2001 (Lohr 2001f).

At a time in her mandate when HP employees found it difficult even just to requisition pencils, Fiorina acquired two new Gulfstream IV jets and replaced two smaller ones in the corporate fleet. This fueled allegations – no doubt encouraged by Walter Hewlett's remarks – about her regal and detached manner. To these Fiorina responded, 'Why do people comment on my flying on a corporate jet when virtually every other chief executive in Silicon Valley does the same?' (Lohr 2002d). To fight off the image of indulgence in corporate luxury, Fiorina went to the point of clarifying that she had no traveling hair-dresser in her entourage, that she did her own laundry and grocery shopping, and that she drove herself to work, except when she hitched a ride with her husband, Frank. Moreover, her office was just a first-among-equals version of the classic Silicon Valley cubicle, fenced-off by shoulder-high partitions, albeit larger and in a corner space (Lohr 2001d). For Walter Hewlett, nonetheless, she was some sort of mercenary, the epitome of 'a professional manager, not someone really committed to HP' (Lohr 2001c).

Two weeks before the final proxy vote, another veteran HP stalwart and former CEO, Lewis Platt, announced that he would also vote to block the Compaq purchase, effectively siding with Walter Hewlett and the other heirs (Lohr 2002b). The rumor was even floated that Platt could takeover Fiorina's job, occupying the post of interim CEO, if the merger were aborted.

Finally, on 19 March 2002, after an exchange of brutal attack ads and vigorous campaigning by both parties, costing them over $180 million in total, shareholders approved the HP–Compaq merger by a 'slim but sufficient margin' (Gaither and Lohr 2002). Crucial to the outcome was the vote of institutional investors, particularly the recommendation of Institutional Shareholder Services (ISS), a firm that accounted for 23 per cent of HP shares (Lohr 2002c). In its report ISS declared that 'while Mr Hewlett makes a credible case that the risks associated with the transaction are real and material, we believe that management's upside scenario is achievable'. Despite Fiorina's victory, she was greeted with timid applause mixed with boos and hisses when she spoke from the dais at the shareholders' meeting, while Walter Hewlett got a standing ovation when he addressed the crowd briefly from the floor (Lohr and Gaither 2002). In effect, unlike the institutional investors, most of the employee share-holders of HP voted against the deal, following Walter Hewlett's lead (*The New York Times* 2002).

The winning margin was indeed slim, concretely, a mere half a percentage point (*The Economist* 2002b). This encouraged Walter Hewlett to file a lawsuit on 29 March 2002 at the Delaware Chancery Court to try to overturn the results (Gaither 2002). He claimed that HP management had used corporate assets to 'entice and coerce' a large institutional investor, Deutsche Bank, to a favorable vote in the 19 March 2002 meeting. A few days before the polls, HP announced that it had secured a $4 billion credit line to defray merger costs with Deutsche Bank as co-arranger. Deutsche Bank stood to earn as much as $2 million in fees from the transaction. Apparently, however, Deutsche Asset Management had already cast 25 million votes against the takeover. Deutsche Asset Management was then led to understand that future business with HP would be in peril if it failed to switch votes. The bank immediately arranged for conference calls with HP on the voting day itself. In the end, Deutsche Bank's asset management arm changed up to 17 million votes in favor of the Compaq purchase.

On 23 April 2002, the HP merger trial opened (Quinn 2002). A few weeks earlier, the HP board released a statement informing that it would not nominate Walter Hewlett as candidate for director because of his lack of candor and adversarial behavior towards his colleagues (HP 2002). Sam Ginn, chairman of the HP board's nominating and governance committee explained how he tried to re-establish – upon Fiorina's encouragement – a constructive working rela-tionship with Walter Hewlett immediately after the shareholder meeting. As a result of those representations, the board had at first unanimously decided to renominate Walter Hewlett. But then came the lawsuit.

> My fellow board members and I were therefore shocked when just hours later Walter Hewlett filed a spurious lawsuit against the company, continuing his assault on the integrity of the HP Board and management team. His recent actions have again violated basic principles of trust, and his ongoing adversarial relationship with the company undermines the board's ability to effectively conduct business (HP 2002).

Aside from bribing or coercing Deutsche Bank into a yes vote, Walter Hewlett likewise accused the HP board and management of withholding important financial information detrimental to the promerger cause (Gaither 2002). HP had publicly released statements where cost savings amounting to

$2.5 billion were supposed to be reached by 2003. Walter Hewlett and his team discovered that such a target would not be accomplished until 2004, and that it would be financed largely by the dismissal of as many as 24,000 employees, instead of the 15,000 previously projected. Also, the estimated earnings per share of the combined company – at a little more than 30 cents – would be $1 billion less than the HP board and management had earlier claimed.

On this count, Jeffrey Clarke, Compaq's chief financial officer, testified in court that one broad internal estimate of the possible cost savings reached nearly $4 billion, significantly more than the $2.5 billion figure released to the public (Lohr and Ross Sorkin 2002). However, Carly Fiorina specifically wanted to be conservative, so the more modest number was disclosed.

Regarding the vote-buying allegation, the basis turned out to be a taped exchange of phone messages between Carly Fiorina and HP's chief financial officer, Robert Wayman (Quinn and Seipel 2002). Fiorina expressed her concern over the votes of two large institutional shareholders, Deutsche Bank and Northern Trust, saying 'we may have to do something extraordinary for those two to bring them over the line here'. For his part, Wayman admitted that 'we did in fact make extraordinary efforts to present the merits of the merger to our investors, including dozens of presentations in the final days'. Although he also hastened to add that 'we never acted improperly, as we will prove in court'.

On 30 April 2002, Chancellor Wílliam B. Chandler III of the Delaware Supreme Court resolved to dismiss the case presented by Walter Hewlett against HP (Lohr 2002f). In his 43-page decision Judge Chandler explained that he found the testimony of HP executives credible and that Walter Hewlett was simply unable to prove his allegations beyond the evidentiary threshold. He wrote that 'nothing in the record indicates that HP lied to or deliberately misled shareholders'.

After the ruling, Walter Hewlett seemed to have undergone a change of heart and issued the following statement:

> I will therefore now do everything possible to support the successful implementation of HP's acquisition of Compaq and encourage others who have shared my views in the past several months to do the same ... My involvement with HP will not end today. I will continue to monitor the company's performance to ensure that it acts in the best interests of all stockholders (Lohr 2002f).

However, despite having prevailed both in the polls and in court, it seems that Fiorina's woes are far from over. She would always have Walter Hewlett and the rest of the heirs with their large swathe of shares as a thorn in her side, although not on her board. And as if delivering on her post-merger promises were not tough enough, she would have to do so knowing fully well that 48.6

per cent of her shareholders voted against the deal. Can she really re-invent the HP way, or was it lost and gone forever?

II. THE LEGACY OF CHARACTER

In the last couple of decades, fabulous fortunes have been made, almost overnight, by participating in the merger or acquisition of publicly traded companies like Hewlett-Packard and Compaq. However, not all corporate unions have been equally blessed with smooth sailing. Oftentimes, an acquiring company has found itself with nothing else but the valueless mortal remains of a firm that just a few months earlier seemed brimming with opportunities. Business analysts and management consultants tend to agree that a major reason behind the failure of such deals was the clash of cultures among the firms or the incompatibility of their corporate characters. Perhaps abstract financial projections were given too much weight, and considerations arising from 'soft' human factors were deliberately ignored.

Character had always been attributed primarily to persons, long before it was ever applied to organizations and businesses under the guise of corporate culture. Character describes an individual's personality, moral type or identity; as culture does in turn, for organizations. As we may recall, character is what results from habit – or from the combination of different habits that a person develops – as its name in Greek suggests (cf. NE 1103a). We also know from these same sources that the Greek term *ethos* stands for both character and culture. Character – like its corporate counterpart, culture – represents, therefore, another level superior to habits in the constitution of moral capital.

Initially, there may be some confusion as to whether virtue of character – which constitutes moral capital – is a feeling, a capacity or a state of the soul or mind. For indeed virtue of character is what allows us to experience certain feelings, positive or negative, with regard to a particular class of objects or actions. Yet we never seem to know for sure if such virtue of character lies in the feeling itself, in the capacity for such feeling, or in the acquired, more or less permanent state from which that capacity derives. Aristotle carefully explores all of these possibilities in the *Nicomachean Ethics* before giving us his response.

By feelings, Aristotle understands 'appetite, anger, fear, confidence, envy, joy, love, hate, longing, jealousy, pity, in general, whatever implies pleasure or pain' (NE 1105a). But he quickly disqualifies feelings as the proper condition for virtue of character. We are neither praised nor blamed for merely experiencing feelings because feelings arise in us by nature, that is, without the concurrence of any decision or consent on our part. And virtues – as well as their opposites, vices – are character traits for which we are rightly praised or blamed, because they are the products of our own independent and conscious volition. Furthermore, in the case of feelings we play a passive role and are moved, while with the virtues we are active and take the initiative in acquiring and developing them.

Aristotle's reasons for precluding capacities from the proper condition of virtues of character are very similar to the above: 'the virtues are not capacities either; for we are neither called good nor bad in so far as we are simply capable of feelings. Further, while we have capacities by nature, we do not become good or bad by nature' (NE 1106a). In effect, an essential trait of virtue of character is that it is acquired, not something that is innate or that appears spontaneously. If only in this respect virtue of character cannot be a natural capacity for feelings or actions.

Aristotle arrives at the choice of character states as the genus or proper condition for virtue by elimination or defect of the other options: 'If, then, the virtues are neither feelings nor capacities, the remaining possibility is that they are states' (NE 1106a). He then continues to explain that virtue is a good state that causes its possessor to perform his specific function well. By extension, 'the virtue of a human being will likewise be the state that makes a human being good and makes him perform his function well' (NE 1106a). Unlike other forms of capital which are valued exclusively for their instrumental or extrinsic worth, moral capital or virtue is desirable not only for this; it makes one perform his function well, but also for its absolute or intrinsic worth; it makes a human being good.

Just as in the case of habits, where the right sort of habituation equally avoids actions in excess as in defect, the right character state also expresses a mean. However, virtue of character is not a numerical mean in respect of the object itself, but rather one that is relative to us, the human subjects or agents. Virtue of character is an intermediate state that eschews both what is superfluous and what is deficient: 'virtue is concerned with feelings and actions, in which excess and defect are in error and incur blame, while the intermediate conditions is correct and wins praise, which are both proper features of virtue. Virtue, then, is a mean, in so far as it aims at what is intermediate' (NE 1106b).

Having virtue of character is not so much a matter of feeling or acting, as doing so 'at the right times, about the right things, towards the right people, for the right end, and in the right way, [that] is, the intermediate and best condition, and this is proper virtue' (NE 1106b). Understandably, hitting the mark on all of the above-mentioned circumstances surrounding feelings and actions cannot be the result of any abstract theory or deliberation. Rather, it could only be achieved contingently, on a case to case basis, after following a minimum of general guidelines or orientations. That is why Aristotle hastens to add that although in its 'substance' or 'essence', virtue of character is a mean, in the measure that it depends on a host of contingent and subjective conditions, 'this is not one, and is not the same for everyone' (NE 1106a). This means that outside of actions or feelings that automatically include baseness – handed down to us in the theory of 'moral absolutes' (cf. NE 1107a) – it is up to each one's invention to discover the character state most appropriate for him.

Delving deeper into the doctrine of virtue of character as a mean, Aristotle clarifies the relations between it and the extremes. Firstly, virtue or the intermediate state is contrary to either one of the two extremes.

> For the brave person, e.g., appears rash in comparison to the coward, and cowardly in comparison to the rash person; similarly, the temperate person appears intemperate in comparison to the sensible person, and insensible in comparison with the intemperate person, and the generous person appears wasteful in comparison to the ungenerous, and ungenerous in comparison to the wasteful person (NE 1108b).

However, the extremes themselves are more opposed to each other than to the mean: 'For they are further from each other than from the intermediate, just as the large is further from the small, and the small from the large, than either is from the equal' (NE 1108b). But in certain cases, due to the object of the character state itself or due to our own natural tendency, one extreme is more opposed to the mean than the other. For example, cowardice, or the vice of excess, is more opposed to the virtue of bravery than rashness, its corresponding vice of deficiency. In like manner, granted that on the whole we have a greater natural tendency to drift towards pleasure, intemperance or the vice of excess is more opposed to the intermediate state or virtue of temperance than insensibility, which is the vice of deficiency.

In the same way that virtue of character consists in an intermediate state or mean, when it comes to corporate culture, what we seek is an equilibrium or balance. For HP, as with most other companies, neither the past as past nor the future as future is valuable in and by itself. Rather, they acquire value only insofar as they positively contribute to the company's present situation and its long-term trajectory. Too much emphasis on tradition leads to stagnation, while obsession with the future causes distraction in the affairs at hand. Virtue lies in reconciling wisdom from experience with entrepreneurial spirit and innovation.

Similarly, there is nothing intrinsically wrong with job security and profit-sharing – they could do wonders for company loyalty – except when employees and managers succumb to complacency as a result. In that case, performance-related pay and stock options may do the trick and introduce workers into a more competitive mode. Yet there is also danger in excessive competition and allowing oneself to be blinded by quarterly performance reports. Again, the solution would then lie in the 'golden mean'. From the viewpoint of corporate culture, what HP really needed was, perhaps, a client-focused Internet strategy as Carly Fiorina propounded. But definitely not at the cost of giving up its solid engineering dependability, however boring, nor of losing its veterans – represented by Walter B. Hewlett – who made it all possible. Theoretically, these two ingredients for success imply no contradiction and one could have them both. But as experience has sadly revealed for HP, that is easier said than done. Character conflicts make for corporate culture battles and uncivil intra-company wars.

An individual person's character is like a piece of fabric that is composed of at least three kinds of strands. In the first place we have the physiological elements. These refer to an agent's bodily traits or attributes insofar as they influence, in a more or less permanent or stable way, his manner of being and acting.

As we have seen in the HP–Compaq merger story, Carly Fiorina's being female was a major issue both in her being chosen to head HP and in the particular manner that she endeavored to re-invent the HP way. This happens to be so despite her strong insistence that 'my gender is interesting but really not the subject of the story here' (Castillo 1999). At least, her being the first woman to ever hold the top position in a Dow Jones 30 company usually receives the same emphasis as her being the first outsider to occupy the helm at HP, the grand old dame of Silicon Valley institutions. Her celebrity status as arguably corporate America's most powerful female executive is further enhanced by her youthful vitality, eloquent charm, cover-girl attractiveness and, not least, by her well trimmed bob of blonde hair. How else could we explain the interest in her grooming habits, such as the rumor that she included a hairdresser in her jet-set traveling entourage? Her critics have always striven to draw a link between this or similar feminine details, be they fictitious or factual, and her purported love of luxury at the company's expense. The argument was, of course, that such ostentation and frivolity were not in keeping with the sober original HP way of the founders.

But the ever prepared Carly Fiorina was more than equipped to turn this charge about her gender on its head. In her address at the Goldman Sachs Technology Conference she recounted:

> During another time and place, at the dawn of another era in computing, a woman named Grace Murray Hopper offered a piece of wisdom that applies to us today. Grace Murray Hopper was not only one of the first women software engineers in America – she was also a Rear Admiral in the U.S. Navy. One day, she was asked why she liked to be in the middle of action at sea rather than docked in safe waters at home. She replied: 'A ship in port is safe. But that is not what ships are built for.' HP can sit idly in its port and watch the rest of the world go by. It can choose the still waters of inaction over the rough waves of competition. But that is not what Hewlett-Packard was built for. Ours is a legacy of invention and values that are worth preserving. Sustaining our company requires moving forward with courage and determination. And that is exactly what we do (Fiorina 2002).

Another strand in the fabric of character comes from a person's feelings, affections and emotions. They represent the psychological component of an individual's personality. They have in common that by themselves they are rather unstable, coming and going on the spur of the moment, and that they do not strictly follow reason, frequently erupting as gut reactions rather than as thoroughly meditated responses.

This was precisely the way in which the HP board and management tried to discredit the heirs' – especially David W. Packard's – opposition to the merger with Compaq. They were supposed to be dizzied and overcome by the sheer speed of change dictated by the combined forces of technology and the market; they were reacting from the 'heart', rather than from the 'head'. That is, the founding family members were acting on the basis of heated, irrational passions instead of cool, calculated reasoning and planned, logical thought. That was certainly no way to steer the course for a company like HP. Although on the other hand, as some members of the HP board would have it, how else could a group of people without comparable management experience proceed in their decision making?

Unfortunately for the heirs' opponents, however, Walter Hewlett did prepare – with the help of investment experts and management advisers – a carefully reasoned position. Such was his credibility that in the end he managed to pull over to his side almost half of the shareholders' votes. And with respect to the jibe that all Walter Hewlett did was to reject Carly Fiorina's initiatives without proposing a plan of his own to bring the company forward, we should in fairness say that the jury is still out on whether the HP board's projections for the merger will eventually hold. What is important is to underscore that Walter Hewlett's stand against the merger was indeed a reasonable – and not a purely emotional – one, based on the company's and the sector's past trajectories. Equally reasonable were the heirs' concerns regarding the negative effects of the massive layoffs and the shift to performance-based pay plus options on employee morale and overall performance. The repercussions of these changes on corporate culture cannot be ignored.

Lastly, a host of sociocultural elements such as a person's family, work, economic and political backgrounds also contribute to determine the kind of character he forms. Aside from nature (psychological and bodily elements), nurture too plays an important role in crafting one's personality. An individual's upbringing is of course influenced by the kind of education received, initially at home from parents and siblings, the socioeconomic class to which his family belongs, and its political sympathies or affiliations, in a wide sense.

Hence the depiction of the Hewlett and Packard brood as rich heirs who never had to work to keep body and soul together. They had always had the luxury to dedicate themselves primarily to their leisure, to academic and artistic pursuits, with the concern over the way HP was run taking a mere second place. In fact, Susan Packard Orr even remembered her father as saying that the company's mission was not to make a profit, but to make a 'contribution'. They had a greater incentive to preserve the wealth they already possessed than to risk it in new ventures that could, however, bring hefty returns.

For similar reasons, without exactly being a rags to riches story, the media played up on Carly Fiorina's struggle to rise up the ranks. Never mind that – like several of the founding family heirs – she too enjoyed the privilege of an education at Stanford and MIT. The difference was that she had to work for everything that she came to possess and that nothing was given her for free or as a birthright. Her life was an updated version of the American dream: someone who started out as a receptionist and wound up as the chair, president and CEO of HP. Perhaps being a 'professional manager' was not so bad at all: rather than an 'executive for hire' with hardly any commitment to the firm, it could instead mean plain competence. Her profile would also come closer to that of most other shareholders, friendlier to risks, because that was the way the could maximize returns on their investments.

The political undertones of the HP proxy fight did not escape the public's notice (Lohr 2002e). Some say that Carly Fiorina's image as the young and dynamic executive who boldly endeavored to bring HP to a position of leadership in the computer industry owed much to Bill Clinton's 1996 presidential campaign. While Walter Hewlett's message of restoring decency and honor to the executive office – in contrast to Fiorina's purported bequest of greed and megalomania – had reminiscences of George W. Bush's 2000 election strategy.

Therefore, a person's character could be described as a unique mix of these three main elements, the physiological, the psychological and the sociocultural. At the same time we could also distinguish between a person's natural temperament or *pathos*, and his acquired character or *ethos*. *Pathos* refers to a personality that is innate, spontaneous and thus, pre-moral; that is, by itself it is not subject to praise or blame. *Ethos*, on the other hand, results from deliberate and intentional acts, and for this reason it is the object of moral responsibility. The transformation from *pathos* to *ethos*, from natural temperament to acquired character, is carried out through a lifelong process of learning and practice. This means that a person could deliberately change, alter or reform his character through the cultivation of different habits.

In his classification of the virtues of character, Aristotle enumerates five main groups. The first concerns virtues related with feelings: bravery is the virtue that governs fear and confidence, whereas temperance allows us to have the proper response to pleasures and pains (cf. NE 1107b). The second group refers to virtues that describe our relationship with external goods. Generosity or magnificence is the desirable character trait with regard to the giving and taking of money, while magnanimity is the mean with respect to honor and dishonor (cf. NE 1107b). The social life requires its own set of virtues of character. Among them we find mildness, which indicates an intermediate state between an excess and a deficiency of anger; truthfulness, which lies midway between boastfulness and self-deprecation; wit, which holds the middle ground between buffoonery and boorishness; and friendliness, which is halfway between being ingratiating or flattering, on one hand, and quarrelsome or ill-tempered, on another (cf. NE 1108a). Next comes a group indicating desirable intermediate states which are not exactly virtues. For example, having just the proper dose of shame, without being ashamed about everything or having no sense of disgrace; or proper indignation, which middles between envy and spite (cf. NE 1108a–b). Lastly comes the virtue of justice, which is highly complex and demands a fuller explanation in its double dimension of lawfulness (general or universal justice) and fairness or equality (particular justice) (cf. NE 1129b).

How are we to acquire these virtues of character and thus invest in moral capital bonds? Aristotle recognizes that hitting the mark between two vices entails hard work, and for that reason it is something rare and praiseworthy: 'getting angry, or giving and spending money, is easy and anyone can do it; but doing it to the right person, in the right amount, at the right time, for the right end, and in the right way is no longer easy, nor can everyone do it' (NE 1109a). Nevertheless, he does venture to offer some bits of practical advice.

Considering that virtue of character lies in the mean, Aristotle admonishes us, in the first place, to avoid the more opposed extreme: 'For since one extreme is more in error, the other less, and since it is hard to hit the intermediate extremely accurately, the second-best tack, as they say, is to take the lesser of the evils' (NE 1109a). With regard to the virtue of courage or bravery, for example, it would be better to err on the side of rashness, or its excess, than cowardice, which is its defect, because cowardice is the more contrary extreme. Secondly, Aristotle suggests that one avoid – depending on his natural inclination or drift – what happens to be the easier extreme. 'For different people have different natural tendencies towards different goals, and we shall come to know our own tendencies from the pleasure or pain that arises in us. We must drag ourselves off in the contrary direction' (NE 1109b).

Aristotle also warns that we be extremely careful with pleasures, 'for we are already biased in its favor when we come to judge it' (NE 1109b). Indeed, for the majority of people, in the matter of pleasures, the tendency towards intemperance is greater than towards insensibility. As a final note, Aristotle tells us that the rules laid down do not, however, give exact and detailed guidance for action. This is not due to any defect in the rules themselves, but is somehow imposed by the very nature of the objects on which they verse. Virtues of character deal with concrete, contingent actions and feelings not covered by general, theoretical accounts: 'for nothing perceptible is easily defined, and [since] these [circumstances of virtuous and vicious action] are particulars, the judgment about them depends on perception' (NE 1109b). We are remitted, in the end, not to perception in itself, but to the perception of an already virtuous person: he alone is the competent judge in each and every concrete situation.

These pieces of advice to achieve virtue of character are like tips on the best investment strategies in moral capital bonds. They may not guarantee the highest of all possible returns, but they are, realistically, our best bet. By following them, we can almost be certain to see our investments in moral capital grow and thus reap benefits now and in the future.

III.   IN BRIEF

- Character results from the unique combination of habits that each person develops. It denotes a permanent state of being that is more stable than feelings or mere capacities for action. As such, character is a better expression of a person's mind and will, and entails a deeper sense of moral responsibility and identity than individual actions or habits.
- What character is for individual persons, that is culture for organizations and firms. A company's culture rests on its core competencies, its portfolio of goods and services, and the standard operating procedures it follows in the delivery of these products.
- Efforts to develop virtue of character are like investments in moral capital bonds. Risks of loss and liabilities are low, practically inexistent, and rates of return are high, even growing exponentially. Furthermore, virtues of character – like moral capital bonds – are readily convertible into good habits and actions.
- Character describes an individual's personality, moral type or identity. It uniquely integrates physiological, psychological and sociocultural elements in a dynamic state or condition. We could distinguish between a person's natural temperament or *pathos*, and his acquired character or *ethos*. An individual experiences greater moral responsibility and identification with his *ethos* than with his *pathos*.
- Virtue – or moral capital formation with respect to character and culture – consists in achieving an intermediate state or mean in one's feelings and actions. Virtue is opposed to the two extremes, the excess and defect, of a given tendency. The intermediate state at which virtue aims is not a numerical mean, but one relative to the agent. It is not the same, therefore, for each and every agent.
- There are several kinds of virtues of character depending on their objects: feelings, external goods, social life, certain desirable intermediate states such as shame and the highly complex virtue of justice.
- To give exact, detailed rules for developing virtues of character is impossible. This is due, among other reasons, to the contingent nature of the objects of virtue. Aristotle, nevertheless, furnishes us with some guiding principles to better achieve the mean: avoiding the more opposed

extreme, steering clear of what is subjectively easier, and being careful with pleasures. These same indications are sound strategies for investment in moral capital bonds.

REFERENCES

Aristotle (1985), *Nicomachean Ethics*, trans. Terence Irwin, Indianapolis, IN: Hackett Publishing.
The Associated Press (2001), 'HP Director discusses Compaq deal', *The New York Times*, 19 November.
BBC (2001), 'Profile: HP's Carly Fiorina', *BBC News*, 4 September.
Bloomberg News (2001), 'Hewlett urged to abandon Compaq merger', *The New York Times*, 16 October.
Burrows, P. (1999), 'Making a new HP way', *Business Week*, 2 August.
Burrows, P. (2002), 'What's the truth about Walter Hewlett?', *Business Week*, 11 February.
Burrows, P. and P. Elstrom (1999), 'HP's Carly Fiorina: the boss', *Business Week*, 2 August.
Burrows, P. and A. Park (2002), 'Compaq and HP: what's an investor to do?', *Business Week*, 18 March.
Castillo, S. (1999), 'Carly Fiorina. Makeover artist', www.time.com (Digital 50).
Economist, The (2001a), 'Hewlett-Packard and Compaq. Sheltering from the storm', 8 September.
Economist, The (2001b), 'Families in the boardroom. Under the influence', 17 November.
Economist, The (2001c), 'Face value. In the family's way', 15 December.
Economist, The (2002a), 'Hewlett-Packard and Compaq. Carly v. Walter', 26 January.
Economist, The (2002b), 'Hewlett-Packard and Compaq. Hanging chads, corporate style', 23 March.
Foley, J. and K. Scott (2001), 'One on one with Carly Fiorina', www.information-week.com, 23 July.
Fiorina, C. (2001), 'Message to HP employees', www.freeedgar.com, 14 November.
Fiorina, C. (2002), 'The case for the merger', www.hp.com, 4 February.
Gaither, C. (2001), 'Hewlett heir in new action against merger', *The New York Times*, 28 December.
Gaither, C. (2002), 'Hewlett heir files lawsuit to overturn merger vote', *The New York Times*, 29 March.
Gaither, C. and S. Lohr (2002), 'Compaq shareholders approve sale to Hewlett-Packard', *The New York Times*, 21 March.
HP (2002), 'HP board does not nominate Walter Hewlett as Director candidate, finds litigation spurious', www.hp.com, 1 April.
Knowledge at Wharton (2001), 'Family matters: are Fords, Hewletts and Packards right to exercise their clout?', 22 November.
Lohr, S. (2001a), 'Relatives may spoil deal between Hewlett-Packard and Compaq', *The New York Times*, 8 November.
Lohr, S. (2001b), 'Executive bonuses included in the Hewlett–Compaq deal', *The New York Times*, 16 November.

Lohr, S. (2001c), 'Clash over legacy fuels computer merger battle', *The New York Times*, 18 November.

Lohr, S. (2001d), 'Hewlett chief battles for her deal and her career', *The New York Times*, 10 December.

Lohr, S. (2001e), 'The man behind the curtain in the Hewlett–Compaq merger', *The New York Times*, 12 December.

Lohr, S. (2001f), 'Hewlett heir issues letter denouncing planned deal', *The New York Times*, 14 December.

Lohr, S. (2002a), 'At Hewlett, new anger in run-up to the vote', *The New York Times*, 27 February.

Lohr, S. (2002b), 'Former chief of Hewlett urges rejection of merger', *The New York Times*, 4 March.

Lohr, S. (2002c), 'Hewlett-Packard gains key backing for Compaq merger', *The New York Times*, 6 March.

Lohr, S. (2002d), 'He said. She said. It just gets uglier', *The New York Times*, 17 March.

Lohr, S. (2002e), 'In Hewlett deal, corporate life imitates politics', *The New York Times*, 19 March.

Lohr, S. (2002f), 'Suit against Hewlett deal is dismissed', *The New York Times*, 1 May.

Lohr, S. and C. Gaither (2001a), 'A family struggle, a company's fate', *The New York Times*, 2 December.

Lohr, S. and C. Gaither (2001b), 'Foundation deals setback to Hewlett-Packard's plans', *The New York Times*, 8 December.

Lohr, S. and C. Gaither (2002), 'Hewlett-Packard declares victory on merger', *The New York Times*, 20 March.

Lohr, S. and A. Ross Sorkin (2002), 'Hewlett's chief scoffs at accusation of coercion', *The New York Times*, 26 April.

Markoff, J. (2001), 'William Hewlett, a pioneer of Silicon Valley, dies at 87', *The New York Times*, 13 January.

New York Times, The (2002), 'What price merger?', 21 March.

Nicomachean Ethics (see Aristotle).

Norris, F. and A. Ross Sorkin (2001), 'Wall St. finds fault with computer merger', *The New York Times*, 5 September.

Plato (1981), *The Republic of Plato*, trans. F.M. Cornford, Oxford: Clarendon Press.

Poletti, T. (2001), 'Meaning of "HP way" defines fight over Compaq deal', www.BayArea.com, 26 November.

Quinn, M. (2002), 'HP merger trial starts today', *Mercury News*, 23 April.

Quinn, M. and T. Seipel (2002), 'Fiorina voice mail reveals late scramble', *Mercury News*, 9 April.

Reuters (2001), '"HP way" and Fiorina's way may diverge', *The New York Times*, 7 November.

Richtel, M. (2001), 'Can Hewlett–Compaq Succeed beyond PC's?', *The New York Times*, 5 September.

Ross Sorkin, A. (2001), 'Hewletts vow to oppose Hewlett-Packard merger with Compaq', *The New York Times*, 7 November.

Ross Sorkin, A. and Norris, F. (2001), 'Hewlett-Packard to acquire Compaq in $25 billion deal', *The New York Times*, 4 September.

Schonfeld, E. (2001), 'Carly Fiorina has a Hegelian moment', *Business 2.0*, 5 September.

6.   Lifestyles and moral capital estates

A frequent recourse in the moral education of the young consists in upholding a model whose virtuous character is to be imitated. This is the figure of the hero, an indispensable element in all children's stories that try to instill virtue. We know, however, that no matter how hard one tried, he could never completely imitate another person's character. There are several reasons for this. Firstly, because we all possess different habits, which furthermore have been developed in varying degrees. Secondly, because the physiological, psychological and sociocultural strands constituting each one's character are all very diverse. Even in the case of identical twins there would always be variations in their acquired character or *ethos* sufficient to offset the similarities in their natural temperament or *pathos*. The ultimate distinguishing principle in character, therefore, is the use that each individual person makes of his own free will in the myriad of situations that life presents to him. And the most complete and lasting testament of a person's decisions regarding these matters could be found in his lifestyle choice.

The choice of lifestyle is arguably the most influential factor in the way an individual feels, behaves and lives; it is also the key element in understanding his biography. A person's freely chosen lifestyle gives unity and texture to everything he does: the feelings he experiences, the actions he performs, the habits he cultivates, and the unique character he forges; it lends structure and meaning to his existence. The final goal or end that a human being pursues throughout his entire existence finds its best expression in the lifestyle that he effectively carries.

An organization's corporate history is the equivalent to an individual's lifestyle and biography. It represents a level of moral capital that is superior to corporate culture because it includes the evolution of that culture or its story, from beginning to end. Whereas corporate culture gives us a snapshot of the firm at a specific moment, corporate history provides us with a full-length motion picture. A firm may experience radical transformations in its culture due to abrupt shifts in market conditions, a thorough reorganization of management or a major transfer of ownership, but as long as it remains one and the same firm these changes would be mere chapters in its ongoing narrative or corporate history. In the level of corporate histories we also find proof of how closely the lives of organizations and individuals are intertwined.

The significance of individual lifestyles and corporate histories may be assessed in terms of estates of moral capital. An estate refers to the property or the beneficial interests in property that a person acquires and accumulates throughout his lifetime. More strictly, it designates the wealth that someone bequeaths to his heirs at the moment of death, his patrimony or legacy. Apart from land, buildings and the things contained therein, it could also include other forms of wealth such as bank, brokerage and mutual fund accounts, pensions or life insurance policies. In sum, any legally protected right subject to economic exploitation that one possesses and which he may transfer to another forms part of his estate.

Concern about a person's estate normally arises at the moment of death. Only then could an estate be considered in its totality, as a finished whole, since the capacity to earn or acquire more disappears with the deceased. So it is, in a sense, with a firm's corporate history. Once most of its protagonists have already retired or severed their formal employment ties with the organization, then its corporate history can be written. At that point, at least insofar as the protagonists are concerned, the organization's corporate history may be said to have already concluded. As retired employees, they are no longer expected to contribute to the firm's stock of moral capital. Supposedly, whatever they could provide has already been given to the firm. In the same way that the deceased person is the one least affected by whatever happens to his estate, retired employees are also the ones least affected by the corporate history in which they have been protagonists. The passage of time finally allows for a definitive judgment of their actions and contributions.

The big question in such instances is how to carry out the transfer of an estate according to the decedent's will. Although the owner has died, he still somehow exists in the collective memory, and there certainly is value in safeguarding his reputation. His estate would then have to be divided among competing claimants, as his creditors and the beneficiaries of his estate.

In general, there are two ways to carry out the transfer of an estate. One is by doing so voluntarily, making use of a will or testament, and another, involuntarily. This second one is something like a default mechanism that governments keep in place to protect legitimate third-party interests in an estate. With regard to the voluntary mechanisms, there are various methods aside from wills admitted by the nonprobate system, such as gifts and trusts. These institutions often function as will substitutes. A gift consists in the giver's parting with a title of personal property in the present, in an absolute and irrevocable manner. It requires, aside from the donor's intent and delivery, the acceptance of the gift by the receiver. A trust, on the other hand, is a fiduciary relationship in which a person, the holder of the title to property or trustee, is subject to an equitable obligation to keep or use the property for the benefit of another, the beneficiary. Unlike a gift, a trust does not require delivery in order to be effective, it only needs a declaration by the settlor.

What is important here is to realize that despite a decedent's intention and the law's assistance, an estate in fact acquires a life of its own and becomes practically impossible to control fully. Something similar happens with the legacy of a personal lifestyle or a corporate history. Oftentimes, one cannot even imagine the impact of his consistent, over-arching choices and decisions on those whom he leaves behind. Although one has gone and therefore could no longer participate in transactions, he would still somehow share in the responsibility and take part in the eventual praise or blame for actions performed. Ironically, we find a situation in which someone would receive praise or blame for something he no longer controlled.

In the remaining portions of this chapter we shall consider how an estate of moral capital can be built or destroyed by a firm and an individual. Concretely, we shall examine the corporate history of Andersen, formerly one of the Big Five global auditing firms, in the aftermath of its involvement with Enron. Later on, we shall proceed with an assessment of Jack Welch's tenure at General Electric (GE) and the impact of his lifestyle choice or legacy on the firm. Finally, we shall have a chance to review and evaluate these corporate legacies and lifestyles, in terms of moral capital, from the viewpoint afforded us by Aristotle's *Nicomachean Ethics*.

I.   ANDERSEN: NO FAIRY TALE ENDING

The Arthur Andersen auditing firm was founded in 1913 by an accounting professor of the same name. After Mr Andersen's death in 1947, the firm found itself on the verge of collapse. But in the end it was saved thanks to the efforts of Leonard Spacek, who convinced partners to remain together despite looming uncertainty. Spacek, who was Andersen's chief executive from 1947 to 1963, had the reputation of being the 'conscience' of the auditing profession (Norris 2002a). He was among the first to warn that the auditing profession's very existence could be put in danger if it did not show sufficient independence from clients. He also complained whenever the US Accounting Principles Board yielded too quickly to pressure from companies which thought that auditing rules would significantly reduce profits. Spacek always insisted that Andersen provide above all high-quality accounting, in accordance with its corporate motto, 'Think straight. Talk straight'.

In 1965, with Spacek already retired, the US Accounting Principles Board delayed action on the treatment of deferred taxes on installment sales, for fear of offending retailers. Andersen took the initiative of bringing the matter to the attention of the Securities and Exchange Commission (SEC), and moved to have a tough rule adopted. In the late 1970s, Andersen once more spearheaded reforms in accounting for pensions, despite their being unpopular among companies which feared negative effects on profit margins.

Since then, however, Andersen's reputation had gone downhill. First was its bitter and distracting corporate divorce from Andersen Consulting – later rebranded as Accenture – between 1997 and mid-2000 (*The Economist* 2001). Although an arbitrator granted Andersen custody of the brand name, it was only awarded $1 billion in damages, far short of the $15 billion it had demanded. Furthermore, because of the break-up, Andersen slipped from the top to the bottom of the ranking among the Big Five global accounting firms. In 2001, Andersen reported revenues of $9.3 billion, less than half of those earned by PriceWaterhouseCoopers, which occupied the first place.

During the late 1990s, Andersen found itself desperately embroiled in some very costly auditing scandals. In the Waste Management and Sunbeam cases it had to disburse close to $120 million in combined penalties and settlements. One of Andersen's own studies revealed that between 1998 and 2000, the number of earnings restatements made by the firm had increased from 158 to 233; that is, a full 47 per cent rise over three years (Coffee 2002). Even then, the quality of Andersen audits was still to reach its nadir.

This was the sorry state of affairs at Andersen when Joseph Berardino took over as CEO in 2001, replacing Jim Wadia (*The Economist* 2001). Compared to his predecessor, who was given to managing through consensus, Berardino generally followed a more direct and straight-talking style. Among his first moves was that of pruning Andersen's management committee from 17 members to 5, reinforcing its powers and attributions. Berardino was likewise known – aside from his professional competence – for two other outstanding traits, his trustworthiness and his ability to listen.

When asked about the strengths that differentiated Andersen from other professional service firms, Berardino cited in first place the cohesiveness of its culture: 'There is one name over the door. We're not an alphabet soup.' While its rivals struggled with a complicated array of country-specific partnerships, Andersen partners enjoyed the benefits of a unique pay system, with each one receiving a list of what he had earned in the previous year. This transparency or openness – at least, at partner level – together with the emphasis on team-building, contributed to Andersen's rapid growth in recent years. This was the reward for the 135 hours of formal training that the firm invested on the average per employee each year. The optimism at the beginning of Berardino's tenure at Andersen was such that some partners had even began to expect an average income growth of 15 per cent a year indefinitely.

Then came Enron. There is no question that some management teams will always overstate their income, or understate their liabilities, or massage their earnings reports. Enron was not unique in this sense. The issue was how

Andersen, as an independent auditor, failed to detect Enron's shenanigans, not withdrawing its stamp of approval until barely a month before the energy company folded up. That Andersen provided Enron with both auditing and consultancy services, gaining $27 million from the former and $28 million from the latter in 2001, made it too beholden to its client. In relationships like these, where there is so much room for serious conflicts of interests and loyalties, auditors are forced to become extremely friendly with their clients, making a mockery of their so-called 'independence'.

How did Andersen react to the Enron imbroglio? After informing the SEC and the Justice Department that Enron-related documents had been disposed of, and after a series of testimonies by some of its key executives, including Joseph Berardino, before the US Congress, Andersen announced the formation of an Independent Oversight Board to steer the firm through the crisis (Andersen 2002a). Paul A. Volcker, the former US Federal Reserve chairman, was appointed head of the board. The board was granted full authority to mandate revisions in Andersen policies and practices, and the means to implement them. More specifically, it was conferred the right to make decisions regarding the dismissal, assignment and retention of key personnel with which Andersen would be obliged to comply.

In a previous appearance before the US Senate Banking Committee, Volcker expressed his desire that accounting firms change their priorities and attitudes, putting greater weight on ethics and the quality of audits (Glater 2001). To achieve this he proposed the introduction of new legislation and new internal procedures. In principle, Volcker could try to change Andersen's structure by tightening its chain of command and opting for greater centralization. For example, he could bring more senior executives to just one location, nudging them to rely less on conference calls and e-mail messages and more on personal contact. Although the board's initial focus was on Arthur Andersen LLP (Limited Liability Partnership) of the US, the scope of its findings and suggestions could be widened to cover the whole of Andersen Worldwide SC (a Swiss Société Cooperative). Andersen Worldwide SC was the coordinating body for autonomous member firms – each with its own governance and capital structure – which shared a common brand and philosophy as well as technologies and practice methods.

Volcker seemed inclined towards the definitive separation of the auditing practice from the management consultancy business. This was in keeping with the board's belief that the auditing profession required such an allegiance to objectivity and independence, that whatever activity in conflict with these values had to be dispensed with. These values should, henceforth, form an integral part of the new Arthur Andersen culture. However, between 1 January 2002 and the time the board first communicated its resolutions a score of publicly-traded companies – Delta Air Lines, Merck and FedEx among them – had already defected from Andersen. In the succeeding months, more were to follow in what amounted to a veritable stampede out of Andersen's door.

On 11 March 2002, the same day the Independent Oversight Board released its preliminary findings, the possible sale of Andersen to Deloitte Touche Tohmatsu, another Big Five accounting firm, was announced (Eichenwald 2002a). Negotiations did not center on the price, unlike most acquisition talks, but on how Deloitte could avoid assuming Andersen's legal and financial liabilities, particularly those arising from the Enron debacle. One possible solution was for Deloitte to buy all of Andersen's assets with the exception of its American operations. The US business would then be left as a stand-alone unit while it negotiated Enron-related problems. People close to the deal said that, in any case, the Andersen name would most certainly have to disappear if the deal with Deloitte were to push through. At that time, Deloitte occupied the number two position behind PriceWaterhouseCoopers, but the purchase of Andersen would almost allow it to catch up. Despite the Independent Oversight Board's efforts to salvage Andersen, the disclosure of the possible sale was interpreted as a sign that the firm was no longer viable as an independent organization (Norris 2002a).

Soon afterwards, separate negotiation teams from other big rivals such as KPMG and Ernst & Young met with Andersen executives to consider their respective takeover options (Eichenwald and Ross Sorkin 2002). KPMG expressed its interest primarily in Andersen's overseas operations, while Ernst & Young soon came to the conclusion that its teaming up with Andersen was going to be particularly problematic. Elsewhere, Andersen affiliates outside of the US were pretty much left on their own. At first, the London practice said that it was not even considering seceding from the global network or merging with rivals, while the Canadian business at once manifested its desire to follow whatever course Andersen Worldwide took. On the other hand, operations in Belgium and Poland, for example, had already initiated talks with other auditing firms such as Deloitte and KPMG.

However, it was the US Justice Department with its charge of obstruction of justice for the destruction of Enron-related documents that hit the nail on Andersen's coffin on 15 March 2002 (Eichenwald 2002c). It was the first ever criminal indictment brought against a major accounting firm in the country. Until then, these firms were almost untouchable, considered as repositories of public trust as they went about the performance of audit functions.

The US Justice Department alleged that from 23 October 2001 Andersen partners working for Enron launched a 'wholesale destruction of documents' at their Houston, Texas office and that in the following weeks they also instructed employees in Portland, Oregon, Chicago, Illinois and London, England to do the same. The claim, therefore, was that Andersen as a firm had

indulged in a coordinated and pervasive effort to get rid of possibly incriminating evidence on the Enron case.

Indeed there was no question that documentation was discarded, but insofar
as Andersen was concerned all this had occurred before receiving any subpoena
from the SEC (Andersen 2002b). Secondly, the disposal was carried out by the
members of the Enron audit team on their own initiative, without any evidence
that they had consulted with other senior Andersen officials, in Houston,
Chicago or elsewhere. Thirdly, the shredding was done according to the firm's
usual practice, in broad daylight, with no effort to conceal the activity or
particular instructions as to what documents to destroy first. Fourthly, the
indictment did not specify the nature of the records destroyed, nor did it
narrowly claim that these referred to transactions involving Enron's chief
financial officer, Andrew Fastow. This was probably because the paper
documents and e-mails were of the type that would ordinarily be destroyed
after an audit assignment had been completed. Lastly, the government's charges
also failed to consider that the vast bulk of Andersen's Enron-related materials
were either retained or had been retrieved thanks to computer backup systems.
Concretely, around 1500 boxes of desk files (containing approximately 3 million
sheets of paper), corresponding to 4800 official files and reports plus hundreds
of thousands of e-mails had been turned over to authorities upon their request.

On the issue of a purported 'firm-wide misconduct', Andersen offered the
following clarifications in its defense (Andersen 2002b). On 23 October 2001,
a member of the Enron audit team in Houston sent a voice-mail to a colleague
in Portland, Oregon leading to the deletion of Enron-related e-mails by that
employee. When this employee forwarded the message to other Andersen
executives in Portland involved with Enron, the practice director ordered the
members of the team to disregard it. There was no proof that any more
documents were destroyed as a result of the request from Houston. During that
same week, two Houston partners called a London colleague previously engaged
in Enron, telling him to purge his Enron files. But no further evidence was
offered by the US Department of Justice as to the nature or amount of the files
purged in London, nor as to who were actually involved in the purging. Finally,
regarding the destruction of records at Andersen's Chicago office, it turned out
that the initiative did not even originate from anyone in the Houston practice
involved with Enron. In late September and early October 2001, Andersen's
Professional Standards Group in Chicago participated in discussions regarding
Enron accounting with Nancy Temple, an in-house legal counsel. At that time,
she reminded Andersen accountants that under the firm's document retention
policy superseded drafts of memos should be disposed of promptly. Thus, in
compliance with Andersen's routine policy and upon Temple's advice,
documents were discarded in the Chicago office. But all of this had happened
before Andersen's receipt of the request for information from the SEC on 17

October 2001. For all of the above-mentioned reasons, Andersen decided to plead not guilty to the charge of obstruction of justice (Eichenwald 2002b).

Upon learning of the indictment, Andersen's potential suitors, Deloitte Touche Tohmatsu and Ernst & Young, withdrew their offers, leaving KPMG alone at the negotiating table, albeit with vastly reduced hopes for a salvage deal. Andersen lawyers found the charges to be 'a gross abuse of governmental power', for although some partners and employees undeniably exercised poor judgment, a criminal prosecution against the entire firm 'would be both factually and legally baseless' (Eichenwald 2002b). The proceedings against Andersen would destroy the firm, denying thousands of conscientious and reputable employees their source of livelihood and substantially diminishing the chances for recovery of the company's claimants.

The $500,000 fine representing the maximum legal penalty that the indictment carried was the least of Andersen's worries (Norris 2002b). Rather, it was the corporate 'death penalty' which came with the charge that seemed virtually certain. Instead of combating charges, Andersen could choose either to disband; eliminating the government's ability to prosecute, or declare itself bankrupt; scaring away the remaining clients and making itself an even less attractive target to potential acquirers (Glater and Brick 2002). Clearly there was no easy way out of the dilemma for Andersen. Even Volcker's plan to salvage the company by transforming it into an audit only firm was put in serious jeopardy (Andersen 2002c). That line of action would require – aside from the government's dropping its criminal case – the commitment of a critical mass of partners to stay, as well as the settlement of a welter of Enron-related SEC proceedings and civil lawsuits. Andersen had already offered $750 million for this purpose, but it had been rejected by Enron investors (Glater 2002c).

Meanwhile, there was a very strong contrast between the reactions of some Andersen employees and clients who stood by the firm, on the one hand (Schwartz 2002a), and those of a certain group of former partners who even sued the firm to protect their retirement benefits, on the other (*The New York Times* 2002).

In an incredible display of loyalty, the members of a certain Andersen audit team, after having been dismissed by Merck & Co., began looking for their next opportunity within the firm instead of participating in a massive exodus (Schwartz 2002b). They formed part of the majority of the 85,000 workers who, in defiance or hope, remained steadfast in their dedication to their jobs. In the succeeding weeks, Andersen employees or 'androids' (as they were often called derisively within the industry) bought full-page advertisements in major US dailies declaring, 'our attorneys are absolutely convinced that no one in this firm committed a crime, and we are confident that our firm will be absolved at trial' (Schwartz 2002c). Rallies were held in support of Andersen in Houston,

Philadelphia and Washington. An internal web page was likewise set up to allow employees to send messages to law-makers and media professionals.

In the past, Andersen partners were guaranteed to receive hundreds of thousands of dollars each year, a result of which they could retire relatively young thanks to the returns on the equity they had invested in the firm (Glater 2002a). But after the Enron scandal, should partners decide to withdraw or join other firms, they ran the risk of being sued for stripping their collapsing organization of money. A further disincentive was that partners normally received their equity investment back only after a period of 10 years from their retirement. But due to Andersen's involvement with Enron, many other individuals and institutions would now have the right to stake their claims first against the accounting firm's capital, leaving the partners' payback in limbo.

What's worse, retired Andersen partners did not have typical pensions backed by the Pension Benefits Guaranty Corporation nor employer-sponsored 401(k) plans. Instead, they were encouraged to invest for their own retirements through Keogh accounts for unincorporated businesses. However, a $3,500 monthly stipend that worked like a safety net was put in place, should those investments go awry (Schwartz 2002d). Through their lawsuit, the retired partners wanted to halt efforts by current Andersen partners to disband, in effect forcing them to guarantee retirement benefits and equity repayment (*The New York Times* 2002). In any case, jumping ship was already harder for Andersen partners in the US than for those from other countries, due to the non-compete clauses in their contracts.

As far as Andersen's foreign affiliates were concerned, it was an altogether different story (Glater 2002b). As an offshoot of the US government's case Andersen's Spanish and Chilean offices announced that they would sever ties with the firm. Branches in Italy, Poland, Portugal and Switzerland admitted considering similar steps, deciding either to operate independently or to be acquired by a rival firm. At around that time, firms such as Sara Lee, Abbot Laboratories and Northeast Utilities – among Andersen's 20 largest and most long-standing clients – revealed that they too would no longer avail of the firm's auditing services.

On 26 March 2002, Joseph F. Berardino declared that he would be stepping down as Andersen's chief executive. Berardino released the following statement upon his resignation: 'I have concluded that my continuing as worldwide CEO could become an impediment to the efforts of Mr Volcker and many others to save the US firm ... While my nature is to keep fighting and protect our clients, the fact is that the improper shredding of documents took place on my watch – and I believe it is now in the best interests of the firm for me to step down' (Glater and Schwartz 2002). When Berardino assumed the top post in Andersen barely 15 months ago he did so with a clear mandate to help the firm recover from a slew of serious accounting scandals. 'We have been prepared to lead some significant change for this firm and the industry, but we have been unable to get that message heard. I only had one more bullet left, and that was the one I used yesterday. But that bullet also sends the message to our people to keep fighting' (Eichenwald 2002e).

Berardino admitted that it was the demonstrations of Andersen staff that prodded him towards his decision: 'Over the last week I have watched our people have rallies, basically crying for their dignity, and I just wanted to help. I just felt the best signal I could give to our people was to sacrifice the only thing I have left to give: my job' (Eichenwald 2002e). It was far from clear, however, whether Berardino's departure provided the troubled firm a better chance for survival or, on the contrary, simply hastened its destruction.

On 30 March 2002, scarcely a few days after the announcement of Berardino's resignation, the already leaderless Andersen was dealt another devastating blow. In a separate case involving the Baptist Foundation of Arizona, Andersen had been accused of faulty auditing in what had become the largest non-profit bankruptcy in the US, costing about 13,000 investors a total loss of $570 million. Andersen had initially agreed to a $217 million settlement, but when the payment was due on 15 April 2002, it notified parties that its insurance carrier, the Professional Services Insurance Company, would be unable to meet those obligations. This was due largely to the fact that Andersen itself had an outstanding bill of more than $100 million towards the payment of its insurance premium, and for this reason the Professional Services Insurance Company was rendered technically insolvent. John P. Coffey, lead trial lawyer for the Baptist Foundation of Arizona Liquidating Trust, offered these words as commentary: 'This is treachery of the highest of the highest order. It's a second stab in the back to everyone who lost money' (Eichenwald 2002f).

It was at this juncture when the idea of a deferred prosecution of an acknowledged wrongdoing was floated (Eichenwald 2002g). Previously, Volcker had tried to persuade the government to drop its charges on the promise of re-engineering a 'new and improved version' of Andersen (Eichenwald 2002d). But the US Justice Department responded that it would not even consider elaborating such a deal unless Andersen was prepared to admit that it had committed a crime. Later on, the US Justice Department gave signs that it could in principle accept deferring Andersen's prosecution if the firm publicly acknowledged the illegal destruction of documents in the Enron investigation and agreed to restrictions similar to those of a 'corporate probation'. Once approved by a judge, prosecution would be deferred for a number of years, after which the indictment would be dismissed. But if the defendant were to commit other misdeeds during the deferral period, the trial would proceed and the admission could then be used against the defendant as evidence. In lieu of Volcker's suggestion of a withdrawal of the indictment 'without prejudice', a deferral without an admission would certainly have been most advantageous to Andersen, but the

US government was unwilling to give in on the requirement of Andersen's admission. This condition exacerbated Andersen's dilemma. The acceptance of precisely that sort of guilt was tantamount to committing corporate suicide for an auditing firm, granted that its integrity and good reputation were by far its most valuable assets.

Meanwhile, an extraordinary pressure mounted on Andersen to admit wrongdoing shortly after David B. Duncan, the former partner in charge of Enron's audits, entered a guilty plea to a single felony: he admitted to having orchestrated a large-scale effort to destroy documents and obstruct a federal inquiry (Eichenwald 2002h). In principle, Duncan's testimony could be used by the government as evidence as it went about Andersen's prosecution. But in the end not even Duncan's defection was sufficient to push Andersen towards an admission of guilt, and on 6 May 2002 the trial began. The basic issues were simple: was the shredding of documents related to Enron's finances done with a corrupt intent of impeding an official investigation? And if so, should Andersen as a firm be held accountable for its employees who committed the crime? (Eichenwald 2002i).

After a six week trial – including 10 full days during which a deadlocked jury agonized over its verdict – Andersen was finally convicted of obstruction of justice in the Enron case (Eichenwald 2002k). Shortly before releasing its decision, the jury was instructed by judge Melinda F. Harmon that it could declare the firm guilty even if it did not agree as to which of the employees had the intent to commit the crime (the 'corrupt persuader'), thus setting a precedent for corporate criminal liability cases (Eichenwald 2002j). Although sentencing was scheduled for 11 October 2002, Andersen announced that it would cease auditing publicly traded companies 31 August. The end of August 2002 would then effectively signal the demise of a once proud, 89-year-old accounting firm.

In the final analysis, the jury reached its verdict on the basis of the deletion of a few words from a single memorandum (Eichenwald 2002k). Surprisingly, the one truly responsible for the removal wasn't even David B. Duncan, the Andersen partner in charge of the Enron audits who had previously admitted committing a felony. Some time in mid-October 2001, Duncan prepared a memorandum for a news release regarding Enron's third quarter earnings. In the draft, Duncan had characterized certain losses reported by Enron to be 'non-recurring'. Upon review, Nancy Temple, an Andersen lawyer, suggested that Duncan remove that specific portion of the memorandum for such a representation could be found misleading. Certainly, this type of advice not to put something in writing was the kind that lawyers routinely give their clients, to protect them from creating documents that could later on be used against them (Gillers 2002).

Just the same, the jury referred to that memorandum as the 'smoking gun'. It concluded that Temple had 'corruptly persuaded' Duncan to alter information for the purpose of impeding an official investigation by the SEC. Temple suggested that Duncan delete the mention of something that could be misleading in Enron's public statements about its financial condition. According to this reasoning, Duncan, who had already entered a guilty plea to obstruction, in effect did not commit any crime.

The jurors acknowledged that the shredding of documents in itself was not an issue. They were convinced that it was done in good faith and not intended to hinder any official investigation. However, in the jurors' opinion, the disposal of records did not cease being a misguided effort on the part of ill-trained employees to comply with Andersen's document-retention policies (Glater 2002e).

By that time Andersen was already but a mere shadow of its former self. Since 1 January 2001, 690 of its 2,311 public company clients had already abandoned it. Moreover, from its original US workforce of around 27,000 employees, only about 10,000 remained, as the combined result of layoffs and defections of entire offices and practices to other competing firms (Eichenwald 2002k). Deloitte had already acquired the bulk of Andersen's tax business in April, 2002 (Glater 2002d), while in May KPMG announced that it had signed a letter of intent to acquire the consulting units of Andersen Worldwide member firms for a total price of $284 million (Andersen 2002d).

II.   NEUTRALIZING 'NEUTRON JACK'

John (Jack) Francis Welch, Jr was born in Salem, MA – a working-class town north of Boston – in 1936. He was an only child. His father worked as a conductor for the Boston & Maine Railroad Company. The biggest influence in his early years, however, came by way of the tough-love lessons he received from his devout and determined mother, Grace.

In the first chapter of his autobiography, *Jack. Straight from the Gut* (Welch and Byrne 2001) he related the following story. Jack used to play for the local hockey team of Salem High, and once, after having been defeated at overtime by their traditional rivals, he blew his top and flung his stick across the rink. A few minutes later, when the team was already in the locker room, Grace Welch suddenly burst in through the door. She then grabbed Jack by the shoulders and yelled at him in the presence of his coach and teammates, saying, 'You punk! If you don't know how to lose, you'll never know how to win. If you don't know this, you shouldn't be playing.' In other emotionally less-charged moments, whenever Jack would express his perplexity over events, she would tell him, 'Don't kid yourself. That's the way it is.' Jack found guidance dwelling on these thoughts each time he faced the challenge of ridding people of false illusions about business: 'I found it hard to get people to see a situation for what it is and not for what it was, or what they hoped it would be. My mother's admonition to me many years ago was just as important for GE.'

Later on, in a fitting tribute to his mother, Jack Welch went as far as saying, 'my basic management beliefs – things like competing hard to win, facing reality, motivating people by alternately hugging and kicking them, setting stretch goals, and relentlessly following up on people to make sure things get done – can be traced to her as well.' When pressed to specify just what exactly was his mother's most important contribution to the shaping of his personality, he responded: 'Perhaps the greatest single gift she gave me was self-confidence. It's what I've looked for and tried to build in every executive who has ever worked for me. Confidence gives you courage and extends your reach. It lets you take greater risks... My mother never managed people, but she knew all about building self-esteem.'

After leaving his hometown, Jack went on to earn a B.S. in chemical engineering from the University of Massachusetts in 1957, an M.S. then a Ph.D. in chemical engineering, both from the University of Illinois, in 1960.

Jack Welch joined General Electric (GE) in 1960, working as a junior chemical engineer for its plastics division in Pittsfield, MA and earning a salary of $10,500 a year. A little over a year later he wanted to quit his job because he felt stifled by the company's bureaucracy, underappreciated by his boss, and somewhat insulted by the $1,000 raise he had just been offered for what he considered to be extraordinary efforts (Byrne 1998). Furthermore, he had recently received an attractive offer at International Minerals & Chemicals, based in Skokie, Ill. Reuben Gutoff, then a young executive a level above Welch at GE, got wind of his plans and desperately tried to dissuade him from leaving. Over dinner at a restaurant with Welch and his wife, Carolyn, Gutoff vowed that henceforth he would protect Jack from being entangled in the web of the GE red tape. He also promised to create for Jack a congenial work atmosphere in GE that combined small-company smugness with big-company resources. Guttoff remembered having pleaded, 'Trust me. As long as I am here, you are going to get a shot to operate with the best of the big company and the worst part of it pushed aside.' Gutoff won Welch over and remained as his boss until 1973. At around that time, Welch had already earned his wings at GE and was bold enough to write in his annual performance review that his long-term goal was to become the company's CEO.

Welch was elected GE's youngest vice president in 1972 and was named vice chairman in 1979. In April 1981, he succeeded Reginald H. Jones as the eighth chairman and CEO in GE's 121-year history. GE traced its beginnings to the Edison Electric Light Company, founded by Thomas A. Edison in 1878 (GE 2002). A merger between the Edison General Electric Company and the Thomson-Houston Electric Company in 1892 gave birth to the General Electric Company (GE), as it began to be called. As of June 2002, GE was the only company from the original Dow Jones Industrial Index of 1896 that still existed. It had become a diversified services, technology and manufacturing firm, operating in more than 100 countries worldwide and employing approximately 313,000 people.

An authority no less than Warren Bennis, from the University of Southern California's Marshall School, affirmed that although it was Alfred P. Sloan who invented the concept of the modern corporation, it was Jack Welch that made it work (Bennis 2002). Bennis wrote: 'It is no exaggeration to say that Welch is at least partly responsible for the amazing resurgence of the American economy over the past 15 years. And few would dispute that he has been the role model for many other CEOs or that his thinking underpins many of the best and most esteemed of today's business practices. His preeminence is well deserved' (Bennis 2002: 96). In heaping accolades over Welch, Bennis was simply joining a roster of business writers who declared Welch to be 'the world's greatest business leader', 'the manager of the century', 'the CEO of the century'; or as *Fortune* magazine would unabashedly say, 'the most widely admired, studied, and imitated CEO of his time' (Walker 2001).

Such claims, of course, would always be controversial. But what seemed beyond doubt was that no other business personality had been the object of as much media coverage and attention as Welch. At least nine full-length books have been written about him. Foremost among them was his autobiography, *Jack. Straight from the Gut*, published in September 2001, which immediately jumped to the number 1 spot on bestseller lists from *The New York Times*, *The Wall Street Journal*, Amazon.com, *USA Today* and the Association of Independent Booksellers. This book earned Welch an incredible $7.1 million author's fee. Other Welch classics included *Get Better or Get Beaten! 35 Leadership Secrets from GE's Jack Welch* (Slater 2001), *Control Your Destiny or Someone Else Will: How Jack Welch is Making General Electric the World's Most Competitive Corporation* (Tichy and Sherman 1999), *Jack Welch and the GE Way: Managment Insights and Leadership Secrets of the Legendary CEO* (Slater 2002), *Business the Jack Welch Way: 10 Secrets of the World's Turn-Around King* (Crainer 2002), *The New GE: How Jack Welch Revived an American Institution* (Slater 1992) *Jack Welch Speaks: Wisdom from the World's Greatest Busiess Leader* (Lowe 2001), *Welch: An American Icon* (Lowe 2002), and the much less flattering *At Any Cost*, by Thomas F. O'Boyle (1999).

Besides all these reams of printed paper, what else was there behind Welch? Did he really have the achievements to deserve all the publicity?

In 1980, the year before Welch became chairman and CEO, GE reported $1.5 billion in profits. From 1981, during Welch's first five years at the helm, he fired one out of every four people working in the firm (Auletta 2001). This earned him the worthy moniker of 'Neutron Jack', referring to his uncanny capability to get rid of people while leaving the company's physical plant intact. Throughout his 41-year career at GE, 20 of which were spent at the top office, he had downsized more than 100,000 employees. By the end of Welch's watch in 2001, profits at the company had grown to $14.1 billion (GE 2002).

For at least the past 20 years, share prices at GE had risen at an average rate of 21 per cent each year. This record was about 50 per cent faster than the Standard & Poor's 500 stock index. The company's market capitalization also grew from $13 billion, in 1981, to almost $500 billion, in 2001 (*Knowledge at Wharton* 2001b). For all of these reasons, GE was Wall Street's darling and consistently ranked first in surveys among the world's most admired and most respected companies. How was Welch able to accomplish all this?

First among Welch's recipes for success was the strategy that every GE product should be 'number 1, number 2 or abandoned' (*Knowledge at Wharton* 2001a). Later on, Welch refined it after he had learned that many of the company's managers were defining their markets so narrowly that practically all of their products became number 1. The revised version then ordered that each product account for no more than 10 per cent of the market share. This simple directive seemed to have opened the door to enormous gains, as what initially appeared to be mature markets were suddenly transformed into astounding growth opportunities.

No less important was the 20/70/10 people management philosophy that Welch instilled in GE (*Knowledge at Wharton* 2001a). The company went through an annual appraisal system in which every manager was ranked in the top 20 per cent, in the vital middle 70 per cent, or at the bottom 10 per cent. After all this effort at differentiation, needless to say, the bottom 10 per cent got fired. The top 20 per cent got a grade of A, meaning that they both 'made the numbers and embodied GE values' (Bennis 2002). The bulk making up the 70 per cent obtained a grade of B, meaning that they either made the numbers or embodied GE values; however, they had the company's commitment that it would help them to achieve both. The official template of executive excellence at GE was comprised of four E's, which stood for energy, energize, edge – the capacity to make tough decisions in the firm's lingo – and execute.

At an Information Technology conference in the spring of 2002, Welch spoke of the need to spot good workers with positive values, while quickly doing away with poor managers, regardless of how much they apparently contributed to the bottom line:

> It's a sin to lose a top performer. The managers who lose top performers should be removed themselves. The way you find out where the horses' asses are is you see they're losing people. In addition, giving false kindness to those workers, especially over age 50, who are not contributors, is unfair. I think it counts so much to let people know where they stand. You have no right to BS people (Russell 2002).

Primarily for this reason, Welch spent at least 60 per cent of his time choosing, developing and of course, firing people (Bennis 2002). So committed was he to the task that he personally interviewed every single promising candidate for the top 500 positions at GE. The company also had a marvelous executive training program that rivaled those of elite business school in terms of quality, intensity and relevance. It maintained a campus, or a 'GE people factory' in Crotonville, NY. And according to a rough estimate, about 3 per cent of its payroll was earmarked for staff development and training.

Welch immediately realized that knowledge and information were the company's primary strategic resources, and that it had to invest in them in order to succeed in the future (*Knowledge at Wharton* 2001a). GE became one of the first global companies to appoint a chief knowledge and learning officer who reported directly to Welch. This move was in line with Welch's initiative to transform the firm into a 'boundaryless organization' where knowledge and information freely flowed. He developed operating procedures that eliminated barriers and helped knowledge to be shared widely, not the least through his famous 'work out' sessions. As he once remarked: 'Taking everyone's best ideas and transferring them to others is the secret. There is nothing more important. But there is also nothing more difficult' (*Knowledge at Wharton* 2001a).

This emphasis on the 'soft stuff' did not mean, however, that Welch did not make use of financial rewards to drive behavior; quite the contrary (Byrne 1998). In 1998, for example, base salaries could rise – depending on one's performance – by as much as 25 per cent, even without a promotion. Cash bonuses could increase by as much as 150 per cent, equivalent to between 20 and 70 per cent of one's base pay. And stock option plans were likewise broadly expanded from very senior executives alone to nearly a third of GE's professional employees.

Finally, Welch also proved to be a consummate master in the art of negotiating deals (*Knowledge at Wharton* 2001b). During his tenure, GE successfully made close to 1,000 acquisitions and more than 400 divestments. His strategy in acquiring new businesses did not always consist in driving the hardest possible bargain. Rather, Welch was always careful to leave something on the negotiating table and try to build on that to have a fruitful long-term relationship with the new subsidiary.

Despite Welch's two acknowledged failures – the pollution of the Hudson River by PCBs released by GE plants and the botched acquisition of Honeywell due to opposition from the European Commission – he left the chief executive's office in September 2001 bathed in an almost supernatural aura. But the business downturn triggered first by the bursting of the Internet bubble, then followed by the Enron scandal invited a more critical revisiting of Welch's supposed merits and accomplishments at GE.

Welch was often painted by hagiographers not only as a 'self-made man', but also as a 'rebel' or 'revolutionary' who single-handedly transformed stodgy GE into a lithe and nimble firm. He was supposed to have been the one primarily responsible for the company's blessed fortune. A few business analysts and commentators, however, begged to disagree.

Contrary to the popular belief that Welch inherited a moribund company from Reginald Jones in 1981, things were already sailing along quite smoothly for GE even then. Between 1972, when Jones began his stint at the top, and 1981, when he handed the baton over to Welch, revenue had already been growing at an annual rate of 12 per cent, and earnings at 16 per cent (Walker 2001). In fact, the average annual earnings growth throughout Welch's tenure at 12 per cent was even lower than Jones's, although it had reached about 15 per cent in Welch's last eight years.

As Stanford Business professors James C. Collins and Jerry I. Porras explained, since the early 1900s GE had enjoyed continued success under a series of extremely competent and innovative CEOs (Collins and Porras 1997). The company was the first to establish a major industrial research lab in the US. In the early 1920s, it blazed a trail in the implementation of enlightened management ideas such as paid vacations for workers. This had allowed GE to attract and retain top talent ever since then. In the 1930s the company made the shrewd move of expanding into home appliances. In the 1950s GE pioneered in decentralizing management, thus encouraging divisional independence and growth in new businesses such as plastics. Its CEO at that time, Ralph Cordiner, founded the corporate university at Crotonville. In the 1960s, the foundations for GE's transformation into a full blown conglomerate were laid: firstly, with the decision to let its credit division offer diversified financial services, and secondly, with the development of its airplane engines business. Despite the recession and the inflation that plagued Reginald Jones' mandate at GE during the 1970s, he managed to hand over to Welch one of the strongest companies in the US, one that – among other things – enjoyed a triple A debt rating.

Another popular benchmark of a company's strength is its return on equity (ROE), or earnings as a percentage of shareholder equity. This figure measures the efficiency with which management uses shareholder capital to create profits. Under Welch, GE registered an average annual ROE of 25.8 per cent. However, when compared to the pre-tax ROE figures of the seven previous CEOs at GE, Collins and Porras found that Welch merely ranked third.

The truth of the matter, therefore, was not so much that GE was the house that Jack Welch built, as GE being the house that built Jack Welch.

Apart from being head of what already was in itself an extraordinary company, another favorable circumstance that contributed to Welch's 'legendary' career was his timing. It so happened that during the 1980s the US stockmarket experienced the greatest bull-run of all time. This was fueled not so much by increased corporate earnings as by an unabated growth in investor willingness to pay for those earnings (Walker 2001). Whereas in 1981 Standard & Poor's 500 stocks traded, on the average, at nine times their earnings, twenty years later it was at 25 times their earnings. Certainly, with Welch, GE shares traded well above the Standard & Poor's average, at 38 times their earnings. This led many to embrace what had come to be the core belief of Welch fans, that he had made shareholders far richer than anyone else ever had. Except for the fact that this just wasn't true, unfortunately.

Even a magazine as favorable to Welch as *Fortune* acknowledged that in the decade of the 1990s GE ranked 55th in annual rate of return to investors (Walker 2001). The same magazine took note that over 17 years, Colgate-Palmolive shares consistently outperformed those of GE. That record was pegged to the tenure of Colgate-Palmolive's CEO, Reuben Mark, who unfortunately for him, was not half as media-friendly as Welch.

Of course there are other better indicators to gauge a company's performance than raw stock market gains. Collins and Porras suggested that one compare the performance of a firm's stocks to that of the market in general during a given period (Collins and Porras 1997). They calculated that between 1981 and 1995, GE stocks under Welch beat the market by a factor of 2.4 to 1. Nevertheless, eleven other companies fared better than GE by this benchmark. Between 1971 and 1991, for example, Kimberly-Clark shares, under the leadership of Darwin E. Smith, outperformed the market by a ratio of 4.1 to 1. So was there really more puff than stuff to Jack Welch's legend?

Hard to say, but one thing clear was that the general public's relationship with business leaders had radically changed during Welch's time (Walker 2001). Aside from Welch, other corporate icons such as Bill Gates and Steve Jobs began to receive far more attention than they used to, thanks to the advent of networks like CNBC, for example, dedicated to live business and stock-market coverage.

What Welch had really mastered was the fine art of having an extraordinarily thriving relationship with Wall Street. Under Welch, GE gave Wall Street exactly what it wanted, predictable increases in earnings, quarter by quarter, without any surprises. When Welch took over, GE was trading at a price to earnings (P/E) ratio of 8, which was broadly in line with the market average (Walker 2001). Normally, a firm's P/E ratio shrank as its revenues and earnings increased. With Welch, however, GE did the exact opposite, with the market apparently believing that the company's growth potential had become greater than it was in 1981. Welch's GE incredibly chalked up this record through more than a hundred consecutive quarters. How did he do it?

Six months after Welch's retirement from GE, serious questions began to surface regarding the veracity of the company's numbers and the credibility of the accomplishments of its former CEO (Brady 2002). First to raise the red flag was Bill Gross, an influential executive of Pacific Investment Management Co., the world's largest bond fund. On 20 March 2002, Gross issued a report in which he accused GE of dishonesty, basically because it used cheap commercial paper and stock to buy growth. In consequence, he said that he would no longer buy the firm's short term debt. Gross wiped off a full 6 per cent of GE's share price and caused the value of its $233 billion debt to plummet, sharply raising the company's interest costs. Those new interest costs were now supposed to reflect the firm's true riskiness more accurately. Whereas GE's superb reputation rested on its industrial powerhouse, with products ranging from light bulbs to aircraft engines, it had in fact become a financial company, according to Gross. But unlike other financial firms, GE's risks were heavily disguised, Gross said.

Gross voiced a common fear that GE was actually 'managing' or 'smoothing' its earnings, rather than reporting them faithfully, so as to keep an impressive record of profit growth (*The Economist* 2002). In other words, the company was – so to speak – merely taking money from one pocket and putting it into another, in order to hide risks in its businesses. More concretely, it used unique gains and restructuring charges to offset each other without disrupting each quarter's earnings flow. Charges associated with the shutdown of the Montgomery Ward chain of department stores owned by GE Capital, for example, could be balanced off by gains from the sale of its stakes in PaineWebber. If these developments were recorded further apart, they could have caused a dip or a spike in earnings growth, difficult to overcome for the following quarter.

'Managing' earnings was one thing, but another more serious charge was that GE was in fact covering up a slump in growth by claiming to earn more money that it actually was. The key to understanding this predicament laid in GE's division into industrial and financial (GE Capital) components (*The Economist* 2002). According to GE accounts, stockholders have two-thirds of their money invested in GE Industrial and one-third in GE Capital. It could be argued, however, that this misstated the true allocation of capital at GE, or that it underrated the true riskiness of GE Capital, for without the support of GE Industrial, GE Capital would in fact need more money for its triple A credit rating. In other words, GE Capital was somewhat being subsidized by GE Industrial. GE however denied that its financial businesses entailed higher risk than its industrial ones. In any case, transparency was certainly needed in GE accounts. For example, a recent balance sheet from the company included an item entitled 'All other current costs and expenses accrued' without any accompanying footnotes or explanations for the amount of $14 billion (*The Economist* 2002).

In August 2000, a month before Welch's departure, GE shares were fetching $60 a piece. As a result of all these doubts raised, by the middle of June 2002, they were going at almost half the price, at $31. Despite the new CEO, Jeffrey

R. Immelt's, offer to give investors more information than Welch ever gave, the market remained skeptical. By the end of the first semester of 2002, GE's share price had fallen by 25 per cent since the beginning of the year, dropping about twice as much as the Standard & Poor 500 index (Leonhardt 2002). A reassessment of Welch's tenure at GE was definitely in order.

In a sense, the same may be said not only of Welch's stint at the GE top office, but also of the impact of GE on Welch's personal life. Welch himself had expressed his regret that due to his work at GE he had 'obviously been marginal on marriage' (Russell 2002). It was a thinly veiled acceptance of his failure to find a balance between career and family life: his professional success had cost him no less than two divorces.

In a chapter on 'Divorce and marriage' in the work *Jack Welch. My Personal History* (Welch 2001) he wrote: 'Unfortunately, while I was doing the biggest deal of my professional career, the biggest merger in my personal life was ending' (Welch 2001). This was in reference to his 28 years of marriage with his first wife, Carolyn. Welch admitted to being the ultimate workaholic throughout his GE years. As a result, the burden of raising their four children fell squarely on his wife's shoulders. At the time of their divorce in April 1987, their oldest, Katherine, was at Harvard Business School, while their other daughter, Anne, was also about to enter the Harvard School of Architecture for her master's degree. Their older son, John, was working through his chemical engineering degree at the University of Virginia, while their youngest, Mark, was already then a freshman at the University of Vermont. On this count, undeniably, Carolyn did a mighty fine job, even without her husband's help.

However, after seeing their children through school, Carolyn wanted to develop a new career for herself, while Welch wanted her to remain at home as a full-time housewife. Welch's having reached the top position at GE did not help their relationship at all and soon enough they parted ways. Eventually, Carolyn became a lawyer and married her former boyfriend during undergraduate years.

In October 1987, six months after his divorce, Welch met Jane Beasley on a blind date arranged by common friends. She was an attorney working in New York, 17 years his junior. Two years later, in April 1989, they were wed. But this did not happen until, in a very Welch-like manner, they first struck out a deal. As Welch himself recounted:

> I told her it bothered me that she didn't ski or play golf. She told me it bothered her that I didn't go to the opera. We made a deal: I agreed to go to the opera if she agreed to ski and golf. I really wanted a full-time partner, someone who would be willing to put up with my schedule and travel with me on business trips. Jane would have to give up her career. She took a leave of absence to try it out and, luckily for me, decided to make this her full-time occupation ... Jane won the club championships at Sankaty Head in Nantucket four years in a row and I won it twice. She's become the perfect partner (Welch 2001).

Whatever happened between Jack Welch and Jane Beasley from then on until March 2002 could be anybody's guess. But the fact was that towards the middle of that month Jane filed for a divorce and hired Raoul Felder, one of New York's top lawyers, to assure her fair half of Jack's fortune, estimated at about $900 million in outstanding GE stock options alone (Hogg 2002). A big factor in Jane's favor was that the once happy couple's pre-nuptial contract had already expired.

The estranged couple's divorce papers revealed that aside from a lifetime retainership of $86,000 a year from GE, Jack Welch would also continue to have – after his retirement – full access to company services and facilities, including a Boeing 737 jet, a luxurious Manhattan apartment with its attendant costs, dining privileges at exclusive restaurants and court-side seats to New York Knicks and US Open games (Fabrikant 2002). It is certainly hard to justify such a lavish outpouring of shareholder money on someone who, like Welch, is already in retirement. Furthermore, the issue remains of who should be paying taxes for such monies. In principle, Welch should be paying and GE could write the corresponding amount off, but only if the company could show that these are ordinary and necessary expenses of doing business (Fabrikant and Cay Johnston 2002).

The 66-year-old Welch's new love was Suzy Wetlaufer, a 42-year-old divorcee and mother of four. They first met when Wetlaufer, the editor in chief of *Harvard Business Review*, requested an interview in October 2001 (Donegan 2002). Over a series of meetings during which Welch revised Wetlaufer's article, the pair found out that they had good rapport. The closeness she had developed with her subject put Wetlaufer's journalistic objectivity in question, so she pulled her story out of the *Harvard Business Review*'s February 2002 issue. Later on, as her affair with Welch became more public, Wetlaufer was somewhat forced to take a leave of absence from her $250,000 a year job. Eventually Wetlaufer got reinstated, although no longer as editor in chief but as 'editor at large', that is, minus the managerial responsibilities. But this was too much for some of her co-workers, two of whom resigned from their posts as senior editors in protest. The normally boisterous and media-friendly Jack Welch surprisingly gave no comments, for he considered these recent developments to be a purely personal matter.

III. LIFESTYLE CHOICE AND MORAL CAPITAL ESTATE PLANNING

Everyone would agree, at least in name, that what we ultimately seek in all our activities is happiness, a good and flourishing life. We engage in whatever it is that we do in the belief that it brings us closer to our goal which is happiness.

Happiness is something that is desirable in and by itself, and everything else becomes reasonably choiceworthy only with reference to it. In a way, therefore, happiness represents the definitive form of moral capital. Happiness is moral capital in its perfect state, where there is only pure gain or accumulation and loss is no longer possible. Even the use or consumption of this form of moral capital does not cause it to diminish, but on the contrary allows it to grow further. Once achieved, moral capital in the form of happiness is no longer subject to future risks and its value becomes more intrinsic than instrumental. The reason for wanting happiness – for accumulating moral capital in this form – is none other than happiness itself.

Despite the terminological agreement, that doing well and living well is the same as being happy, not everyone coincides in the particular kind of life that happiness consists in. Something similar occurs with corporate agents – such as Andersen or GE – with regard to the blanket term 'profit'. The truism was that firms existed in order to maximize profits, but profit is not a univocal term. One could obtain profits by simply buying or selling shares in the market, even when the company whose shares one traded was operating in the red. Furthermore, the strategies that profit making requires in the short, middle or long term could be entirely different from each other. Correspondingly, in the case of individual agents such as Jack Welch, one could suppose a nominal agreement regarding success as that towards which all efforts are aimed. Yet what success means in each individual case is subject to much controversy. For example, would it be alright to sacrifice one's marriage and family life for gains in one's career and profession? Would such an advancement truly qualify as success?

We know that in the case of individual agents, happiness as the ultimate good should not be attributed exclusively to a few isolated actions, some more or less developed habits, or certain outstanding character traits. Rather, true happiness should only be ascribed to a life that is full, complete and entire. It is a characteristic of a person's completed biography. Practically no one ever contested Jack Welch's success while he was CEO of GE. But soon afterwards such judgment began to seem hasty and premature.

Following the analogy we have established between personal and corporate agents, we could say that happiness should only be attributed properly to the whole lifespan of a firm. It is a mark of a particular corporate history, rather than of any specific action, mode of operation, facet of organizational culture or long-term strategy. What took Andersen more than eight decades to build – a reputation for professional competence and integrity – all went down the drain in scarcely five years. We also realize that at GE Jack Welch was extremely lucky to have been able to reap the rewards of the work of his predecessors in what had long been an exceptional company. In other words, he wasn't only cashing in his own chips.

In the *Nicomachean Ethics* (NE), Aristotle explored at least four different lifestyles which vied for a life of happiness according to popular understanding. These would be the equivalent to different planning strategies for the building up of moral capital estates. A choice among these diverse lifestyles would be similar to deciding which planning strategy would be best for one's moral capital estate. And as we already know, moral capital estate planning should be a fundamental concern to both individual and corporate agents.

Firstly, a kind of life that Aristotle considered was one centered on wealth or money: 'The money-maker's life is in a way forced on him [not chosen for itself]; and clearly wealth is not the good we are seeking; since it is [merely] useful, [choiceworthy only] for some other end' (NE 1096a).

Aristotle did not have a positive judgment of a life dedicated mainly to the pursuit of material wealth. This was because money or material wealth belonged to a class of objects that were desirable not in themselves, but only instrumentally or for the sake of another. And a basic condition that Aristotle had established for a life of true happiness was that it be in relation to something that was good in and by itself, preferably the supreme and ultimate or final good for human beings. On this count, clearly, money did not qualify, for its value laid in its use or exchange for some other object which was the ulterior good. In other words, money simply represented a means, not the end that one should be looking for. Such was Aristotle's disdain for a life of money-making that he thought that no one in his right mind and who had the choice would ever commit himself to it. Rather, it could only come about involuntarily, as the result of coercion or force.

One could say that at the root of Andersen's troubles was a conflict of interests in its double role as Enron's auditor and management consultant. Andersen stood to gain more than $25 million a year for each of these functions. By so doing, however, it compromised its objectivity and independence, and eventually its integrity as well. It would certainly have been better if Andersen had earlier given up one of these sources of immediate financial gain to safeguard its professionalism. As for Jack Welch at GE, one could say that he was somewhat consumed by the ambition to become the most successful CEO of all time. What he failed to realize, perhaps, was the ephemeral character of that professional success, currently under revision. Of course, money and success are good things, even great ones, but not at any price.

Elsewhere, we realize that Aristotle's contempt for material wealth was not as absolute as one may have thought, for albeit 'external', he still considered it as a 'good'. He even recognized that a certain amount of prosperity was necessary for happiness:

> happiness evidently also needs external goods to be added [to the activity], as we said, since we cannot, or cannot easily, do fine actions if we lack the resources. For,

first of all, in many actions we use friends, wealth and political power just as we use instruments. Further, deprivation of certain [externals] – e.g. good birth, good children, beauty – mars our blessedness; for we do not altogether have the character of happiness if we look utterly repulsive or are ill-born, solitary or childless, and have it even less, presumably, if our children or friends are totally bad, or were good but have died (NE 1099a–b).

A next contender for the happy life was one of pleasure or bodily gratification (NE 1095b). Aristotle attributed this choice to the majority of humans, and implicitly, to 'the most vulgar', meaning those who never had the chance to cultivate their taste through proper education. Neither did this option convince him, for he found such kind of life to be 'completely slavish' and more proper to 'grazing animals' than to human beings. Not that Aristotle ever questioned the appeal of pleasure to humans. But he likewise thought that despite being biologically the same as other animals, unlike them we happened to be endowed with reason. And reason should lead us to aspire to higher things than the mere and immediate satisfaction of our senses. Otherwise, we would be no different from grazing animals indeed. Similarly, Aristotle linked this choice of life to many people who occupied positions of power. Rather than as leaders of their fellow human beings, they behaved in fact as slaves of pleasure, using whatever means they had to gratify their bodies.

A third option was a life of action, a political life dedicated to the pursuit of honor (NE 1095b). In contrast with a life of pleasure, a political life seemed to be reserved only for the cultivated few in any given society. However, neither did Aristotle completely agree with this choice. For although honor was certainly of a more elevated stature than pleasure, it 'appears to be too superficial to be what we are seeking, since it seems to depend more on those who honor than on the one who is honored, whereas we intuitively believe that the good is something of our own and hard to take from us' (NE 1095b).

The most satisfying kind of life for a human being ought to be based on that person's own doing or making, rather than on somebody else's. We are not entirely responsible for the honor that we receive and instead are largely dependent on other people. For Aristotle, it was just too big a risk to make one's happiness depend mainly on other people rather than on oneself. Furthermore, as Aristotle himself clarified, honor was rendered to one by other people and for a certain reason. We would do well, then, to investigate the basis of that praise. We seek to be honored not just by anyone, but by people who know us; and we seek to be honored by intelligent people rather than by the foolish. Lastly, what we ultimately seek is to be honored for our virtue, rather than for anything else: 'It is clear, then, that in the view of active people at least, virtue is superior [to honor]' (NE 1095b).

Andersen received a terrible lesson in the price of reputation mismanagement. It did not realize soon enough that the main reason why clients flocked to it and availed of its services was the public trust that it enjoyed. By squandering this trust, Andersen had in fact lost its most valuable resource, a good name, and immediately afterwards everything else. Perhaps no CEO received as much honor as Jack Welch during his tenure at GE. Media, Wall Street analysts and the public at large fawned on him. But then, for such honor to be valid, it had to be founded on virtue and truth. And that precisely was what was now being brought into question.

What kind of lifestyle, therefore, is absolutely the best for human beings? For Aristotle, it had to be a life of virtue, or a life of theory (contemplation or study), insofar as it represented the highest form of virtue accessible to human beings:

> If happiness, then, is activity expressing virtue, it is reasonable for it to express the supreme virtue, which will be the virtue of the best thing. The best is understanding ..., and to understand what is fine and divine, by being itself either divine or the most divine element in us. Hence complete happiness will be its activity expressing its proper virtue; and we have said that this activity is the activity of study (NE 1177a).

He enumerated a list of commonly accepted features of genuine happiness. Firstly, it had to be an activity, and one that contained its own end: 'The belief that the happy person lives well and does well in action also agrees with our account, since we have virtually said that the end is a sort of living well and doing well in action' (NE 1098b). Virtue would be of little use to someone if, despite possessing it, he did not employ or exercise it.

Secondly, a life of virtue also had to be pleasant in itself, for being pleased was a condition of the soul included in its own proper activity. Furthermore, 'the things that please lovers of what is fine are things pleasant by nature; and actions expressing virtue are pleasant in this way; and so they both please lovers of what is fine and are pleasant in themselves' (NE 1099a). A life of virtue did not need pleasure to be added to it as if some sort of ornament, for it already had pleasure incorporated in itself, in its own activity which was good and fine.

And thirdly, a life of virtue was one in accordance with reason and sound judgment (NE 1099a). For reason was man's superior faculty, and in a life of virtue it revolved on the noblest objects, the immutable and eternal realities: 'no human achievement has the stability of activities that express virtue, since these seem to be more enduring even than our knowledge of the sciences; and the most honorable of the virtues themselves are more enduring [than the others] because blessed people devote their lives to them more fully and more continually than to anything else' (NE 1100b).

This note on the stability, continuity or permanence of a life of virtue was mainly in response to the issue that happiness required a complete life, one that was no longer subject to reversals of fortune (NE 1100a). Therefore, rather than conclude that we would have to wait until one were dead in order to definitively pronounce him happy – something which would be completely absurd

– we simply have to reason out that virtue itself is the stable and controlling element in a life of happiness: 'the happy person has the [stability] we are looking for and keeps the character he has throughout his life. For always, or more than anything else, he will do and study the actions expressing virtue, and will bear misfortunes most finely, in every way and in all conditions appropriately, since he is truly "good, foursquare and blameless"' (NE 1100b).

The best strategy in moral capital estate planning was one that invested in a life of virtue. Due to its nobility, self-sufficiency, pleasantness and continuity, Aristotle described it as a life inclusive of all good, more proper to the gods than to human beings (cf. NE 1177b). Certainly, this is much easier to see in the lives of individual agents than in firms. But if there is one lesson we could learn from cases like that of Andersen, involving corporate criminal liability, it is that corporate agents are also subject to the opposite of virtue, which is vice.

In both Andersen and Jack Welch's GE, we have cases of failed estate planning in moral capital. Andersen failed to live up to the ideals of its eponymous founder and his first successor, Spacek, who were the beacons of the accounting profession in their time. Never mind its 'cohesive culture' or the erstwhile merits of its decentralized partnership structure. Even after the Waste Management and Sunbeam snarl-ups Andersen still did not pay attention to the writing on the wall and went on with its more than cozy relationships with clients. The Independent Oversight Board formed in response to the Enron investigations promised too little, too late, and was rendered completely ineffective by management's refusal to acknowledge its faults. Honestly admitting one's faults lends credibility to the sincerity of one's amends. As for Jack Welch at GE, it would certainly have been better for him to be more forthcoming with his financial reports. Instead of currying the favors of the media and Wall Street, he could have provided more accurate information about GE's profits and earnings, and left the market to judge and decide on its own regarding his company's merits. Because of Welch's window-dressing his entire corporate legacy at GE has been cast in the shadow of doubt. This – and not seconding Welch's dubious record – was what made his successor, Jeffrey Immelt's, job extremely difficult.

IV. IN BRIEF

- The final end that a human being pursues finds its most complete expression in his choice of lifestyle. A person's lifestyle gives unity to his feelings, actions, habits and character; it lends structure and meaning to his existence.
- An organization's corporate history is the equivalent of an individual's lifestyle and biography. Whereas corporate culture gives us a snapshot of

the firm at a certain point in time, its corporate history furnishes us with a full-length motion picture of how that culture evolves.

- Individual lifestyles and corporate histories determine the moral capital estates of persons and organizations, respectively. We call them 'estates' because they refer to the wealth of moral capital – patrimony or legacy – that individuals and firms bequeath to their successors. In the same way that a person's estate is fixed only at his time of death, so it is – analogously – with a firm. An organization's corporate history could only be written once its protagonists have already retired or departed.

- The transfer of moral capital estates cannot be fully controlled by one's will, and part of it is always passed on involuntarily. One's reputation or image in the collective memory is an important part of that heritage. This element is particularly difficult to control.

- A nominal agreement exists regarding happiness – a good, flourishing life – such as that which human beings ultimately seek in all their activities. Happiness is desirable in and by itself, and we seek whatever it is we choose in the belief that it leads us to happiness.

- Happiness represents the definitive form of moral capital. In its perfect state there is only pure gain and enjoyment, without any risk of loss. The value of happiness as moral capital is substantive rather than instrumental. Happiness is properly attributed to a life that is full, complete and entire.

- In the *Nicomachean Ethics*, Aristotle explored four rival lifestyles that vied for true happiness: one dedicated to money-making and material wealth; another to pleasure; a third – the political life – characterized by the pursuit of honor; and fourthly, a life of virtue or theory (contemplation and study), which is the highest virtue.

- For Aristotle, a life dedicated to virtue was the best life for human beings. It consisted in an activity involving reason that was self-sufficient, most pleasant, and most continuous or permanent. Corporate virtue depends on the individual virtue of its members.

REFERENCES

Andersen (2002a), 'Volcker names independent oversight board', www.andersen.com, 27 February.
Andersen (2002b), 'Updated analysis on the Justice indictment of Andersen: The government's factual and legal errors', www.andersen.com, 15 March.
Andersen (2002c), 'Volcker outlines framework for a "New Andersen" with governing board', www.andersen.com, 22 March.
Andersen (2002d), 'KPMG Consulting Inc. signs letter of intent to acquire Andersen's global consulting practices', www.andersen.com, 8 May.

Aristotle (1985), *Nicomachean Ethics*, trans. by Terence Irwin, Indianapolis, IN: Hackett Publishing.

Auletta, K. (2001), 'Jack Welch: The lion roars', *Business Week*, 24 September.

Bennis, W. (2002), 'Will the legacy live on?', *Harvard Business Review*, February.

Brady, D. (2002), 'The education of Jeff Immelt', *Business Week*, 29 April.

Byrne, J.A. (1998), 'How Jack Welch runs GE. A close-up look at how America's #1 Manager runs GE', *Business Week*, 8 June.

Coffee, J. (2002), 'Accounting for bad accounting', *Multinational Monitor*, January/February, **23** (1 & 2).

Collins, James C. and Jerry I. Porras (1997), *Built to Last: Successful Habits of Visionary Companies*, New York: Harper Business.

Crainer, Stuart (2002), *Business the Jack Welch Way: 10 Secrets of the World's Turn-Around King*, Chichester, UK: Capstone Publishers.

Donegan, L. (2002), 'Neutron Jack and his electric affair', *The Observer*, 17 March.

Economist, The (2001), 'Leading the cause', 3 March.

Economist, The (2002), 'General Electric. The Jack and Jeff show loses its lustre', 4 May.

Eichenwald, K. (2002a), 'Arthur Andersen is said to be near a sale to a rival', *The New York Times*, 11 March.

Eichenwald, K. (2002b), 'Andersen is said to rule out plea', *The New York Times*, 14 March.

Eichenwald, K. (2002c), 'Andersen is charged with obstruction in Enron inquiry', *The New York Times*, 15 March.

Eichenwald, K. (2002d), 'Volcker's plan for Andersen is a long shot', *The New York Times*, 24 March.

Eichenwald, K. (2002e), 'Andersen chief says he resigned to aid workers', *The New York Times*, 28 March.

Eichenwald, K. (2002f), 'Andersen dealt another setback as talks over civil case stall', *The New York Times*, 30 March.

Eichenwald, K. (2002g), 'Deferral talk reported in Andersen case', *The New York Times*, 2 April.

Eichenwald, K. (2002h), 'A guilty plea from Andersen's Enron auditor', *The New York Times*, 10 April.

Eichenwald, K. (2002i), 'A handicapper's guide to the trial of Andersen', *The New York Times*, 5 May.

Eichenwald, K. (2002j), 'Judge's ruling on Andersen hurts defense', *The New York Times*, 15 June.

Eichenwald, K. (2002k), 'Andersen guilty in effort to block inquiry on Enron', *The New York Times*, 16 June.

Eichenwald, K and A. Ross Sorkin (2002), 'Andersen widens effort to find buyer', *The New York Times*, 13 March.

Fabrikant, G. (2002), 'G.E. expenses for ex-chief cited in divorce papers', *The New York Times*, 6 September.

Fabrikant, G. and D. Cay Johnston (2002), 'G.E. perks raise issues about taxes', *The New York Times*, 9 September.

GE (2002), 'GE fact sheet', www.ge.com, 19 June.

Gillers, S. (2002), 'The flaw in the Andersen verdict', *The New York Times*, 18 June.

Glater, J. (2001), 'As Andersen's overseer, Volcker won't settle for nominal change', *The New York Times*, 26 February.

Glater, J. (2002a), 'No rich route for partners in a merger by Andersen', *The New York Times*, 13 March.

Glater, J. (2002b), 'Longtime clients abandon Andersen', *The New York Times*, 16 March.

Glater, J. (2002c), 'Former fed chief outlines proposal to save Andersen', *The New York Times*, 23 March.

Glater, J. (2002d), 'Andersen to lay off 7,000 in sale to Deloitte', *The New York Times*, 5 April.

Glater, J. (2002e), 'Half of jury began deliberations backing Andersen, but support gradually eroded', *The New York Times*, 16 June.

Glater, J. and J. Schwartz (2002), 'Andersen chief quits in effort to rescue firm', *The New York Times*, 27 March.

Hogg, A. (2002), 'Jack Welch's new squeeze', *Moneyweb*, 13 March.

Knowledge at Wharton (2001a), 'Life according to Jack', 8 November.

Knowledge at Wharton (2001b), 'The Jack Welch show', 7 December.

Leonhardt, D. (2002), 'The imperial chief executive is suddenly in the cross hairs', *The New York Times*, 24 June.

Lowe, Janet (2001), *Jack Welch Speaks: Wisdom from the World's Greatest Business Leader*, Chichester, UK: John Wiley & Sons.

Lowe, Janet (2002), *Welch: An American Icon*, Chichester, UK: John Wiley & Sons.

Nicomachean Ethics (see Aristotle).

Norris, F. (2002a), 'Demise of Andersen would leave a dent in the industry', *The New York Times*, 11 March.

Norris, F. (2002b), 'Execution before trial for Andersen', *The New York Times*, 15 March.

The New York Times (2002), 'Andersen's ex-partners sue', *The New York Times*, 25 March.

O'Boyle, Thomas F. (1999), *At Any Cost: Jack Welch, General Electric, and the Pursuit of Profit*, Maryland, US: Alfred A. Knopf.

Russell, J. (2002), 'Jack Welch on success, regrets and values', *VAR Business*, 21 March.

Schwartz, J. (2002a), 'Andersen crew baffled but happy for hugs', *The New York Times*, 15 March.

Schwartz, J. (2002b), 'Sense of loyalty keeps many at auditing firm focused', *The New York Times*, 16 March.

Schwartz, J. (2002c), 'Arthur Andersen employees circle the wagons', *The New York Times*, 22 March.

Schwartz, J. (2002d), 'Andersen's retired partners fear benefits may slip away', *The New York Times*, 3 April.

Slater, Robert (1992), *The New GE: How Jack Welch revived an American Institution*, Berkshire, UK: McGraw-Hill.

Slater, Robert (2001), *Get Better or Get Beaten! 35 Leadership Secrets from GE's Jack Welch*, Berkshire, UK: McGraw-Hill.

Slater, Robert (2002), *Jack Welch and the GE Way: Management Insights and Leadership Secrets of the Legendary CEO*, Berkshire, UK: McGraw-Hill.

Tichy, Noel M. and Sherman Stratford (1999), *Control Your Destiny or Someone Else Will: How Jack Welch is Making General Electric The World's Most Competitive Corporation*, New York: Bantam Doubleday.

Walker, R. (2001), 'Overvalued: Why Jack Welch isn't God', www.robwalker.net, 11 June.

Welch, J. (2001), '26. Divorce and marriage. Jack Welch. My personal history', www.nni.nikkei.co.jp, 27 October.

Welch, Jack and John A. Byrne (2001), *Jack. Straight from the Gut*, Boston: Warner Business Books.

7. Measuring and managing moral capital

I. MANAGING TO MEASURE

Moral capital or virtue can be found on several levels that are closely linked with each other. In the case of individual agents, we have seen how moral capital builds up through one's actions, habits, character and lifestyle. Similarly, corporate agents also develop moral capital through their products, protocols or standard operating procedures, corporate culture and history. Each of these levels corresponds to what we have called the currency, interests, bonds and estates, respectively, of moral capital.

Likewise we have seen two different ways in which virtue or 'personal excellence' behaves as capital. One is through its capacity for unlimited growth or accumulation, as long as the proper investments in virtue-producing assets are made. A business leader could always 'sharpen the saw', not only of his own professional skills and competencies, but also of his positive character traits such as truthfulness, honesty, fairness, compassion, and so on. The sky is the limit in cultivating virtue. Some of the means a person could use to increase his moral capital are, to name a few, constant practice with zero-tolerance for defects and participation in continuing education programs. Secondly, virtue could be assimilated to capital due to its usefulness to individuals and companies. More concretely, a firm profits from virtue – just like from any other form of capital – through the positive influence that virtuous workers exert on corporate culture. At the very least, virtuous workers diminish the legal, social and financial risks and liabilities – which may prove very costly to a corporation – that are associated with corporate wrongdoing. On the more positive side, virtuous employees and managers work better, contributing more to a company's bottom line.

For some people, however, claims about the benefits of moral capital for business carry little weight unless supported by facts and statistics. The reason behind their stand is not so much the value or importance of measurement itself as its usefulness for moral capital management. For in the case of moral capital, just as in any other asset, the dictum according to which 'you can't (properly) manage what you can't measure' invariably holds. Once we've established our aim or goal, the general direction towards which we'd like to be heading, it is imperative to have clear reference points along the way. That's how we know how near or far away we are at any given time with respect to our goal. Within an organization, this effort translates into the establishment of projections and schedules, performance standards or benchmarks and guidelines for the allocation of resources, for example. Measurement provides us with this sort of information which is vital to keeping our course and reaching our objective.

By this moment it should be fairly clear that moral capital indicates a very special kind of human capital. Moral capital is peculiar in that in one sense it forms part of human capital, and in another, it does not. It forms part of human capital because a free will – which determines moral capital's value – constitutes just a part of an individual person's faculties or endowments. Aside from a free will, a person also possesses reason or intelligence, memory, imagination, feelings, sentiments, passions and other capacities. On the other hand, moral capital is not just a part but rather covers the whole of human capital, because the moral dimension extends to everything that a person is capable of and does that is humanly significant. Put in another way, there's no escaping the moral dimension in any truly human endeavor. It is precisely this moral dimension that lends to any human activity its unique value, as the self-determination of a free and sovereign will.

Human capital is usually mentioned in the same breath as physical and financial capital, and all three are considered among the major factors of economic production. As we have found out, however, human capital alone is what really produces wealth. Without the work of people, neither the most cutting-edge technology nor any amount of accumulated wealth or property will ever produce a significant improvement in human welfare. In other words, it is not the money locked up in a bank that creates wealth and well-being, but the work that people do while making use of that money. At best, technology and money – when properly employed – could only help to increase a person's productivity at work, but never be a substitute for work itself. Strictly speaking, productivity should be attributed exclusively to a person's work, and not to the technology nor to the money that he uses. 'All the assets of an organization other than people are inert. They are passive resources that require human application to generate value. The key to sustaining a profitable or a healthy economy is the productivity of human capital' (Fitz-enz 2000:1).

The establishment of the knowledge economy in the more advanced societies has served to underscore our dependence on human work, particularly on human intelligence, as the motor of development and welfare. It has also shown us the difficulty of measuring the productivity and value of intellectual work. This is because the main products of the human mind – such as ideas and concepts – are immaterial or intangible. Therefore they are not as readily measured as the nuts, screws and bolts at the end of a manufacturing chain or the cars that come out of an assembly line. It is hard to count exactly how many ideas a knowledge-worker comes up with while sitting at his desk; and even if we could and actually did, we wouldn't know for sure how to gauge the value – economic or otherwise – of those thoughts. We could simply intuit that they are the most important ingredients in the creation of wealth and welfare, a fact reflected convincingly by the salaries the market is willing to pay those who generate innovative and useful ideas.

The development of the knowledge economy to a position of prominence has heightened our perception of a work-related dilemma. On the one hand we've come to realize our ever growing dependence on human intellectual work, but on the other we've also become increasingly aware of how hard it is to objectively measure the productivity of such work. 'The great irony is that the only economic component that can add value in and by itself is the one that is the most difficult to evaluate. This is the human component – clearly the most vexatious to manage' (Fitz-enz 2000: xii). The problems and difficulties that arise in measuring the impact of intellectual capital on the modern economy also hold true in the case of moral capital.

Aristotle offers us some guidance to the solution of this problem through some of his considerations on the nature or purpose of measurement. In one of the early chapters of the *Nicomachean Ethics*, after having established politics as a rational activity or form of knowledge, he immediately adds that it is not, however, an exact science (cf. NE 1094b). But this lack of accuracy should not be taken to detract from the excellence of politics, because the same degree of precision or exactness (*akribeia*) could not be expected in all sorts of discussions. Rather, in the case of politics, it would be sufficient to give an account that adequately captured whatever amount of clarity the subject matter itself allowed.

It used to be that we took to audited accounting reports almost like Bible truths based on verifiable facts. But our experience with cases like Enron and Andersen has rid us completely of that illusion. We've now come to realize that even the numbers that appear in financial statements merely represent – at the very best – a combination of conventional agreements, hopes and expectations as expressed by fallible accountants and auditors.

In other words, in our investigations in politics and ethics – and by extension, in our research regarding moral capital, its productivity and contribution to the economy – we should be content with arriving at a broad outline of the truth, 'since we argue from and about what holds good usually [but not universally]' (NE 1094b). We should be satisfied to draw from such propositions conclusions that are similarly qualified. For as Aristotle himself reasoned out, 'the educated person seeks exactness in each area to the extent that the nature of the subject allows; for apparently it is just as mistaken to demand demonstrations from a rhetorician as to accept [merely] persuasive arguments from a mathematician' (NE 1094b).

Accepting the limitations on precision which the very nature of an object to be measured imposes should not imply a renunciation to measurement itself, nor – by extension – a renunciation to its usefulness in management.

With regard to moral capital, two measurement strategies may be carried out in parallel. One consists in indirect measurement, which measures the absence or lack of moral capital and its consequences. The other engages in direct measurement, which detects the presence of moral capital and its effects. As we shall soon see, it is often easier to make an indirect measurement of moral capital than a direct one. This may be due largely to the fact that it is less troublesome and controversial to reach an agreement or consensus as to what constitutes wrongdoing and harm than it is to define virtue. What is inevitable, however, is the need to reason logically from a case of dearth or abundance of moral capital to its consequences; or inversely, the necessity of interpreting certain situations as caused either by the presence or absence of a given amount of moral capital.

The consequences of a moral capital deficit on individuals and companies immediately make themselves felt. In attempting to make an indirect measurement of moral capital – that is, of its absence or lack – we may establish two kinds of indicators: some are quantitative and could readily give rise to numbers in terms of costs, capacity and time; while others are qualitative, resulting in figures that reflect value perceptions.

Among the quantitative indicators we may include, for example, the rates of turnover, absenteeism and tardiness in a company's employees. High figures alone for these items at some particular point should not lead us to conclude necessarily that there is a dearth of moral capital among a company's workers. But consistently elevated numbers should be taken as a flashing red light with respect to the moral capital level of workers in that particular organization. We only have to recall the experience of airport screening contractors such as Argenbright and ITS in the US prior to 9-11. A major reason employees come in late, absent themselves or quit their jobs could be an unconducive work environment or corporate culture that takes its toll on their health and well-being. Employees are simply uncomfortable and could hardly stand working for such a firm, to the point that they would rather risk job loss regardless of its dire consequences.

Not only workers, but employers and companies themselves also suffer enormously from high rates of turnover, absenteeism and tardiness (Fitz-enz 2000: 34). Considering that – in the knowledge economy – employee costs easily run into 40 per cent of corporate expenses, this should be one of the first items that we check for returns. Rapid employee turnover rates make a firm incur high termination, replacement and vacancy costs, aside from an inevitable productivity loss as the new employee works his way up the learning curve. Orientation and training expenses should then also be charged against a company's accounts. All of these factors amount to the equivalent of at least 6 months of pay for a staff member or a year's salary for a manager. Afterwards, we'd also have to make allowances for the negative effects resulting from the disruption of activity and the drop in employee loyalty and morale. High rates of absenteeism – and similarly, of tardiness – always prove expensive for a company, despite the coping mechanisms it may have in place. This is because the work ascribed to a certain job is not done by the person supposed to do it; someone who, nevertheless, may still be receiving pay.

Another set of quantitative indicators for the absence or lack of moral capital refers to the incidence of illegal and criminal activity among a firm's workers. The legislation of the different countries where corporations operate is a helpful guide in determining this. We should keep an eye not only on the occurrence of violent personal crimes, such as battery, assault or homicide within company premises or affecting company personnel, but also on those crimes committed against property, such as theft, pilferage or the misuse of company resources, either intentionally or due to neglect.

Two investigative journalists, Russel Mokhiber and Robert Weissman, have compiled a list of 'The Top 100 Corporate Criminals of the Decade of the 1990s' (Baue 2002). Included are corporations that have pleaded guilty or no contest to crimes, thereby receiving fines and sentences. Quite a number of these firms are recidivist. Exxon, for example, entered a guilty plea to charges from the Exxon Valdez oil spill in 1991, for which it paid a $125 million fine, then once again for the Arthur Kill oil spill in New York and New Jersey, which cost it the maximum penalty of $200,000. Another such infamous corporate criminal was Rockwell International. In 1992 it paid an $18.5 million fine for illegal storage and treatment of hazardous waste at a nuclear plant near Boulder, Colorado, and in 1996 it once more disbursed $6.5 million in penalties – even as two of its scientists perished – for disposing of hazardous materials illegally. Both journalists call our attention to the fact that while, according to the FBI, around 19,000 people in the US are murdered every year, a whole lot more, some 56,000 all in all, die either at work or due to occupational diseases such as black lung and asbestosis.

A different category altogether may be dedicated to the so-called 'white-collar crimes' covered, for example, in the case of the US, by the Sherman Antitrust Act of 1890, the Foreign Corrupt Practices Act of 1977 and the Federal Corporate Sentencing Guidelines of 1991, to name a few (Sison 2000). Aside from these general norms there are also other laws that target specific industries, such as the Securities and Exchange Act of 1934 and the Insider Trading Sanctions Act of 1984 for the financial sector; or some pieces of legislation that address special concerns, such as the Environmental Protection Act of 1995. At the baseline of moral capital growth and development is the condition of being a law-abiding individual or corporate citizen.

Certainly there are laws – once more, in the context of the US – governing workplace conditions, such as the Occupational Safety and Health Act of 1970, and workplace procedures, such as the Equal Opportunity and Employment Act of 1972. However, many of the abuses committed in these areas are mere infringements of generally accepted public manners or of implicit social rules. Without falling into the category of law violations, nevertheless, they still are symptomatic of insufficient moral capital, and we should in consequence keep account both of their number and of their kind.

For example, although there has been an Omnibus Drug Initiative Act in the US since 1988 concerning the use and sale of habit-forming and mind-altering substances, its provisions are not necessarily applicable to work conditions in many European countries, which may have more permissive laws or different notions of privacy and well-being altogether. Nevertheless, given the harmful effects of substance abuse (including alcohol and tobacco) on individuals and their work, we could still consider it as one of the quantitative indicators of a low level of moral capital. The same could be said of the occurrence of any form of disruptive or antisocial behavior at work. In fact, according to a 2001 survey by the Walker Information group, the most common integrity lapses in the workplace do not necessarily constitute crimes: lying to supervisors, unfair treatment of employees and improper or personal use of company resources (Walker Information 2001).

Next come the qualitative indicators of moral capital deficiency. We call them qualitative, because the information they provide does not usually come in the form of absolute numbers or statistics but in descriptive observations and normative inferences. We gather data basically by way of value-surveys and in-depth interviews administered among a firm's different shareholders or constituencies. In carrying out these studies we may inquire about issues related with quality of home-life, rest and leisure, involvement in volunteer work and community out-reach programs, religious observance, and so on.

For example, out-of-wedlock births and single-parenthood are generally recognized as both personal and social problems, especially for teenagers and young adults. This is because the burden of raising children in these circumstances falls exclusively on the shoulders of a single person, usually female, who as it is, already suffers from a disadvantaged social, economic and professional condition. Something similar may be said of workers and employees who undergo difficult times in their relationships, with marriages that end up in a separation or a divorce. 'People who have family and personal problems cannot be productive. They go through the motions, worrying about what they are facing outside...' (Fitz-enz 2000: 101). As we know, work-related factors and company policies are a major influence, for the good as well as for the bad, in lifestyle decisions. As people spend a greater part of their time at work, they also expect to receive an increasing amount of support, moral and otherwise – as they previously would from a community, a church, a neighbor or a family member – from the company. Moreover, it just so happens that a person's professional, public life cannot be completely shielded or detached from his private pain.

This truism also works the other way around, however; that is, personal, private joys often translate into public, professional successes. Take, for example, the sense of happiness or fulfillment that comes from a good and stable marriage, or the joy that one experiences with the arrival of new offspring. Workers tend to be more stable and dependable once they're married and with children. In this respect, the findings of a recent work by Linda J. Waite and Maggie Gallagher about the transformative effect of marriage on individuals are very enlightening. In *The Case for Marriage. Why Married People are Happier, Healthier and Better Off Financially* (Waite and Gallagher 2000), the authors compellingly argue about the benefits of marriage on the basis of the special-ization and mutual trust that it affords couples due to their long-term 'until death do us part' commitment. Contrariwise, failures in marriage and family life seem to have a way of unavoidably sapping the energy – of which moral capital forms part – out of people.

At this point, one may contend that in our attempt to measure moral capital we may be too happily crossing the line between people's public and private lives. We discover, however, that such a division in a person's existence is never really hard and fast. Markets and the general public are seldom able to distinguish between a corporate executive's public and private life when it comes to concrete situations. That's why when Phyllis Redstone – the wife of Sumner Redstone, the Viacom chief – initiated divorce proceedings after 52 years of marriage, alleging adultery and abusive treatment, a full-blown corporate crisis ensued (Jones 2002). After all, she was claiming no less than $3 billion in shares and conjugal property in her suit, regarding some supposedly personal and private issues.

In terms of the direct measurement of moral capital, much headway has been gained thanks especially to the work of Dr Jac Fitz-enz, the acknowledged father of human performance benchmarking and assessment. He is also founder and chairman of the Saratoga Institute based in Santa Clara, CA. For over 20 years, his organization has provided a comprehensive and integrated approach to human capital management in organizations, summarized in his book *The ROI of Human Capital. Measuring the Economic Value of Employee Perfor-mance* (Fitz-enz 2000). Although he focused mainly on traditional human capital (HC) measurements, his indicators could safely be extended – with proper adjustments – to moral capital as well.

Fitz-enz considers – among others – as direct quantitative indicators of human capital at the corporate level, items such as human capital revenue, human capital return on investment (ROI) and human capital value-added (VA) (Fitz-enz 2000: 279–80).

In order to arrive at these figures, one should first of all calculate the so-called 'full-time equivalent' (FTE) of a firm. The FTE represents the ratio between the total number of hours actually worked by all employees in a firm and the standard number of hours that they – in theory – should have worked within a given period (Fitz-enz 2000: 31). Take for example a company that employs 10 people, each of whom have in principle a 40-hour work week. The perfect FTE for that company would be 1.0, meaning that all of its employees have worked all of their projected hours. But if – for instance – two of its employees checked in two hours late one day on any given work week, its FTE for that week would then be calculated thus: $((8 \text{ employees} \times 40 \text{ hours}) + (2 \text{ late employees} \times 38 \text{ hours}))/(10 \text{ employees} \times 40 \text{ hours}) = 0.99$.

A company's human capital (HC) revenue is its total revenue divided by its FTE for a given period. Its human capital return on investment (HC ROI) is equivalent to (revenue – (expenses – total labor costs))/ total labor costs; where 'total labor costs' stands for employee pay and benefits. On the other hand, its human capital value added (HC VA) could be arrived at by calculating its (revenue – (expenses – total labor costs))/FTE (Fitz-enz 2000: 31–5).

Helpful as these metrics may be, we should however use them with caution. They indicate general trends which are best interpreted in the light of other data or observations. These numbers are the result of a wide range of activities carried out by the firm, which at the same time are subject to various external influences. For example, although HC revenue per employee is widely used by government and business analysts, it is still a rough tool in that by itself it does not allow us to distinguish between the effects of human capital and the leveraging of other assets. Improved HC revenue per employee may have been caused by external factors, such as a series of mistakes committed by one's competitors or extraordinary customer loyalty. But then again, it could also be due to internal factors, such as having a great sales force, launching a highly effective advertising campaign, engaging in an aggressive price-discounting strategy or simply having the best product available on the market.

A further step would be to relate these enterprise-wide measures to the level of the individual worker. With the HC value added figure we could determine the profitability of the average employee; find out whether he has really created economic value, as opposed to a mere bluff on financial statements. But it would also be interesting to discover who among the workers has actually contributed most to the creation of that value. And for this, we may have to take recourse to complementary instruments which compare the HC value added of – for example – full-time and part-time workers, or permanent employees and contingent staff.

As for direct qualitative indicators, Fitz-enz explores – in a company-wide scope – the human capital competence level, the human capital commitment level, the human capital satisfaction percentage and data on corporate climate, among others (Fitz-enz 2000: 148–9). These are also helpful in attempting to detect and measure the amount of moral capital present in individuals and firms.

Justice demands that a worker has professional skill and competence (human capital competence level), and beyond this, loyalty requires that a worker gives a bit more of himself – at least in terms of goodwill or benevolence – to his employer or firm than what is strictly entailed in a purely commercial transaction or exchange (human capital commitment level). And if it is true that virtue is its own reward, then competence and commitment should contribute greatly to one's own sense of satisfaction or self-fulfillment (human capital satisfaction percentage). Lastly, since virtue is not to be lived or practiced in a void, but rather, in a community, it is extremely important that the surrounding corporate environment or climate be one that is conducive to virtue (positive data on corporate climate). As a minimum, it should acknowledge and reward good behaviors, while discouraging the bad.

The HC competence level indicates the percentage of employees who have met established competence standards. These are the workers who have demonstrated the skill and knowledge that permit them to meet the current and near-term performance requirements or demands in their jobs. The HC commitment level refers to the percentage of employees expecting to remain in a firm for at least three years. In this regard, nothing helps to retain talent in a firm as much as addressing its employees' personal issues.

There is a consensus among human resource specialists that the best predictor of overall excellence in a company is its ability to attract, motivate and retain talent (Fitz-enz 2000: 51). The key personnel in the firm would then act as leaven to develop a distinctive corporate culture. However, as every CEO knows, a company's corporate culture is precisely its most important resource in recruiting talent; and this is what in the end permits us to close the loop among a company's recruitment policies, its culture and its performance.

Regarding top performers, studies reveal that they usually have in common the following set of priorities: an emphasis on teamwork, a sharp consumer focus, a keen appreciation for the fair treatment of employees, a penchant for innovation and lots of initiative (Fitz-enz 2000: 51–2). They also strive to develop a strong commitment to the values and culture of an organization, trying to keep their decisions and actions consistent with them. Similarly, they display the following 'structural traits': partnering, which consists in regularly looking outside of the firm for organizations with which they can leverage resources; collaboration, which involves seeking the cooperation and involvement of several sections within a function; innovation, or the willingness to assume and manage risks; and communication, which means keeping channels of dialogue open with all stakeholders. By contrast, average or mediocre performers seem to be primarily interested in just minimizing risks, respecting the chain of command, supporting the boss and making the budget.

The HC satisfaction level indicates the percentage of employees who figure in the top quartile of a job satisfaction survey. Employees have a range of expectations which include receiving job-related training and career-development support, having an opportunity for advancement, being treated as contributing adults, having their knowledge and experience put to use, being kept informed about company matters and changes, and being compensated fairly and equitably (Fitz-enz 2000: 237). Special attention must be paid to the employees' training and development. By spending time and money to help workers learn and grow professionally, a company simultaneously makes huge deposits in these employees' loyalty accounts, an investment from which it could expect to draw enormous returns in the future. In this manner, a high HC satisfaction level has a beneficial impact on the HC commitment level.

A high HC satisfaction level also positively affects a company's HC competence level. A happy employee is a productive employee. However, an employee's positive feelings and dispositions are basically a function of his relationship with his supervisor or manager. Employees who have a good relationship with their supervisor and are content with their jobs will also take care of keeping customers well served, satisfied and loyal. Employee dissatisfaction, on the other hand, could manifest itself in any of the following ways: by being absent, by leaving early or right on time, by working at a slower pace than normal or by not volunteering for projects (Fitz-enz 2000: 150).

Finally, data on corporate climate reveal the percentage of employees who manifest a positive concern with the culture and climate of their work environment. As we can infer from the foregoing, a good corporate climate is the end result of high HC competence, commitment and satisfaction levels.

These pieces of information could be complemented by a company's rating in 'employer of choice' surveys (Fitz-enz 2000: 140). The rationale behind this is that the ability to attract and retain top talent ultimately reflects on organizational effectiveness and financial performance. By making it unusually pleasant and convenient to work for a certain company, the idea of transferring to another firm is kept away from employees' minds. A supportive and caring corporate culture not only makes employees more focused and energetic, but it also nurtures in them a lot of positive morale and an enormous amount of goodwill towards the firm.

Bruce Tulgan, a management consultant, enumerates three major areas that should be addressed in order for a company to qualify as 'employer of choice': family support, wellness services and concierge services (Tulgan 2001: 178–83). The family happens to be the top priority for most people, who would really appreciate flexible work hours in order to be able to respond better to the needs of their children, elderly parents or sick relations. Workplace-sited day care would certainly be a big incentive, especially for working mothers. Wellness services would cover whatever is necessary to keep workers healthy in mind, body and spirit – athletic facilities and fitness programs, counseling, faith-centered activities. As we have already said, the happier employees are the more productive they will most probably be in their jobs. And finally, concierge services refer to the small ordinary tasks which inordinately occupy a lot of room in people's minds, such as grocery shopping, dry cleaning and laundry, home and car repairs and travel arrangements. These little things have an uncanny ability to chip away at employees' productivity to the extent that it could really be best to have them taken care of at an institutional level, given the opportunity.

Another approach at measuring moral capital directly could follow from the initiatives promoted by the Walker Information group. This company engages in the research and measurement of nonfinancial aspects of business, such as ethics, corporate reputation, employee commitment and customer satisfaction, in a manner that facilitates their combination with traditional financial indicators for more effective management. It carries out business integrity assessment programs through which one may gauge the effectiveness of corporate ethics and compliance procedures as perceived by employees. Both its 1999 National Business Ethics (Walker Information 1999) and its 2001 Integrity in the Workplace (Walker Information 2001) studies reveal that corporate ethics programs effectively prevent misconduct and enhance organizational reputation. A sterling corporate reputation is vital not only to customer retention but also, and more importantly, to employee commitment and loyalty. And a loyal and committed workforce is what is primarily responsible for producing higher returns to a company's shareholders in the long term.

A third source of ideas for the direct and qualitative measurement of moral capital could be provided by the AccountAbility 1000 framework – analogous to the 'Generally Accepted Accounting Principles' or 'GAAP' – designed by the Institute of Social and Ethical Accountability (2002). The Institute has generated indicators, targets and procedural systems for the accounting, auditing and reporting of a company's social and ethical performance, along the lines of a 'corporate citizenship' oriented research. Its framework purports to merge these instruments with other traditional financial indicators and strategic planning tools such as the 'Balanced Scorecard' (Kaplan and Norton 1996). The Balanced Scorecard technique is based on the premise that conventional accounting is too insular, focusing exclusively on past financial performance. By contrast, this method proposes that other matters such as learning and growth, customers and business processes be added to the data considered in evaluating a firm.

While recognizing that accountability in social, environmental and ethical issues almost always goes beyond mere compliance with the law, Account-Ability 1000 nevertheless concentrates on 'second-order' dimensions as transparency and responsiveness in a company's reports. By emphasizing procedural aspects, this approach definitely gains in practicality and apparent usefulness. But it somehow leaves lingering doubts as to the more substantive values on which such protocols or procedures are to be anchored, such as com-mitments to a shared vision of the good or virtue. Furthermore, this approach does not seem to go very far beyond the problems arising from the dichotomy between compliance-based and integrity-based programs (Paine 1996). Faced with this alternative, AccountAbility 1000 decidedly settles for the former, allowing itself to be blindsided with respect to the advantages of the latter.

II.   MEASURING TO MANAGE

Although initially the strength of the argument in favor of moral capital derived from its positive contribution to worker productivity and economic success, this, however, is not the main point of our proposal. Our concern is not simply to discover what leads to economic growth, but to reason out why economic growth is desirable for human beings in the first place.

Whereas human capital literature, for example, normally focuses on the instrumental value of education, on increasing or improving worker produc-tivity, moral capital emphasizes the intrinsic value of character education itself, as constitutive of a worker's overall development, flourishing and happiness. In this sense, moral capital is closely related to Amartya Sen's (1999) notion of 'human capability' or 'substantive freedom' (as opposed to 'instrumental freedoms' or socioeconomic and political opportunities, which are linked to a more limited understanding of human capital). Substantive freedoms are those which allow people to lead the kind of life they have reason to choose and value; they are important not so much for their effectiveness as for their own worth, from a holistic standpoint of human development. Reflected more by the quality of life than by income per capita, substantive freedoms are the true goal of development, understood – in the manner of Sen – as the expansion of freedoms:

> economic growth cannot be sensibly treated as an end in itself. Development has to be more concerned with enhancing the lives we lead and the freedoms we enjoy. Expanding the freedoms that we have reason to value not only makes our lives richer and more unfettered, but also allows us to be fuller social persons, exercising our own volitions and interacting with – and influencing – the world in which we live (Sen 1999: 14–15).

Our position regarding the production and distribution of moral capital is influenced by the fact that virtue – like lighthouses, knowledge and ideas – behaves very much in the same way as the so-called 'public goods' (Kaul, Grunberg and Stern 1999: xx). That is, virtue is a 'positive externality', a good that is non-rivalrous and non-excludable in its consumption. This means that whatever gain one makes in moral capital or virtue does not detract from any other's; and it would actually cost everyone more if somebody were to be excluded or barred from the benefits of moral capital or virtue than the contrary. If at all, someone else's virtue could only serve to facilitate the exercise of one's own and to magnify its effects. Also, its being a 'public good' could somehow explain the dearth of investments in virtue. Market mechanisms alone could not provide it, since it would always be easier to freeload on the benefits of other people's virtue than to take the pains of developing it oneself. Likewise, as in a classic case of the so-called 'prisoner's dilemma', the lack of cooperation between agents, particularly in the effort to cultivate virtue, eventually leaves everyone worse off.

The various approaches and techniques so far discussed should already allow us to measure moral capital quite well. We must not forget, however, that the whole purpose of measuring moral capital lies – rather than in the measurement itself – in being able to manage it correctly.

The very first step, of course, consists in producing enough moral capital assets in individual workers and firms; that is, in fostering the right human actions or in coming up with the right products, both of which we have called the 'basic currency' of moral capital. This means avoiding certain activities either because they are illegal or because they inhibit the growth of moral capital and destroy it. Such are, for example, dealerships in drugs, arms and pornography, engagement in the flesh trade, and so on. Or they could also be businesses that indulge in corrupt practices or corporations that fail to respect basic human rights.

Some investment funds or investment fund indexes such as Domini (www.domini.com), Jantzi (www.mjra-jsi.com) or FTSE4Good (www.ftse4good.co.uk) already take care of screening companies on the basis of social and environmental criteria apart from profitability. The rules that these institutions follow in their investments play a similar role to that of 'moral absolutes' in traditional ethical reasoning; they are prohibitions that admit no exception. Domini, for instance, flatly refuses to invest in companies that manufacture tobacco or alcohol, as well as in firms that produce nuclear power or provide services to gambling operations. It even establishes that a corporation derive no more than 2 per cent of its gross revenues from the production of military weapons in order to form part of its portfolio.

The main virtue to be practiced in the production of basic moral capital assets or currency is, therefore, that of justice: the constant and firm will to give to each of one's associates – or to every one of a firm's stakeholders – his due in accordance with law. Justice disposes the agent to respect the rights of others and to establish harmony in human relationships such that equity and the common good are promoted.

Once we have produced – and will foreseeably continue to produce – sufficient moral capital currency in terms of the right actions and products, we would then have to look for the best rates of interest for our assets. As we have explained, personal habits and corporate standard operating procedures are the equivalent of the compound interest of moral capital. This is a concern that to a large degree practically takes care of itself, so long as one does not give up what he has started and keeps the effort not only of doing the right things, but also of doing them correctly. The temptation to be led by a mistaken sense of urgency, by short-termism or by an obsession with quarterly financial results, for example, will always be present and one will have to be on his guard. It is imperative that he be constant and persevere with his proper time-tested habits or protocols even if, on the immediate face of it, they do not appear to be as effective as other methods.

The key virtue here, then, is temperance or moderation; the control of the desire for instant gratification and of the attraction towards pleasures. For immediate short-term gains often ought to be sacrificed to obtain a greater, more durable good which nevertheless takes longer and greater effort to produce. Temperance provides balance in the use and enjoyment of goods; more importantly, it ensures mastery over one's instincts and tendencies, keeping them within the limits of what is honorable.

In the third place comes – for proper moral capital management – the necessity of choosing the appropriate investment bonds. These moral capital bonds are represented by a person's character and a corporation's culture. One should not forget that in his professional work he is planning for the long haul, both personally and corporatively. So he would do well to maintain an integral and holistic view not only of his own inclinations, actions and habits, but also of the compentencies, products and procedures of the organization for which he works.

The virtue that this requires is, above all, that of courage or fortitude. Embarking on long-term and worthwhile projects entails assuming lots of risks and overcoming many obstacles, the most formidable of which, perhaps, arise from within the person himself or from the very organization. Courage ensures firmness in difficulties and constancy in the pursuit of the good. It strengthens an agent's resolve to conquer fear and all sorts of trials or temptations.

Finally, after having decided on the most appropriate investment bonds, one would then have to think of one's moral capital estate or legacy. These are influenced primarily by an individual's lifestyle choice or the corporate history of an organization. In administering one's resources, he would have to consider the influences or effects of his actions on others beyond himself, especially on those who are somehow dependent upon or subject to him. He would have to govern his assets or patrimony with a view to the common good, which includes the welfare of others who may even be spatially or temporally distant. (He may not even be alive any longer.) He must be able to balance the inevitable conflicts of interest among collaborators and other parties. To do this, he would have to review his commitments, the ends that he has vowed to pursue, and the means that he has at his disposal here and now – which will always be limited – to achieve those ends. Such is the function of the virtue of prudence – the 'right reason in action' – which disposes practical reason to discern the true good in every circumstance and to choose the right means of achieving it.

In the end, managing moral capital amounts to practicing the virtues of justice, temperance, fortitude and prudence, not the least in the exercise of one's work and throughout the course of one's life.

III. IN BRIEF

- Due to its intangibility, moral capital or virtue is inherently difficult to measure. However, we have to attempt to do so to be able to manage it properly. Aristotle provides us with a certain leeway in our measurement by saying that we should only look for precision or exactness to the degree that the subject matter itself allows.
- Two parallel strategies may be carried out in gauging moral capital. One consists in indirect measurement, which indicates the absence or lack of moral capital, and the other in indirect measurement, which accounts for its presence.
- Both indirect and direct measurement strategies in turn make use of quantitative and qualitative indicators. Quantitative indicators give rise to absolute numbers that could readily translate into costs, while qualitative indicators produce figures that reflect value perceptions. For indirect moral capital measurements, some examples of quantitative indicators are high rates of turnover, absenteeism and tardiness, and a high incidence of illegal and criminal activity; whereas among the qualitative indicators we may include the prevalence of a dysfunctional family life among workers. For direct moral capital measurements we may consider human capital revenue, human capital return on investment and human capital value added among the quantitative indicators; and human capital competence, human capital commitment and human capital satisfaction

levels – together with a positive perception of the corporate climate –
among the qualitative indicators.

- These moral capital measurements could be complemented by information from 'employer of choice surveys' and data gathered by other
initiatives – such as the metrics of the Walker Information Group or the
AccountAbility 1000 framework of the Institute of Social and Ethical
Accounting – which incorporate socioethical and environmental concerns
into conventional financial data.
- Aside from its instrumental, productivity-related benefits, moral capital
or virtue is also desirable in itself, as an expansion of our 'substantive
freedoms' (Sen) or in representation of integral human development. In
this regard, the economic behavior of moral capital is similar to that of
the so-called 'public goods', which are non-rivalrous and non-excludable
in their consumption.
- The proper management of moral capital or virtue could be summarized
in four steps:

1. producing enough moral capital currency or assets by fostering the
   right actions and coming up with the right products; practicing the
   virtue of justice understood as adherence to the law;
2. earning the right interest on moral capital assets by investing in proper
   personal habits and corporate procedures; practicing the virtue of
   moderation or controlling one's desire for immediate gratification;
3. choosing the appropriate investment bonds for moral capital resources
   by fostering an upright character and corporate culture; practicing the
   virtue of courage that sustains one in long-term worthwhile projects
   despite difficulties and obstacles;
4. instituting a worthy legacy or estate of moral capital by cultivating the
   proper lifestyle choice and giving a correct orientation to a firm's
   corporate history; practicing the virtue of prudence which disposes one
   to do what is good here and now without losing the final end from view.

REFERENCES

Aristotle (1985), *Nicomachean Ethics*, trans. by Terence Irwin, Indianapolis, IN: Hackett
    Publishing.
Baue, W. (2002), 'Journalists list corporations found guilty of crimes throughout the
    1990s', www.SocialFunds.com, 29 May.
Fitz-enz, Jac (2000), *The ROI of Human Capital. Measuring the Economic Value of
    Employee Performance*, New York: AMACOM/ American Management Association.
Institute of Social and Ethical Accountability (2002), 'AccountAbility (AA) 1000 series:
    Making stakeholder engagement work. Consultation brief', www.accountability.
    org.uk, March.

Jones, D. (2002), 'CEOs find marital bliss tougher than business', *USA Today*, 15 May.

Kaplan, Robert S. and David P. Norton (1996), *The Balanced Scorecard: Translating Strategy into Action*, Boston, MA: Harvard Business School Press.

Kaul, Inge, Isabelle Grunberg and Marc A. Stern (eds) (1999), *Global Public Goods. International Cooperation in the 21st Century*, New York and Oxford: United Nations Development Program and Oxford University Press.

Nicomachean Ethics (see Aristotle).

Paine, L. (1996), 'Venturing Beyond Compliance', *The Evolving Role of Ethics in Business*, New York: The Conference Board.

Sen, Amartya (1999), *Development as Freedom*, Oxford: Oxford University Press.

Sison, A.J.G. (2000), 'Integrated risk management and global business ethics', *Business Ethics: A European Review*, **4** (4), October, 288–95.

Tulgan, Bruce (2001), *Winning the Talent Wars*, London: Nicholas Brealey Publishing.

Waite, Linda and Maggie Gallagher (2000), *The Case for Marriage: Why Married People are Happier, Healthier and Better Off Financially*, New York: Doubleday.

Walker Information (1999), National Business Ethics Study, www.walkerinfo.com.

Walker Information (2001), National Employee Benchmark Study, www.walkerinfo.com.

Index

Cay Johnston, D. 138
Chandler, W.B. III 107
character 35–42, 94–116
    Hewlett-Packard 97–108
    legacy 108–15
charisma 35–42
Chile 126
Ciulla, J.B. 36, 37
Clark, J. 75
Clarke, J. 107
Clinton, B. 113
CNBC 135
Coase, R. 19
Coffee, J. 121, 127
Colburn, D. 75
Coleman, J. 18
Colgate-Palmolive 135
Collins, J.C. 134, 135
Compaq Computers 72, 74–5
    character 97–9, 102–8, 111–12
Condor 28
Cordiner, R. 134
Corel 79
craftsmanship 88–9
Crainer, S. 131
cultural capital 17
culture 96–7
customer capital 15–16

David and Lucile Packard Foundation 99
de Soto, H. 6–8
Dell 97, 98
Deloitte Touche Tohmatsu 123, 125, 129
Delta Air Lines 122
Deutsch, C. 47
Deutsche Asset Management 106
Deutsche Bank 106, 107
Digital Equipment 98
direct measurement 150
Disney 78
doing 88–9, 91
Domini 159
Donegan, L. 138
Drew, C. 1
Drucker, P.F. 15
Duncan, D.B. 29, 30, 128–9

Eaton, L. 3
Edison, T.A. 130
education 9–12

Egypt 7
Eichenwald, K. 25, 29, 30, 123, 125, 127, 128, 129
Elstrom, P. 100
emotions 40–41
employer of choice surveys 156–7
employment 90–91
Enron 24–30, 60
    lifestyles 121–9, 133, 140, 143
    management of moral capital 149
    Online 26, 60
Environmental Protection Act (1995) 151
Equal Opportunity and Employment Act (1972) 152
Ernst & Young 123, 125
eSpeed 55–6, 59, 60
ethnic Chinese 17
ethos 40, 108, 113, 118
eudaimonia 31–2
eunoia (good will) 41
Europe 2, 152
European Commission 133
Excel 75
Exxon 151

Fabrikant, G. 138
Farber, D. 77–8
Fastow, A.S. 25–6, 27, 28, 30, 124
fear 37
Federal Aviation Administration 1
Federal Corporate Sentencing Guidelines (1991) 151
Federal District Court 80
Federal Government 48
Federal Trade Commission 71
FedEx 122
feelings 108–9
Felten, E. 77–8, 84
Fifth Amendment 30
fine arts 88–9
Fiorina, C. 97–107, 110–3
Firestone, D. 2, 21
Firestone, H.S. 52
Fisher, I. 5–6, 8, 9
Fitz–enz, J. 148–50, 152–6
Foley, J. 102
Ford, H. 52
Ford, W.C. 52, 53
Ford–Firestone 46–54, 63–5
Foreign Corrupt Practices Act (1977) 151